This book is the standalone sequel to

A Cactus Called Ironside

Excerpts from reviews posted on Goodreads

Loved it! I really enjoyed the story and the tender characters within. Amusing and engaging – I would have read it without stopping if I'd had the opportunity.

Full of funny moments plus aspects from the 1980s, many of which I had forgotten but to read about them in this book reminded me of many happy (and embarrassing) moments of my own.

A hilarious roller coaster ride with many twists and turns along the way, Brilliantly observed.

A superbly written story with a heroine you feel is chatting to you from her armchair in the same room. You will laugh out loud.

Clever plot which I never guessed.

A hilarious account of student life in the 80s set against a wider context of family intrigue, evasion and falsehood with an engaging cast of eccentric characters spanning the social and generational spectrum. A hoot – not to be missed.

A Feather Between the Lines

Kath Crew

First published in 2025 by Fuzzy Flamingo
Copyright © Kath Crew 2025

Kath Crew has asserted her right to be identified as the author of this Work in accordance with the Copyright, Designs and Patents Act 1988.

ISBN: 978-1-0684468-9-4

All rights reserved.
No part of this publication may be reproduced, stored in a retrieval system, or transmitted in any form or by any means, electronic, mechanical, photocopying, recording or otherwise, without the prior permission of the copyright owner.

Editing and design by Fuzzy Flamingo
www.fuzzyflamingo.co.uk

A catalogue for this book is available from the British Library.

For the enthusiastic and complimentary readers of A Cactus Called Ironside who encouraged me to explore what happened next.

Remembering Boris (2010 – 2025) whose walks gave me the peace and focus to work things out.

Footfalls echo in the memory
Down the passage which we did not take
Towards the door we never opened.

Burnt Norton, Four Quartets
T S Eliot (1888 – 1965)

God pity them both! and pity us all,
Who vainly the dreams of youth recall;
For of all sad words of tongue or pen,
The saddest are these: 'It might have been!'
Ah, well! For us all some sweet hope lies
Deeply buried from human eyes.

Maud Muller
John Greenleaf Whittier (1807 – 1892)

We must find our duties in what comes to us, not in what might have been.

Daniel Deronda
George Eliot (1819-1880)

We can never know what might have been but what is to come is another matter entirely.

C. S. Lewis (1898 – 1963)

She began now to comprehend that he was exactly the man who, in disposition and talents, would most suit her. His understanding and temper, though unlike her own, would have answered all her wishes. It was an union that must have been to the advantage of both: by her ease and liveliness, his mind might have been softened, his manners improved; and from his judgement, information, and knowledge of the world, she must have received benefit of greater importance.

Pride and Prejudice
Jane Austen (1775-1817)

ALEC: But there must be a part of you, deep down inside, that doesn't feel like that at all – some little spirit that still wants to climb out of the window – that still longs to splash about a bit in the dangerous sea.

Still Life
Noel Coward (1899 – 1973)

"Hope" is the thing with feathers,
That perches in the soul,
And sings the tune without the words
And never stops – at all

                                            Emily Dickinson

Reflection

I'd been lurking down the bottom of our freezer with some unlabelled grey lumps, half a portion of turkey curry from several Christmases ago and various rogue peas and sweetcorn kernels making a futile bid for freedom. Not much progress for over thirty years. I hadn't even realised until I heard that song last November.

I rarely listen to music in the car. It distracts me. I once went the wrong way round a roundabout because I was joining in with The Proclaimers asking for a letter from America. If white van man hadn't swerved, I'd have left this world shouting the names of some places in Scotland I'd be hard pushed to place on a map.

I can't take all that talking on Radio 4 either. I'm not a regular listener. I like a good play or something amusing, but I'm irritated by programmes featuring people asking questions about begonias or how to avoid inheritance tax. Most of all I can't put up with those earnest voices raking over people's problems, telling you how awful the world is. Who wants to wallow in misery whilst doing the ironing? I prefer silence so I can daydream.

When I turned on the engine the song blasted out at full volume. I should have known: chocolate wrappers and discarded coffee cups. The clues to check the radio first. My son Arthur can't drive without a constant infusion of sugar and caffeine accompanied by several thousand decibels of music. I should have worked out that he'd been the last person driving the car.

It was quite a catchy tune, so I sat and listened to it for a bit and, as the heater slowly revealed the world beyond the misted windscreen, I thought about the envelope I'd just received and the letter which it contained. There was no hint of sadness in the jaunty melody, so it caught me by surprise when I heard the lyric about a girl who got frozen in time, unable to forget. Immured in a fantasy aged twenty-three whilst all around her everyone else got on with it – it was a song about me. I have been fantasising since I was twenty-three – how did Taylor Swift know?

I'd been down the bottom of that freezer, dolloped into an old ice cream tub with 'Roni McNamara 1985' scrawled on the lid in thick black marker pen. Undisturbed, unaware and largely unbothered.

Of course, I didn't see myself as a twenty-three-year-old last seen in 1985 – all big hair, shoulder pads, legwarmers and pixie boots – but the truth remains a shock. I'm sixty. Fuck me, how has that happened? I get a teacher's pension and free prescriptions. Surely some mistake?

Other people had got older (often surprisingly) but I had remained the same. For me, ageing and counting birthdays stood still while everyone else sped towards decrepitude. I might have noticed it a bit more if I ran marathons, climbed mountains or lived on the top floor of an apartment block without a lift. If you sit on your arse all day reading books like I do and don't look critically in the mirror, then the years don't matter. My age-ometer had stopped, like a fixed clock on a dodgy second-hand motor.

There was an explanation, I realised that autumn morning. Sitting in the car, as the windscreen cleared, I recognised that, unbelievably, Taylor Swift and I were alike – in one respect at least. I had frozen aged twenty-three after he left me, when I realised he wasn't coming back and when I made the choice that meant I feared his return. Since the arrival of the letter, I'd felt a thaw begin in myself.

A mountain shepherd known as the Tyrolean Iceman spent five thousand years in a glacier before he began the big defrost.

A Feather Between the Lines

I'm a rookie melter by comparison. I admit long-distance treks (with or without accompanying goats) at high altitude aren't my thing and I've emerged from the ice a better colour than he did, but we too have something in common. After thawing we'd both have to admit that we couldn't ignore the years in between and hope to resume where we left off.

Nine months ago I received a letter which began the end of my own personal ice age and I'm back where I was before my time in the freezer. If I was an interviewee on one of those cod psychology radio broadcasts I try to avoid, I'd be going on about 'my journey', having 'baggage', making 'connections' and doing a lot of 'unpacking' before arriving at a destination called Resolution or Closure.

Fortunately, no one is asking me to talk about it. I can only write things down anyway. I'm a sixty-year-old woman who's spent thirty-seven years not going anywhere. *Right Where You Left Me* – just like the song. Not much of a journey.

1

Oxford. 10th May 2023
Predictably somewhat later than planned

The jeans were tight, cutting across my middle as I drove into the city. Why on Earth was I wearing them? Hastily bought in an optimistically small size, apart from bisecting me when in a sitting position they weren't noticeably different from the other pairs I own. They had no secreted chocolate wrappers or half-used Kleenex poking out from their pockets, neither did they conceal solid pellets of hardened tissue indicating a previous heavy cold and subsequent history with the washing machine. The hems were definitely mud-free – but they were just another pair of jeans. A very uncomfortable pair.

I subscribe to the mantra of the self-deceiver: if I can squeeze in to a size 12 then I must be a size 12 and look like one. But who will fail to recognise the over-inflated balloon, the denim blimp, taut and poised to pop? Why am I bothered? Sixty years old but behaving like a fifteen-year-old – you'd think I would have learned. Deep down I knew. I wanted to be my youthful self or at least appear to be like her.

I was in a hurry. Once in the underground car park I'd spent too long peering into the mirror on the back of the sunshade trying to assess the seepage of eyeliner on my lower lid caused by the eye-watering tightness of my waistband. I'd taken too long gurning in the rear-view mirror with my lipstick, not helped by the feeble interior light in the car.

Out of the car I'd had problems with the parking app. Which idiot at the council decided not only to dispense with coins for the meter but also make contactless payment impossible when there is no Wi-Fi signal below ground level? My phone is full of parking apps but rarely the right one for the place where I'm trying to leave my car. If by amazing coincidence the correct one is loaded onto my phone, I will guarantee that there will be no signal.

I was late – one of my worst characteristics. The one which I was keen to impress had changed. I wanted to show I could now keep time and not make people hang about waiting for me. *I am the same as I was then in so many ways, but I have improved in this particular area of irritation.* But already it was obvious that neither of these statements was true.

I'd only climbed up a few steps to the outside, but it was clear that I wasn't going to be able to move normally, let alone have a conversation at the same time. I suppose it was fortunate I discovered this before I'd got too far. Holding my stomach in was not going to be an option for the short walk to the end of the road, let alone for any more of the afternoon

The pain in my stomach wasn't just the jeans. I decided to breathe out and give up on trying to control my muscles. The button stud at the waist flew off like a bullet fired from holster level by a pistol-toting cowboy. As I stooped to pick it up from the kerbside, the jean's zip began to slide rapidly down. Before I pulled it up again, willing it would miraculously stay there, I acknowledged that the ache remained. A nervous grip, good old-fashioned butterflies.

I could have turned round and gone back to the car, driven home and opted out. Perhaps I should have. Thirty-seven years is a long time. Things and people change. Relationships change.

A Feather Between the Lines

They mature, sometimes they disintegrate, and even those which just pootle along unchallenged don't stay the same. How foolish would it be to assume any former liaison would be simmering away on the back burner either waiting to be re-lit or extinguished completely without complication?

Scuttling along Beaumont Street, late as usual, in a pair of jeans a size too small, the zip descending lower with every step, I looked every one of my sixty years. Another wakeful night rounded off by oversleeping in the morning and a face full of car-park-applied makeup did not show me at my best.

Maybe it was just as well. Looking alluring was unnecessary. Appearing as a grotesque version of my former self, an apprentice at Madame Tussaud's first attempt to capture the mature woman, might solve issues with prospective flirtations.

The pain in my guts was real. Despite the tight waistband being freed by the popping of the button, there remained a visceral agony which I associated with departure lounges at airports, the half hour before exams and standing on the top board at a swimming pool contemplating diving off.

Just short of the hotel entrance, I stopped and caught my breath. Last chance to run back to the car. Well, probably not run given the state of the jeans. My stomach was spilling out beneath my carefully chosen sweater – an item of clothing I would not now be able to remove casually if the temperature rose because it would expose the waistband and its inability to meet in the middle.

Would he recognise me? Would he look straight past searching for the twenty-three-year-old version of me to come through the door? That would be devastating. Even if he was bald and grossly overweight, sallow skinned and dressed like an American tourist in elasticated waist cargo shorts and a T-shirt with a lurid logo, I wanted the upper hand. It would be hard to achieve that, given how I presented.

I took a deep breath, zipped the jeans up to the top and stood under the glass canopy at the entrance. Three outsized Union Jacks waved from poles jutting out from a balcony directly above me. The saints, Patrick, Andrew and George, combining to herald the lunatic intention and undoubted folly of what was about to happen. Gripping a handrail, I tightened my stomach muscles and walked up the few steps through the grand portal which led to the open door of the hotel. It was a Hogwarts experience, Victorian Gothic architecture at its best. The sorting hat lay somewhere inside, about to welcome me to 'Bloody-Idiots', the house for people who have lost not only their sense of reality and proportion but also self-respect. Eight months previously I'd only imagined this reunion was a possibility. It's one thing inhabiting a dream world, but what happens when reality crashes into that dream? I was about to find out.

2

Six months earlier

Sunday 13th November 2022

"Whore!" Just the one word. It was clear it was me who was being addressed. I was alone.

"A whore with a flair for drama!" a woman's voice continued, shouting up to the window. "Tell me it's not true." I ignored the cacophony reverberating between the houses in the lane outside. "A sexually alluring adulteress, a femme fatale who lures her lover to share a debauched lifestyle. Don't deny it."

That's not what you expect to hear in a village near Abingdon, not a place known for its depravity and loose morals as far as I am aware. Not yet. My mum used to say, "Still waters run deep," with enough of an air of authenticity to suggest she may have had proof. Suburban gossip was always her speciality. There is always hope something exciting might happen round here.

The voice was projecting way beyond our doorstep. Those at the end of our lane and in the roads beyond could tune in to the full-volume broadcast. Something to make a dull Sunday afternoon pass with a fizz.

I hoped she'd think I was out because the car wasn't there. She couldn't have seen me in my upstairs eyrie, but she sensed I was there. "It's you. A predatory and wicked husband deceiver who seduces anyone in her path. A seductive and immoral beauty. It's got to be you!"

Her voice had risen. There was now no one in the county who could be in any doubt about exactly what she was shouting about and to whom. Had I dared look out of the window, I'd probably have seen the neighbours lined up in their front gardens taken by a sudden desire to put something in the bin. Weekend gardeners, leaf blowers suddenly silenced, would be idly dead-heading a rose bush, ears cocked and turned towards our house, alert for the next accusation. They'd be loving this, nosey bastards.

"Mercurial strumpet. Come on, open the door!"

I folded the letter up, carefully replacing it in its envelope. She's an expert at projecting loud, clearly enunciated information. All those years marshalling hormonal teenagers to lessons they didn't want to attend and forcing knowledge into heads that would rather be filled with moronic TikTok challenges and Instagram poses. They've left her with a voice which could penetrate reinforced concrete bunkers and ancient and solid stone castle walls.

If Angela thought you had something interesting to tell her, she had the ability to swoop from a great height like a bird of prey targeting a tiny field mouse. That intuition and nose for the truth should have been used by Thames Valley Police. Crime solving and successful prosecutions would have risen exponentially if, at the end of a fruitless week of sleuthing, they'd asked her up to the station for a quick flick through some scanty evidence. You don't spend a career dealing with schoolkids and their parents, navigating a staffroom peopled with prima donnas, shirkers, sociopaths and mentally unstable hysterics, without picking up a few vibes about what makes folks tick. If anyone could sniff out a drama, a scandal or, significantly, the truth at ten paces, it was Angela. But even she couldn't have known I was reading the letter – still less what its contents were.

This room, that day lit by a low-level autumnal sun, had

A Feather Between the Lines

become my refuge. I can't call it a secret hiding place – because I'd admitted to her that I had a comfy den, my son's bedroom, used as my retreat when he's not there. I mentioned it unguardedly, just once, whilst I was distracted ensuring I wasn't left with only a Rich Tea on the breaktime biscuit plate. You can't face *Of Mice and Men* with year 10 without an injection of several chocolate digestives mid-morning. She's clearly a woman who doesn't forget. You should keep secrets to yourself. Sharing one is like letting a chocoholic know you're keeping a box of truffles in the back of the cupboard to eat one by one. There's no chance any will be left next time you fancy one. I used to be an expert on secrets.

I'd ignored the doorbell, but she knew I was hiding. "I know you're up there," she called. Stupidly I chanced a peek out of the window coinciding with her stepping back from the door so she could look up and catch me. I was discovered.

She was drawing conclusions about something which hadn't yet happened and potentially never would. She couldn't possibly know, could she? I hadn't seen her for several weeks and certainly not since the letter had arrived, unexpected, bringing a shock wave of self-realisation which consumed me with guilt and excitement at the same time.

As soon as I went downstairs and opened the door her suede moccasin was inserted over the threshold so that shutting her out again would involve a deliberate act of violence on my part. "Don't deny it," she continued. "I know you too well. Grand passion. Immortal longings. It's so obviously you." I considered spoiling the cerise pink footwear (clearly new) and inflicting some GBH on the foot inside, but I reckoned she knew I'd never dare. She was right. She's a former colleague who does know me well and she wasn't going to give up. "An erotic enchantress who is charismatic and volatile. Come on, Roni, you can be all those things."

"Angela, I thought I'd explained," I said feebly. "It's not me." She remained silent giving me an old-fashioned look suggesting she wasn't having any of that. "I'm too old for one thing. I'll be sixty next month."

"Are you telling me mature women don't have feelings and can't have passionate affairs?" I didn't have an answer for that. I knew only too well that it was true. Did Angela know I'd acknowledged that? She is, after all, a mind reader who probes the innermost thoughts of other people. "The woman in question is certainly older, not some fly-by-night youngster after a sugar daddy. It's not about power or material goods, it's about passion." Angela's voice rose to the kind of crescendo which formerly could only have culminated in an invitation to the Head's office or a term of detentions. "This affair is about things money can't buy. Raw sex."

"I think you'll find money can buy that. Fairly easily," I answered back, the sure-fire way to get yourself in deeper trouble when up against a teacher.

"And who can resist death by a serpent's bite?" She'd changed tack. "On stage! It's a gift."

"I've got a phobia about snakes. I'll look old and ridiculous."

"Ellen Terry last played Cleopatra aged 75 at the Old Vic. Stick on a black bobbed wig, loads of slap and bright lights. You'll look like Elizabeth Taylor from the stalls."

"That was a film with a multi-million-dollar budget and clever photography. This is the Marketplace Theatre. I wouldn't even look like Elizabeth Taylor from the gods – if there were any."

The Marketplace Theatre sounds grander than it is. It's one up from a village hall in that it's made of brick not wood, but it is still full of the same earnest amateurs and serial organisers who live out their theatrical dreams on a smaller stage than they would really like.

"Roni, please. You're the only one that can learn the lines."

This was true. And flattering, even though I knew it was part of her game plan. I could feel the words 'OK, I'll do it – if you can't find anyone else', which seem to be implanted in small LED lights on my forehead, flashing furiously, illuminating the front porch. I'm just a girl who can't say no. And not saying no at the appropriate time had landed me in an ill-advised production of *South Pacific* singing a song entitled just that some years ago. Cavorting about the Marketplace Theatre stage with a chorus of arthritic sailors and pensioners in grass skirts wasn't the highlight of my theatrical career. Realistically, it's hard to say what has been.

So here was the truth. It was my memory she wanted for her ridiculously self-important, pretentious production. Who in their right mind wants to see an amateur production of any of Shakespeare's plays? They can go on a bit when there are famous actors you've seen on TV in them. You only stick it out because you've paid so much for the ticket.

I have turned into a philistine. I don't mind admitting it. We're barely into Act Two these days before I'm thinking about my gin and tonic in the interval and whether I can be bothered to queue up for peanuts because I forgot them on my pre-interval drinks order. I've had it with dressing Richard III up as a Nazi or having *Julius Caesar* set in contemporary Burkina Faso; I like a musical or a bit of light Coward. Short, un-taxing, plenty of time in the bar and in a theatre with sufficient lavatories so that you don't spend half the evening queuing for the two that the Victorian architect thought was sufficient for female playgoers.

"I'll let you know," I said lamely.

Angela had got a bit above herself, if I was honest. It's one thing having the vasty fields of France up on stage in the school hall where Henry V and his band of brothers recruited from the lower school are crying "God for Harry, England, and Saint George," with unbroken voices like castrati at La Scala. You can't help it, not in a school where the head teacher thinks a mix of Shakespeare and patriotism is what kids want. You can't do *Oliver!* every year.

However, the hiatus of lockdown had given her grandiose ideas about Shakespeare and the mixed bag of ageing, dubious talent that comprises The Isis Mummers.

I'd suggested a name change, but she wasn't having that. If you live near Oxford or have a passion for waterways, then you know that Isis is a name for the part of the Thames which runs from its source to round about Dorchester where it is joined by the Thame. Those not in the know, coming upon a poster on a lamppost or the society online, frequently confuse it with something to do with Iraq and Syria. We receive a huge amount of hate mail as well as the odd offer of support.

"I'll text you the date of the read-through." She was still talking as I pushed the door up to the moccasin and gently closed it. I wanted to get rid of her but not dirty the footwear. Our front door is bound to be muckier than Angela's, particularly in autumn when leaves and the last of the rose petals blow up against it, queuing for admission as soon as it's opened a chink. Fallen foliage wouldn't dare congregate by her entrance, still less seek to invade.

I didn't want to play Cleopatra. Not just because attempting Shakespeare with a cast of mainly geriatrics still looking for the bright lights on a stage the size of a small front room was lunacy. The Isis Mummers should have been doing an Agatha Christie or Tom Stoppard at best. It wasn't because I really am a 'whore with a flair for drama' and I can't come to terms with it. I'm not sure I have a flair for drama any longer and I'm certainly not a whore. I'm not even an adulteress but I was just worried that I might become one. The Queen of the Nile might rub off on me and give me, like Angela, ideas above my station.

"You should be so lucky!" my friends might have said. I'm not Cleopatra, Helen of Troy or any other female icon of the ancient world. I haven't got a face that could launch a thousand ships, not even a small dingy or rowing boat. Any woman of my age will

A Feather Between the Lines

tell you she has become invisible to men. I'm like an outdated, dog-eared magazine in the dentist's waiting room. In the absence of choice, someone might have an anxious flick through but find I'm out of date, tatty as hell and they've read it all before. If they seriously want some entertainment, not just something to stop them thinking about root canal work, then they'll invest in a newer edition.

But to my foolish mind something about that letter suggested the possibility of reconnection. I was probably deluded. I should have ignored it.

3

Back in my eyrie, I watched from the window to check she was really leaving. Unseen she pushed a remote button which lifted the boot lid of her soft-topped two-seater. It revealed a trunk completely devoid of old bits of newspaper and packaging, plastic bags of jump leads and spanners and the bits of garden which have managed to return home despite being destined for the dump. She placed her compact handbag, isolated and lonely, into the void and closed the lid without having to touch any metal. You can have a car like that if you're unmarried, childless and in receipt of a generous pension and inheritances.

I'm not bitter. Our boot is my fault. Phil tries, with his cordless vacuum and endless patience, to keep some order inside the glory hole at the back of our long-serving and ever reliable Toyota. I load it full of shopping and stuff I don't know what else to do with. I can't be bothered to keep it unsullied, and although he never accuses me directly of slovenly boot management, it's implicit. He knows I hate throwing stuff away and he loves nothing better than what he refers to as 'a clear out'.

After Angela had gone, although I'd only been down to the front door and back and was alone in the house, I returned immediately to the letter. I had to be careful where I stashed it. I certainly didn't want it accidentally dropping into the bin, slipping into a pile of newspapers and going into the recycling – or worse being found by anyone else. The letter was one secret no one knew about. Yet.

Phil would have had something sensible to say on the matter. He always has a rational comment ready to make me feel even

A Feather Between the Lines

more ridiculous. He'd have an opinion about Cleopatra and about the unexpected communication.

In Arthur's room I looked at the books which form a cocoon of literature in which both he and I could happily stay forever. No need to emerge into the real world with butterfly wings, you can explore the universe through words in his bedroom, caterpillar-like, without shedding your chrysalis dressing gown. Ideal for a daydreaming slob like me.

Phil says this is pretentious rubbish. He's probably right, voicing the kind of analysis you'd expect from the most commonsensical man on the planet, who only reads fiction when he is sitting in a deckchair on a foreign beach.

Arthur's huge collection lines the shelves that cover all four walls of his room and the landing. Like me, he never gets rid of a book. This drives Phil mad. "You'll never read them all again," he says logically, "and if you did want to look at one, you can get anything on an ebook." He has a point. "When did you last read this?" he asks, to prove it. Then he'll pick up a random yellowing paperback with an impossibly cheap £2.99 on the back and a spine which would crack making the pages spew out like propaganda leaflets dropped from an enemy plane if you did try to reread it.

He doesn't understand that the book represents so much more than the story its words tell. Its price and cover design reveal the period of its publication. Its title reminds me not only the first time I read it but often subsequent visits all recalling what else was happening in my life at that time. Holidays, exam revision, feeding babies in the middle of the night, hospital stays, moments of sadness and times of extreme joy: they are all accompanied by books. Sometimes a lingering bookmark adds to the memory: a ticket, leaflet or receipt which helps root a reading place to the story inside. Phil doesn't reread fiction. He says there's no point because he can remember the plot. For him they are just stories and even the name scrawled inside the front cover is irrelevant.

'V. McNamara 6B' tells me everything I need to remember: an A level set text and memory of Mrs Taylor, who taught me to appreciate it. 'Happy birthday, Ron, love Mum'. The careful handwriting brings her back immediately. 'Roni McNa, Cambridge 1983' finds me back at the Sidgwick site sitting next to my college friend Mary and as far away as possible from Perfect Penny, always on the lookout to point out my failings as a student compared with her own impeccability. 'Barking Lending Library' gives me a pang of thief's guilt. 'Webster Ferris'. Well, that's always a hard one, his distinctive script not only claiming ownership but making spidery annotations in the margins. More guilt, multi-layered this time, mixed with the shock of static recognition of his name and the reminder of him it provokes.

Unusually, with my children, it's my son who is the reader. I spent my career trying, mostly unsuccessfully, to get boys to read. My girls rarely have their noses in fiction.

World Book Day at school was always a challenge for Jessica, who is like her father, neat and organised with her feet firmly grounded in real life and facts. Dressing up is not something she is comfortable with. Finding a costume to represent *The Guinness Book of World Records*, her favourite bedtime story, was a task I dreaded year after year. There are only so many times a school will accept a child in regulation games kit half-heartedly pretending to be the world's fastest runner.

Katie was easier. Her favoured childhood books were full of dragons and mystical heroes with vaguely rude-sounding Scandinavian-type names like Tyrdkrapp, Aasstynk or Fylthewenkka. It's easy to portray the high priestess Dyrefartar with an old curtain and some dangly beads. Nowadays, if she ever delves into a book, it will be returned to the Oxfam bookshop looking for another reader and saving the planet from over production of paper seconds after she has finished the last word.

A Feather Between the Lines

She mostly favours tortuously written self-help books concerning healing, energy cleansing and spiritual balance.

Arthur's book collection includes those he has written himself. He thinks I have read them but I'm lying about that too. I've started them with good intentions. He writes experimental literature which is supposed to play with form and conventions. There is no set style or way of presenting the words, there's certainly no plot. Arthur is very successful, I'm pleased to say, although he never has any money. My latest secret is that I can't finish any of his work. Mum called me Barking's Biggest Bookworm (not a title she necessarily thought was flattering) and I still read all the time, but I can't read my own son's work. Luckily a degree in English Literature equips you with convincing critical bullshit, designating motive and intent to any theme or imagery you attribute to the author, without fear of contradiction. This can be applied whether you have read the book or not. My critiques are entirely spurious and, because his work is so impenetrable, whatever I say, it's bound to have some validity.

That afternoon, of course, I hadn't been reading a book, I'd been transfixed by the letter. A proper letter: one with news and opinions, which had come in the post with a stamp and an envelope and all the exciting old-fashioned accessories that used to arrive with mail that was written by hand.

Even if it is a scrawl in Biro and not cursive script attractively drawn by a fountain pen and ink, a personal letter is always more exciting than a bill or a speeding fine and certainly superior to anything which arrives on a screen. You probably know who it's from before you even slit the envelope open. I knew who had written to me. The distinctive handwriting heralded his message and set my heart racing even before I'd read a word.

I hoped Phil's ability to ignore emotion and consider the facts would help when I did finally disclose the letter's arrival and its contents. Thirty-seven years is a long time to sit on an undetonated bomb and the truth was I had more than one in my armoury – the most explosive of which would be news even to the letter writer. I'd got used to them lurking around, like unexploded ordnance on a French farm in the Somme or whopper 1000 pounders from the Blitz waiting to be discovered during building works in the City. I was hoping their fuses might have decayed making explosion impossible. I thought I was going to get away with it until technology caught up with me and, paradoxically, an old-fashioned letter came through my letterbox.

I don't know why I kept rereading it. I knew its contents off by heart. I suppose I had to remind myself that it really existed, that it wasn't some daydream I'd had whilst nodding off after lunch or something I imagined in a vivid nightmare. I didn't want to drop my bombshell unnecessarily and put the biggest cat in Oxfordshire amongst my family of pigeons for no reason. But it was real and I was going to have to deal with it – not that I really wanted to. I'd have preferred to keep things how they were, how they looked before the wretched college reunion. Life was so much simpler when I just had to keep my little secrets to myself.

I slotted the letter back into *The Chamber of Secrets,* which I thought was an appropriate hiding place. Arthur loved all the Harry Potter books as a boy. He rereads books but I decided if he came home for the weekend he would be unlikely to choose the second Harry Potter as his bedtime story. The letter could remain undiscovered for a bit longer whilst I decided how to deal with it.

There was no denying the truth was coming, and I would have to let it through the door along with all the fallen leaves, dried-up rose petals, twigs and junk-mail leaflets holed by wandering snails making a beeline for our threshold.

4

Predictably, as it was Sunday afternoon, Phil was at the dump when Angela was shouting about Cleopatra in the lane outside. I wondered if she would have given such a display if he had been there. Phil knows Angela. He has provided technical help for previous performances, both for the Isis Mummers and various school productions. He would have answered the door and, of course, I wouldn't have been upstairs reading the letter in the first place. She'd chosen her time carefully.

Visiting the amenity refuse facility, as the tip is now known, is his weekend treat. He loves that place. It's his spiritual home, a place where a cathartic karma descends upon him as he tips unwanted possessions into designated containers.

Unfortunately, as it turned out, I'd opted out of that trip. I break out into a cold sweat and have a panic attack at the thought of throwing any of my possessions away. I spend as little time as possible at the dump to avoid the painful, jabbing doubt, 'might that still be useful for something?'. If I go, I have to stay in the car to try and take my mind off any permanent separation between me and a cherished item that is undoubtedly occurring. Yet I'm compelled to watch out of the window, like a one-woman SOS rescue service, so I can pre-empt the loss of something vital.

There are three employees at the site. The short, elderly one must be the boss. He has raised a rescued garden table and parasol up on wooden blocks and positioned a couple of barstools and a few reprieved garden gnomes and ornaments alongside. This lookout post is stationed in the centre of the tipping area and from it, aloft, he surveys the scene rarely moving except to change barstool when the sun moves round.

A second man ferrets about amongst the trash, occasionally pulling out an item and putting it in a separate pile. These must be treasures whose value had remained unrecognised by their former owners.

The third is an officious sergeant major type who berates the casual dumper who doesn't adhere to the strict regulations about what goes where. His zealous and sharp-eyed surveillance misses nothing. Heaven help you if you put wood into the metals container or try and deposit your garden waste in 'fabrics and clothing ABSOLUTELY NO PILLOWS OR DUVETS'.

If I was outside, paralysed in poised-to-chuck position, this fanatic might take a view and consign me to one of the bottomless pits of mysterious items that lurk in the large hoppers. I'm sure there's a sign on one of them inviting collection of 'clapped out menopausal women who can't be arsed'. This jobsworth, whose name badge not only tells me he is called Ryan but also jokily boasts 'Recycling – See you again!', would love to tip me in.

After Phil left, I'd performed a pointless check to ensure the letter hadn't somehow made its way into the pile of random but to my mind vital items he had selected for disposal. I didn't mean to spend such a long time rereading it, but I couldn't resist.

I was warmed by the sudden bright sun spilling through the window. Looking out at the piles of leaves which the wind had blown onto the verges at the side of the lane reminded me of that autumn in Cambridge. That afternoon when, as the evenings arrived earlier, I had kicked my way through piles of swept-up foliage towards the old-fashioned comfort of that ancient room – his just for the year. It was the moment when we had finally acknowledged our attraction to and longing for each other. I always thought of him in autumn. I thought of him most of the time, but particularly in autumn, longing still.

A Feather Between the Lines

It was a fantasy, of course – something to keep my imagination active during dull staff meetings or boring car journeys, something to think of in bed as I drifted off to sleep where, like all good fantasies, I could control the narrative. No hideous shocks or disappointing plot lines, it was all under my control. I was the star part, still with the body and inquiring mind of a girl in her early twenties, and he my co-star, retaining the sparkling intellect and bullish and unpredictable personality that frightened and excited me in equal measure. In my fantasy scenario I could ignore the fact that he disappeared from my life, suddenly and completely and, to my mind, unreasonably. He was selfish and he'd hurt me badly but like a film adaptation of a book where scenes and characters are manipulated for the change in medium, I ignored all that in my sanitised version. Perhaps he wasn't that person anymore. Maybe he was worse. But that didn't use to matter because it wasn't real.

That was until I had received that up-to-date piece of him. The letter which showed he was still alive, still in the USA and still thinking about me too. A useful update for fantasy purposes that it might have been, it also told me that he was coming here. Not just to the UK but to Oxford – right up the road within cycling distance not only for Phil but, with a tail wind and an uncharacteristic surge of energy, for me as well.

Why hadn't I told Phil? I could have done. I could even have said, "You'll never guess who's written to me?" We could have had a laugh about it and about the sender. Phil would have been reasoned and clear in his response.

I should have mentioned it, but I hadn't. He is the kindest and most understanding of men, my husband. Throughout our long marriage his gentle support and common sense have allowed me to get away with being the quirky, slightly useless but fun one. "Honestly, Ron, how does he put up with you?" people ask when I'm entertaining everyone with a story about my knickers being flown from a flagpole. I haven't really had to grow up fully.

Roni, the perfect foil to practical Phil. We're a low budget double act: Yin and Yang, coming to an anecdote near you soon. He has allowed me to inhabit the world of daydreams and fantasy that characterised my childhood and adolescence, way beyond the time when most people have to get a grip and start playing the adult.

I knew why I'd kept it quiet, why I'd hidden the letter amongst the books in Arthur's bedroom and not left it on the table downstairs for him to see. Realistically, I could have done so. Phil is so honourable that if I'd left the opened envelope lying about he wouldn't have had a little sneaky look to see what was inside. I would have done.

What kind of person reads the last chapter of a book before they get to the end? Which bastard winds up a sister-in-law who takes everything at face value, or takes advantage of her mother-in-law's hearing loss for her own amusement? Who finds a neighbour's obsession with finding a partner hilarious? Me. I'm despicable and I have taken advantage of Phil's understanding nature over the years. There are things I haven't shared with him which I should have.

Those unappreciated bedrocks which formed the foundation of my childhood and adolescence, Mum and Dad, Nan, Gran, they would have forgiven me even if they didn't understand or approve of what happened. I never told them either. Besides, Mum wouldn't have wanted me to be the subject of the gossip she rolled out with hairpins and curlers at her salon. And Gran would never have told Father O'Connor at confession – he only received carefully filtered sins. They're all gone now anyway, consigned to anecdotes and fading photographs. I got away with it. But Phil would have every right to complain; his support was not guaranteed.

He returned from the dump invigorated. It has a strange effect on him, cleansing and rebooting his life, a kind of colonic irrigation of unnecessary possessions. I'm so envious. I'd love to be able to shake off the accumulation of nearly sixty years of stuff. I know that if a huge sinkhole opens up under our house and the whole lot disappears for ever, life will go on. Phil will have wise words to say, probably pointing out that we can get a much nicer replacement on the insurance. But it worries me.

I met Phil when he was doing technical things, shining lamps at people and sticking fat electrical cables to the stage with gaffer tape. The Pared-Down Players were my university equivalent of The Isis Mummers. When we took a show to the Edinburgh Festival, Phil and I began our relationship.

We didn't dwell on past liaisons either of us had had. Best not to. They don't always paint you in a good light. I don't suppose he had any dirty linen to wash, in public or in private, but my personal soiled laundry remained well and truly concealed.

From Arthur's window I watched Phil vacuuming the boot and then getting his bike out for its weekly maintenance check. I took him out a cup of tea, recognising that this was the ideal moment to mention the letter, casually, in a chatty, gossipy kind of way, whilst he felt evacuated and unencumbered, high on his tip trip.

He grinned at me when I gave him the tea. "Dump was busy," he chortled as if to preclude any of my sarcastic comments about visiting the household waste and recycling centre being a popular thing to do on a day off. "The bossy one went ballistic at some woman who was trying to put a toaster in scrap metals. He has a very unpleasant manner. There's no need. I was able to explain to her that although the toaster was metal on the outside, it should be disposed of in small electricals. It's an easy mistake to make if you're new to waste disposal." You can't accuse Phil of not being helpful or committed to recycling and correct refuse management.

"What's for supper?" he asked in a tone implying that he probably already knew the answer.

"Chateaubriand with beurre maître d'hôtel, duchesse potatoes, a bouquetière of legumes and béarnaise sauce."

"OK. I might just make the supermarket before it shuts if I go now," he replied. One of the nice things about being with someone for nearly thirty-eight years is that much can be communicated by reading between the lines.

He's at his best as a man with a mission. Thank God for the Phils of this world. I have the hugest admiration for him, not only for dealing with my poor housekeeping but also for the flow chart of decision making that he uses in all circumstances. The military and government need people like Phil. They don't want people faffing about deciding which cushions look best on the sofa in the Oval Office, indecisive about treaty signing ("Oo I don't know, it might upset some people…and have we used an appropriate font?") or delaying employment of rescue attempts in disaster zones ("Hang on, I've got to pack, what's the weather like at this time of year?"). Not when there are evil despots and natural catastrophes to respond to.

He was back in the car, off to make the 4 o'clock closing deadline between us and beans on toast. And I hadn't mentioned the letter. I decided I wouldn't have to disclose exactly when it had arrived. No hurry. Up to my old tricks – lying by omission. My top-scoring sin amongst the large selection Gran made me aware were available to fallible mortals just like myself. Perhaps I'd send a reply first.

It would have been irresponsible to do nothing, given what I had learned and what I had suspected all along. It wasn't just about me anymore. I got out a piece of paper, excited to be writing a real letter for once. How hard could it be? I planned to write Ferris a brief response, tell Phil what he needed to know and hope for the best.

For almost the first time, since I had first held a pen to paper, I, the writer, the reader, the wordsmith, was without words. There

A Feather Between the Lines

was not a single inky mark on the sheet, just a large tear which had fallen centrally on the page. A well-aimed water bomb producing a series of ripples, which spread out rapidly towards the edges of the page like a dropped pebble invading a previously still pond.

5

A week later
Sunday 20th November 2022

Despite constantly turning the possibilities over in my mind and acting through scenarios in which I delivered the news with varying levels of brutal honesty, I remained conflicted about what to do.

I almost came straight out with it when Phil was eating his breakfast one morning. "You'll never guess what," I began.

I didn't continue because Phil's attention had been grabbed by news which had arrived via an alert on his phone. It concerned a one-way temporary traffic light system in place on the bridge in Abingdon. He regularly points out how cyclists as well as motorists need to check for traffic snarl-ups and plan their journeys accordingly, never missing an opportunity to illustrate that advice with a real-life situation.

I choose four wheels over two at every opportunity and, in Phil's eyes, just set off aimlessly on a wing and a prayer – even when only going the short distance to the shops or the station. He is frustrated by this lack of planning and organisation for even the simplest of journeys. No amount of downloaded apps and real-time traffic updates helpfully suggested by him improve what he considers to be my casual attitude to time management and

A Feather Between the Lines

devotion to the car. He's not a man to give up where common sense is involved. When technology is spurned, information about contraflows and roadworks (and suggestions for avoiding both) are imparted face to face in the vain hope that I might avoid adding an extra ten minutes to my journey and will be on time.

Phil's obsession with traffic issues reminds me of my dad. When we got a television which had Ceefax, an early teletext information service, Dad was delighted. Once he had worked out how to use it he spent hours checking in with the news, keeping up with the racing and other sports results and looking at last minute holiday bargains for trips which he had no intention of going on. However, his obsession with country-wide traffic issues bordered on the fanatic. From his armchair in our front room in Barking, he would announce with an unnecessary level of urgency, "There are terrible hold-ups in the city centre in Dunfermline." Undoubtedly this would have been helpful information if Mum or I had been gripped by a sudden desire to drive 450 miles up to Fife and explore the ancient capital of Scotland.

"Steer well clear of Bridge Street," Phil advised, which I took as a suggestion to avoid other things too.

I had stayed away from peeking at the letter during the week. I had even resisted the 'just check it's still there' routine. It's embarrassing, but this is the maximum level of self-control I can muster.

I'm feeble when faced with a tin of Celebrations or a newly opened pack of Jaffa Cakes. I'm drawn to the words 'spoiler alert' in any context and the one genre of fiction I should not be allowed access to is twisty plotted crime.

I often drive past the house where Agatha Christie lived and think how furious she'd be if she knew how I'm compelled to read her novels in a deliberately non-sequential way. All that planning she must have done to lay red herrings and hints in her plots and here is someone who reads them determined to discover who dunnit often even before the 'it' has been done itself. Is it a hangover from deconstructing literature when I was a student? Or just a proclivity to give in to temptation and ruin everything for myself? I waste a lot of time thinking about this kind of conundrum – a good example of lack of discipline. Time wasting has always been one of my major suits.

I was picking out a book in Arthur's room to enjoy on my Sunday home alone when there was a knock at the door. Not Angela again, please.

I'd managed to last the week without responding to her plea to stand in front of a poorly-painted backdrop of an Egyptian palace in a nylon Claudia Winkleman-style wig on the stage of the Marketplace Theatre. The irony of a tragedy pitting love against duty with a cast of eight and an audience of not many more was not lost on me. Yet I couldn't even bring myself to say no to this ridiculous proposal.

Angela firstly was a colleague, the Head of the English and Drama department at the school where I taught. She had become my friend yet even in retirement there is still an unvoiced but recognised acknowledgement of rank between us.

Free of school, rather than retreat to a warm room with a good book and a packet of Tunnock's teacakes, Angela follows a self-directed programme of museum and theatre visits, cultural activities and long-haul holidays as well as pouring more of her boundless energies into the Isis Mummers. As with her pupils, she gets the best out of an untalented and self-deluded company of what even the most charitable might struggle to call performers. Saying no to Angela required reserves of grit and resolution which I lack.

"Roni, it's cold out here!" a voice pleaded. Not Angela, thankfully, but Mandy, our neighbour. As soon as I opened the door a chink, she and a trail of fallen foliage blew in uninvited.

"Is Phil here?" she asked although she knew the answer

because when he was bagging up her garden waste before he left, he'd briefed her about the section of the Coastal Path route he would be undertaking the following weekend.

Mandy prefers to come over when Phil is out. He's useful for mending things and tackling her hedge with his battery-powered super loppers but he is also superb at getting rid of people he thinks have overstayed their welcome. It's a skill I've never mastered. Discussion about accessories and colour wheel theory and the suitability of several swatches of fabric and samples of paint that all look the same colour is pointless to his mind. She'd barely have a biscuit poised for dunking in her cup before Phil would have got her out the door.

Mandy went straight into the kitchen. She filled the kettle with water and switched it on. "I'm having second thoughts about the Moroccan souk," she confided, looking in the biscuit tin to see if there was anything inside. "No Hobnobs?" She has an addiction to these treats and considers not being offered one to eat with her cuppa the height of domestic ineptitude. It's one of the many areas in housekeeping where she considers I fall short, an opinion where she is allied with my mother-in-law. And presumably my husband – although he's too nice to say.

Mandy has a trio of obsessions: her ex-husband and his parsimony, her search for 'a new man', and what she calls 'refresh and refurb'. This involves redesigning the fixtures and fittings in her home and complete redecoration. She is never happier than when delivering a monologue about one of them whilst dunking an oaty biscuit.

To my mind, the lack of funds from the ex, constant wish for a fresh look and a new partner are easily solved. "Put in your profile that you are looking for a painter and decorator," I once suggested when the conversation rotated to the online search for love. "Save what you spend on those glossy design magazines and you'll be able to buy the materials and he'll do the work for nothing."

When she first moved in next door, before her divorce, she and her ex cohabited with what she described as 'Rustic Provencal'. A description which put me in mind of expensive artisan loaves rather than the lavender fields and olive groves of Southeast France.

Shortly after their house had been transformed into a 3D Cézanne experience, he left her for a twenty-five-year-old with a brand new top-of-the-range BMW and no interest in interior design.

Impulsively, as a way of expunging every trace of him, Mandy replaced rural Ménerbes with a brief foray into 'American Abstract Expressionism' – migraine inducing blocks of red and yellow.

Most recently, she'd been through an interminable period of 'New England Shabby Chic'. Everything was painted shades of cream and white then immediately sanded down to look like it needed repainting. She obsessed over a colour chart consisting of rectangles of what looked like the same colour. Unadvisedly she asked Phil his opinion. "Go for the cream one," he exclaimed exasperated.

"Which one is that? 'Cornish Curd' or 'Old Bones'? Or are you calling 'Milky Whey' cream? I'm not sure it is."

Phil chooses paint by a quick mental calculation about quality versus price and durability and then picks the least offensive colour. "Curdled Codswallop! They're all off white. Any one will do. I can't tell the difference," he added, hoping that would help without realising it might annoy her.

Mandy is never rude to Phil. He might refuse to change her tyre next time it's flat or not take her bins out when he notices she's forgotten. Phil's obsessed with getting the correct bin out on the right day. He has no time for people who mix up recycling with general rubbish or put the wrong things in the food waste canister, not when the council send an easy-to-understand leaflet.

Phil had spent a very long time writing names like COWPARSLEY in big black letters on the lids of her collection of half-used paint. I'd have written CREAM on all of them for a laugh, but Phil is much nicer than me. 'Off Milk', 'Rancid Yoghurt', all those pretentious names belong in the bin, though, as all responsible householders know, paint must be taken to the dump for specialist disposal. I hadn't yet told Phil that it looked like all the half-full tins he'd carefully labelled and stored in her shed were headed that way.

Inspired by the Moroccan Souk, her house was relocating to a fragrant market whose scents and vibrant colours were as far from that previous insipid colour chart as a paint manufacturer in search of new trends could travel. She was considering drenching everything in what she called 'jewel colours of the Sahara'. I told her that any desert gems are buried under ever shifting dunes of sand so she'd just need to paint everything yellow. She said I was being facetious. Again.

"I was expecting Angela," I admitted as Mandy realised that a stale cream cracker with poor dunking potential was all there was in my tin. "Has she asked you about Shakespeare?"

I introduced Mandy to the Isis Mummers. Although she gets stage fright and can't learn the lines, she comes along because one day a man who is under seventy who is in search of a relationship might join.

"She said something about *Antony and Cleopatra*," Mandy replied, rooting through my cupboard for a heavy-duty biscuit supply she foolishly thought I had hidden and not eaten immediately. "If there are no Hobnobs, I fancy something with chocolate. Where've you hidden the Tunnock's wafers? I bet you've got some of those teacake ones somewhere."

"I'm trying to lose weight," I explained truthfully. Mandy's diets always coincided with potential new partners. She gave me a look which combined suspicion with a conviction that this was likely to be a fruitless project. I certainly didn't want Mandy getting wind of the contents of my letter.

"Apparently it's a big cast with lots of non-speaking but vital roles and tons of male parts." Angela's transparent recruitment policy was obvious.

"That's the problem. Well, two of them."

"I've been messaging someone online," she announced, dipping a bendy Jacob's cracker into her cup. This was not news. Mandy spends a lot of her time contacting potential lovers. "He lives in Scotland."

I tried not to react and point out the geographical hurdle which was going to be the first impediment to true love. He didn't just live over the border, a mere change from the M6 to the A74 at Gretna Green, but 'not far' from Drumnadrochit – about 250 miles further on. "It's not as far as Inverness," she protested when I raised an eyebrow, "and it's where the monster is." It took great and unusual self-discipline on my part not to fill the pause with an obvious quip about what kind of beast she had been talking to. But Mandy was going to find out herself because she then told me she was going to visit him. She doesn't hang about.

"What do you think of tartan carpets?" she asked in all seriousness. "I saw a picture of Balmoral once and they're everywhere. Queen Victoria had them all over." It seemed likely that the potential Loch Ness lover had diverted the restyle from Cape Cod to the Highlands rather than Marrakech.

Friends' chatter about long-term relationships is boring and confined to moans about not putting dirty washing in the linen box, reluctance to remove the core of a spent loo roll from the holder or walking over freshly hoovered carpets with muddy feet. Phil does none of these things, I might add. I'm capable of all of them and more. There was little doubt that Mandy would fill me in on every passionate detail of her visit. It was good to live vicariously through her frolics in the land of love.

6

Another two weeks later
Saturday 3rd December 2022

Whilst Mandy was having her highland fling, I was headed for Reigate and Phil's ancestral seat – always a treat. Now I was no longer working I wasn't able to complain about this being part of my Saturday.

I'd stopped teaching at the end of the previous summer term. My sixtieth birthday was in sight and my pension beckoned. Hoo-bloody-ray! Phil loves work but he could see I'd had enough. He sits in a quiet, carpeted office with a coffee machine and a water cooler, occasionally going 'on site' and seemingly taking as much time off as he wants. He doesn't spend weekdays trying to convince TikToking adolescents with tiny attention spans that they might find reading a book a more rewarding use of their time.

Phil's elderly parents were pandered to by his older sister Paula, who lives near to the family home and is unmarried and retired. First call for everything parent-related, she bore her cross with a thinly disguised irritation and a realisation, too late, that location and circumstance had handed her the short straw. Phil did his share – but that didn't get in the way of over sixty years of sibling rivalry. He was endlessly helpful, but it was never enough and Paula bore an unreasonable grudge against her brother, who spent hours on a Saturday queuing in traffic so that he could take his mother out to the local garden centre for her weekly question about the cheese scone.

A car journey would be a good time to bring up the matter of the letter. Its arrival anyway. Casually throwing it into the conversation as Phil navigated driving down the M4 and round the M25 would be an easy way to introduce the concept of renewed contact, assuage some of my guilt and prepare the ground for any further revelations I might be considering.

"Remember that college alumni magazine that arrived a few weeks ago?" I asked casually, aware that as a conversation starter it was somewhat random.

"With the cover photo of you with a lurid coloured drink and cocktail umbrellas in your hair? How could I forget? Did you give permission for them to use it?"

"I don't even remember them taking it. I expect I signed something at the reunion without realising."

"Why do people travelling at 40 miles per hour think the middle lane is the place to be? I've left a gap for him to come into the inside lane."

"Those magazines get sent all over the world to past students."

"The wonder of the web. Honestly, I really don't want to undertake; that's a very dangerous manoeuvre."

"Some people may have recognised me, even though I did look ridiculous."

"Now a truck is having to overtake him in the fast lane. Professional drivers should know better."

I abandoned the conversation. Phil's focus was on correct driving procedures as detailed in The Highway Code. He was busy avoiding an accident. I didn't want to distract him by mentioning a name which could well spark a lapse in concentration, however brief.

When the danger zone was passed and traffic had thinned, Phil

A Feather Between the Lines

asked me if I minded him practising his French. He connects his phone to the car's audio system and responds to various questions from a language app he has downloaded ahead of a cycling trip to France. He is an intelligent man but his abilities lie in what are now known as STEM subjects. Opportunities to mention the letter were prevented during the rest of the journey by Phil announcing, 'Wee, jepron due pane seal vue plate,' 'Be-ann sure, eel fate showed oh zure dwee,' and other impenetrable phrases to passing motorists.

Pamela was ready in her coat, sitting on a chair in the hall at 39 Meadowmead Close, when we arrived. She had probably been there for most of the morning, even though Phil calls his mother ten minutes ahead of his arrival (never from a moving vehicle, naturally). Her party trick is opening the door before your finger has left the bell push and greeting you with a face suggesting a strong level of irritation about lateness – warranted or not.

Next stop: the garden centre café for the question of the week.

"Philip, ask them what kind of cheese is in this scone. I hope it's not Stilton. Those blue veins are mould you know."

The fourteen-year-old behind the counter is barely aware that it contains cheese at all – let alone that there might be different varieties. She never knows.

"Cheddar, Mother," Phil replies without asking anyone. When I'm there, I have a bit of fun.

"It's Queso de l'Alt Urgell i la Cerdanya this week, Pamela. It's a Catalan cheese." I was proud of this internet discovery, the cheese with a ridiculously long name. I varied it – sometimes I suggested Tibetan yak cheese or Italian Casu Marzu, which is served with live maggots and has a long-lasting aftertaste.

"What did Veronica say, Philip?"

"It's cheddar, Mother," Phil confirms ignoring me.

Next stop: the nursing home. Phil's father, a quiet and kindly man, used to be an older version of his son except with a giant potting shed and gardening gloves. Three years previously, Peter Spittal had downed tools, both metaphorically and literally, and gone to live in the local nursing home.

He had run the white flag of surrender up the pole of his marriage years ago, when we were still using pounds, shillings and pence. He existed as a living stereotype who, when he stopped travelling on the 7:29 from Reigate to Waterloo via Clapham Junction and the 17:32 back again, spent much of his time in his well-appointed den at the bottom of the garden.

A miserable serf when inside the house, he was lord of a garden-based outdoor kingdom when in its grounds. Pamela only went outside to hang out washing and very occasionally to sit briefly in a deckchair when the weather was warm enough. Even then 'lounging about' was accompanied by a commentary on how much there was to be getting on with indoors and how she should be doing it. "A house doesn't run itself. Idle hands are the devil's playthings," she'd say looking at me and then her husband in an obvious way.

Peter's potting shed was the fortress in which, when he wasn't getting high on creosote fumes, he listened to Radio 3 and took refuge from Phil's mother and her list of tasks. "That which always has something beyond itself," he quoted, alluding to this catalogue of chores, which were never finished. It was pinned to a cork board in the kitchen and detailed jobs to be done about the home. No sooner had he accomplished one than another filled its place. And, exponentially, something simple such as 'change the bulb' became 'replace light fittings in the hall' before morphing into 'rewire the whole of the downstairs'.

On family visits he would entertain the children and me in his garden HQ, all of us seeking escape from Pamela. We shared his secret supply of wine gums and fruit pastilles, a conspiracy of silence ensuring that his cache was safe from confiscation.

He had a small selection of conversational gambits. One was

A Feather Between the Lines

a comment about family names. "We're all Ps," he'd remark. "Ps in the Spittal pod." I almost believed he wished Phil had married a Polly or a Penny just to perpetuate the tradition. He called me Poni or Peronica – a harmless but intensely irritating 'joke' he never seemed to tire of. I liked to point out that although Phil's name began with a P, phonetically he was an F.

"We should have called him Pill!" He'd guffaw at his own lame and equally annoying response. I got the feeling there weren't many laughs left in Peter Spittal's world.

Now the potting shed had been swapped for a comfortable, list-free existence doused in a cocktail of strong cleaning solutions and faintly medical odours. An initial whiff on arrival served as a signal for me to behave myself.

"Peter, your wife and your son and daughter-in-law are here," announced a care worker to an assembly of elderly residents seated in a circle in the day room. Some looked up hopeful of a visitor whilst others scowled, wishing desperately not to be called Peter so that the interlopers were not destined for them.

My grandmother suffered from dementia, spending her last years confused as to whether the war was really over. Daily life was interspersed with worries about air-raids and rationing and an underlying fear that any minute Hitler might be riding down Longbridge Road in Barking giving a Nazi salute from an open-topped Mercedes. Nan lived with us and Mum took her to her hairdressing salon so she could keep an eye on her whilst she was colouring and perming. No one could take Peter Spittal to work. Not unless they were employed as a football steward or owned a Glaswegian pub.

"Bollocks up your arse!" shouted Peter by way of recognition and a greeting.

Unexpectedly and surprisingly, during the Covid pandemic, Peter Spittal had undergone a potty-mouthed sea-change. Spouting the vocabulary of Malcolm Tucker driving a white van in rush hour, he had been swiftly moved to the dementia wing. Uncharitably, I found it amusing that a man who had previously never sworn or cussed now spoke very few other words. His communications consisted only of vulgar insults and appallingly crude and foul descriptions. It was as if he had spent his whole life saving them up and his finale was letting them all burst out.

"How are you, Peter?" I asked, bracing myself for the reply.

"Piss off!" he grinned welcomingly. It could have been worse; he was saving the heavy-duty language for his wife. "Knackers, goolies, nuts and gonads," he shouted. "Shove them up your arse." Pamela's failing hearing had its advantages. She had no need to curtail a desire to collapse in hysterics like me. I'd love to say that kind of thing to Pamela but have to take pleasure vicariously from Peter's ability to do so.

"Crackers and nuts at Christmas? I'll see what I can do. I'm not promising," she replied. The rest of the residents looked on oblivious.

Naturally, conversation is one-sided. Phil usually tells his father about his week and information about cycle rides, trips to the dump and work projects are usually well received and always commented upon.

"We're working with the architects on a new supermarket in Wantage. It's an innovative design so there are some engineering issues," Phil explained.

"Fuck you, great big dicks!" Peter commented approvingly.

"I've walked another section of the Coastal Path with Geoff and Malcolm."

"Wankers!" Peter shouted loudly, a sentiment I shared heartily but couldn't vocalise for obvious reasons.

Phil is not concerned about his father's vocabulary, but I know it affects him. Even the most rational mourn the loss of the person they once knew. He was quiet in the car on the way home. It wasn't the moment to mention the letter or its author.

7

Too early for my liking
Saturday 10th December 2022

It seemed dawn had only recently broken. As I stepped outside, my breath, like a massive exhalation of vape fumes, formed a con trail so it looked as if a low flying jet had passed through our front garden. No need to lay a trail of breadcrumbs behind me like Hansel and Gretel, my route next door was clearly marked.

Mandy had been insistent that we needed to leave at 8:30 to get to Oxford for our trip to a coffee shop. I had pointed out that there were convenient cafés much nearer to us or, better, that a kettle and jar of Nescafe in our warm kitchen would produce the same drink at a fraction of the price. I was informed in no uncertain terms that the report of her trip to the Highlands was best described in the centre of the city, at a weekend amongst a crowd of Christmas shoppers. Overpriced coffee obviously tastes so much better when you're wearing your thickest coat and have built up a thirst in a traffic jam beforehand. What's more she wanted to go by bus.

"It'll be an experience," she suggested improbably. Travel to another part of Britain had obviously encouraged Mandy to consider putting 'explorer and adventurer' on her online profile.

"Maybe she has 'news'," Phil had suggested grinning. "Church bells may be ringing. Or an appointment at the register office at least."

Surely not this quickly! The short break amongst the heather and whisky was the first time Mandy had met Nessie in person. Would she be so rash? She'd refused to give me any details about how it had gone when we'd fixed up the unnecessary trek for a cappuccino.

I noticed a set of bagpipes in her hall when I peered through the glass in the door. The tartan makeover was obviously on. I surmised with some relief that this might mean the tryst had been successful, but that Mandy was not moving north immediately. I knew I was in for a long session; if she'd had an enjoyable trip, it would make our outing more pleasant at least.

"Och aye!" I shouted when she came to the door. "I hope you're not intending to play those pipes. Not when I'm at home anyway." Mandy ignored me. "Tell you what, I'll send you a surreptitious text when Phil is in full flow about his next leg of Britain's Coastal Path, and you can blow really loudly with my blessing."

"You don't deserve him," she scolded. "I got them in the charity shop. No one wants to play the pipes in Oxfordshire."

"That's a relief!"

It was obvious that the weather near Inverness in winter had been something of a revelation. As we walked down the lane, Mandy nattered on like a teenager being given a lift home from the school disco. She didn't talk me through her wardrobe choices, but the general gist was that she had found her clothing somewhat inadequate. Iain (as I discovered he was called) lived away from the nearest town in a very rural area.

We huddled at the bus stop, a cluster of woolly hats and mismatched gloves, surprised by the sudden cold snap. The bus was silent when we boarded. Mandy's minute by minute broadcast about her adventures north of the border echoed round

A Feather Between the Lines

the downstairs as we travelled towards the city by a circuitous route. The other passengers soon tuned in to her expressive monologue, some choosing to move and sit as close to us as they dared. Although they tried to look as if they weren't at all interested, their gaping mouths showed their fascination.

Mandy was outlining the necessity of spending a great deal of time in bed when you're having a highland fling as we lurched round a corner and a lady across the aisle partly slipped off her seat. Apparently at that latitude in December it gets dark shortly after lunch and isn't light again until about 11 in the morning. The temperature had rarely risen above zero. There was a palpable sigh of relief from the audience when Mandy described how during several severe storms they had been able to huddle romantically beside Iain's very efficient wood burner. The eavesdroppers were clearly disappointed when we got off at our stop just as she was beginning to describe the itchiness of his beard and the pros and cons thereof.

The café was already filling up despite the early hour – a welcome haven from the pre-Christmas onslaught of tinny festive music seeping out of every shop doorway.

Mandy bagged the last empty table whilst I queued up for our order. "Very merry berry Yuletide," the barista droned in an unenthusiastic monotone. "Do you want a frankincense or myrrh syrup in your coffees? It's £2.70 extra." She had tied a piece of tinsel round her head in a half-hearted attempt to invoke some Christmas cheer.

"Whatever is frankincense and what does myrrh taste like?" I asked mischievously.

She looked at me blankly. "It's syrup. For coffee. There was another one, gold, but we're out of that."

"Already? But the infant child has not been born yet." I feigned horror.

A man who I guessed might be the manager interrupted.

"Please accept our apologies. Our seasonal specials are proving popular." He was wearing a headband from which a single star attached to a thin spring projected above his head and he was trying to show his rank by looking important with a milk frother. "Frankincense is kind of piney with cinnamon notes and myrrh is bitter orange. Delish!" He licked his lips and leaned his head to one side coquettishly so that the star, which was a little too heavy for the flimsy spring, orbited his head like a meteor heading for Earth. I declined.

"What names shall I put on the cups?" the girl asked. Her face was totally devoid of expression.

"I'm Balthazar and my friend is Caspar. Melchior couldn't make it."

Mandy had been watching. "What are you up to?" she called. "There's a queue building up."

"I didn't have an Irish Catholic gran for nothing," I replied, adding to her confusion. "Lord, I hate Christmas."

The manager looked puzzled too. For him it clearly was the most wonderful time of the year, despite the fact his Christmas sweater, showing Rudolph's face with a huge red pom-pom for his nose, had been purchased at a time when he was much slimmer.

"You're embarrassing," Mandy complained as I returned from the counter with the coffee. One cup had BRA in big fat black letters scrawled on it and the other MILKIER.

It was a pity Mandy had stage fright and an inability to learn lines, because she could project her voice a very long way indeed and certainly had a flair for the dramatic. She was a free cabaret for the espresso and macchiato drinkers escaping the countdown from the retail brigade informing us just how many minutes of shopping time there were left until the BIG DAY! My hands were wrapped around my second cup of coffee before she got as far as the potential disadvantages of dating a man who lived over 500 miles away.

A Feather Between the Lines

I knew the ins and outs of travelling to Inverness already. Phil had outlined the comparative journeys by rail, road and air to me when he was giving his (as it turns out correct) assessment of the drawbacks of the relationship. In future, should Mandy have chosen to ask, I could have told her about the cost versus time ratio of rail over air, and how this would be altered were she old enough to qualify for an over 60s railcard. The axing of the Cross Country service from Oxford to Edinburgh meant she would now have to go to London and get the train direct to Inverness yet the likelihood of Mandy's ageing Citroen making the lengthy drive there and back in one piece was debatable. A topic for discussion if you run out of chitchat whilst walking round Britain's coast, for example.

Mandy, having bankrupted herself taking the Caledonian sleeper, had arrived bleary-eyed and stiff-necked in Inverness with the clicks of crossing points and assorted coupling-up and station-stopping noises circulating round her head. She may well have been up for advice about comparative travel in the future. She plainly was not to be put off.

"Iain has asked me back for Hogmanay and a ceilidh," she grinned.

"Ooo, another opportunity to look under his kilt and nibble his haggis," I roared.

Unfortunately, there had, by chance, been a collective lull in the conversation in the café. I delivered this line with the level of decibels and projection required for reaching the back of the auditorium of the Edinburgh Playhouse, which, to my recollection, is several miles from the stage.

For the first time since 8:30 even Mandy was silent. The sipping of flat whites, mochas and hot chocolates with whipped cream and marshmallows by those close by who'd been following her narrative stopped. The munching of mince pies was halted.

"Oh, it's alright for you, isn't it?" she snapped forcefully. "Mrs

Happily-Married for God knows how many years. You're alright, with your three kids and Phil doing everything for you. Let's all have a laugh at Mandy."

No one was laughing; my quip had fallen flat with the entire assembly. Eventually a few raised eyebrows and some furtive yuletide shortbread dunking began to thaw the awkwardly frozen moment.

"I'm sorry," I said eventually, offering to buy her a festive flapjack with cranberries as an apology. She turned me down.

My penance was to accompany Mandy to several shops in each of which she took an inappropriately long period of time to choose not to buy Christmas presents or anything else. I stood there in my thick coat, sweltering in the tropical heat of the stores amongst the T-shirt clad assistants as Michael Bublé sang through a collection of seasonal schmaltz. As a punishment it was more than adequate.

Mandy and I get on very well really. I tease her and she takes offence. I apologise and we're back to square one again. "It's nice to have a neighbour you know well," she told me on an occasion when I'd overstepped the mark once again. "No secrets or pretence." How wrong she was. How little she really knew.

"You have to remember," she cautioned when we were back on the bus heading home, "everything has turned out OK for you. You're lucky. It's not like that for everyone."

"Yes," I replied, conscious that the status quo would most probably be upset sooner than she imagined.

"Phil is a good man. He goes on a bit, but he's got a heart of gold. He's not exactly exciting but your interests always come first. You can't ask for much more." Mandy was frank, but she was right about him.

I wondered if Mandy might go for Phil if he chucked me out when he found out how I had deceived him. Perhaps she'd redecorate her house. Out with the tartan and in with whatever theme she could attribute to Reigate. Relandscaping the back garden to suggest the North Downs and running a mock M25 down the hall. How do you represent suburban commuters and potting sheds in soft furnishings?

The bus was slow. The 'quick coffee' had taken all morning. It was almost lunchtime. "Don't forget how fortunate you are to have Phil," she insisted as we got off in our village. She was right. I made up my mind to tell him when I got in. Tell him how fortunate I was to have him and then tack the bit about the letter on to the end. He'd understand. I might have to cry a bit – somehow I didn't think accomplishing that was going to be an issue. No method acting required – it was going to come naturally. Sometime later, when the dust had settled, I'd tell him the other bit. The part he might complain about.

The house was quiet. "Phil?" He wasn't in the kitchen and hadn't said he was going out on his bike. I opened the door to the sitting room. I was unprepared for who was sitting there.

8

"Surprise!"

The noise was deafening. I was flabbergasted. Here, in our front room, were some of my best friends from university. We hadn't been all together for over thirty years, although we had seen each other together on Zoom more recently.

"Happy Birthday!" said Phil. "I know it's not today, but it was easier for everyone to come at the weekend. Mandy's done a marvellous job keeping you out of the way!"

I was speechless. The whole cast of *Arthur and the Knights of the Round Table,* the show we had taken to the Edinburgh Festival in our last year, was in front of me. We were prepared for current versions of ourselves because Zoom had given a preview, but face to face no clever lighting or positioning of tables could hide bulges and sagging. They were all instantly recognisable but slightly different – as if someone had asked me to draw a picture of them from memory and I hadn't got them quite right. Good enough but a variation on a theme.

"Happy Birthday, my darling!" Lovely Neil, my dear friend who I'd seen frequently when we first graduated but who, somehow, when too many children, work and the boring parts of living had got in the way, had slipped out of my life more recently. "Thank God you're finally here. I thought we were going to have to go round Britain's Coastal Path again." He winked.

Mellow Steve, always the conciliator, chipped in. "Phil has certainly done thorough research on the route. I feel like I've walked it myself."

"You should," Phil said encouragingly. "David, Chris and

A Feather Between the Lines

Malcolm have dipped in and out but Geoff and I are hoping to complete all the legs. Do you remember them? They were also theatre techs with me."

"Er, no, 'fraid not," replied Neil in an insincere tone that anyone but Phil would have taken offence at.

"It's been too long," said Danny soulfully. His eyes looked sad and, as he put a friendly arm around Ameerah's shoulders, I wondered if he felt a pang of regret. They had been an inseparable couple at university. Danny had remained single but Ameerah had not.

"It's great to be here. Phil has pulled off a triumph!" Thoughtful Ameerah. She always said the right thing.

Phil grinned as he popped open a champagne bottle and began to fill some glasses he'd laid out on the table. As the technician he'd held our shows together and, true to form, here he was, reuniting us. "You're only 60 once!" He handed me a glass and pecked me on the cheek.

"I'll have you know that I am still 59," I replied.

"I've just been so excited to see you all," gushed Lucy in a way which instantly took us all back to 1985. Where had the intervening time gone? It seemed only a few years since those ridiculous performances in Cambridge and the Edinburgh Fringe where we had performed our final show.

Luscious Lucy had morphed into a replica of her kaftan-wearing mother, who mooned about the house all day occasionally striking yoga poses before refilling her wine glass. Steve, her long-suffering former boyfriend, was looking edgy, presumably wondering how he would get through the afternoon without being inveigled into getting back together with the thrice-divorced needy one. What fun we'd had together and how marvellous it was to see them all again.

"I've missed you soooo much," she continued, draping herself around me and giving me the biggest envelope I'd ever seen. "And

Phil says your son is coming. I'm just dying to meet him. He was a weeny itsy bubba last time I saw him."

Phil grinned triumphantly again. "Yes, more surprises! Arthur rang about coming down this weekend – after all, he is named after that last show in Edinburgh!"

"Hooray! Yea for Arthur!" trilled Lucy.

"Ha, you look shocked, Roni," Phil exclaimed. "I'm not surprised."

Everyone laughed. Everyone except me. My throat was dry. Did Phil suspect? Was he going to put it to the test in front of some people who would remember.

"Arthur is in contact with his mother all the time. He was under strict instructions to keep it from her. It's amazing he did."

I downed my champagne very quickly. Perhaps I was overreacting.

Why hadn't I seen these dear friends for so many years? How had that happened? Where had the middle bit of my life gone? How did I get from 23 to 60 without passing Go and collecting my £200? A huge amount of time working and child rearing had formed into a large midlife blob. Only thanks to Covid and the sudden need everyone felt to re-engage with their friends and relations had we connected again.

"We've had such fun talking about everyone before you arrived." Vivacious Lucy had always been entertaining company. I was disappointed I'd missed it all. "Poor old Roland, master of the abbreviated play, the stick-on moustaches in Romeo and Juliet, the man-biting dog,…"

"And who was that bloke that was hanging around you, Roni, when we were doing *Two Gentleman of Verona*? The dog wouldn't have bitten him! It wouldn't have dared." Danny chuckled and the others joined in. "He had a stupid name."

"Ferris!" Ameerah shouted triumphantly. "Wesley? Warwick? Wycombe? I'll remember in a minute."

"Wycombe Ferris – sounds like a place in the Cotswolds!" Steve was laughing along with the others.

"He was called Webster Ferris," Phil replied, but I noticed he wasn't laughing. Neil shot me a look that made me feel uncomfortable.

Only emotionally savvy Neil knew how close I had been to Ferris. He was the only other person who knew that Webster Ferris came up to Edinburgh that summer. But even the most intuitive man I had ever met didn't know the full details of what happened.

I noticed the photograph of Arthur in his graduation gown on the shelf. Arthur preserved at the age when we had last seen Ferris ourselves. Somehow I had to cover it up. I opened Lucy's monster card and shoved it in front of the picture.

Arthur looked like my uncle Patrick, Phil said. Few children are a carbon copy of their parents. Distinctive features, big noses or prominent chins are often a gift from a more distant relative. Colourings skip generations. There was every possibility that Arthur's unkempt, curly black hair and lean body shape had come from an ancestor the assembled company didn't know. I hoped that when Arthur himself arrived, the fact that he was now thirty-six would disguise any resemblance a little. He often wore a beanie hat which he kept on indoors resulting in a row with his father about taking it off 'as good manners'. It covered up the tell-tale hairstyle. I might be able to persuade Phil to let him keep it on so that there wasn't an altercation in front of the guests, resulting in a revelation which would make the conversation turn in an unexpected direction. I was panicking.

The doorbell rang. It was too late.

9

I hurried to the door and took a deep breath before I opened it.

A coatless Mandy was shivering on the doorstep. "Phil said it was OK if I gate-crashed," she explained. "Do you mind?" I noticed she had changed, re-done her make-up and sprayed herself with perfume. "Which ones are single?" she whispered once she was inside, preening herself in the mirror in the hall.

"What about the Long-Haired Lover from Loch Ness?" I asked. "It's a surprise party for my birthday, not a speed-dating event."

"You never know…"

In the sitting room there was a lot of chat about the deception and some laughing about my reluctance to waste my Saturday morning shopping surrounded by a 1973 time warp soundtrack of Roy Wood and Noddy Holder. "It's Christmas!" they chorused. I grinned feebly, reluctant to give up my position with easy access to the hall so I could jump to it to suggest compulsory beanie wearing next time the bell rang.

"Mandy: not only our neighbour but a stalwart of the Isis Mummers," Phil announced suddenly as if he were a butler in a stately home.

"Isis?" Danny echoed, alarmed.

"It's a tributary of the Thames. I've suggested a name change but Angela won't budge," I explained. There was so much laughing and loud chortling about the Pared-Down Players' similarly stupid name that when the bell rang again I was able to slip out unnoticed to open the door.

A Feather Between the Lines

"Pizza for Spittal," announced a tall stack of boxes with two legs at the bottom. The tower was passed over to me. "It's paid for." In the moment of exchange I could see a man grinning moronically, no doubt because he was wearing a stupid hat – a 12" fabric pizza with a peak. "Is that really your name? Spittal?"

"No. I gave it for a laugh," I said. "Sometimes I use Phlegm or Bile. I even used Snot once."

There was a pause. The delivery man's expression changed to one of dour earnestness. "You shouldn't use fake names when ordering. The pizzas might end up going to someone who really is called Spittal." His tone was one used for speaking to people considered very stupid indeed.

Phil had ordered enough pizzas for every person in Britain called Spittal to eat a whole one with enough left over for anyone with the misfortune to be named Phlegm, Bile or Snot.

"I've got us my favourites. You'll love them," assured Phil as he carefully took the boxes and put them on the table. "Choose between Honolulu – that's ham and large chunks of juicy pineapple, I think it's tinned but I prefer that anyway – or Tijuana, which has got ground beef, thick slices of chilli and hot sauce."

There was a collective silence whilst these delicacies were contemplated.

"Are they gluten free?" asked Lucy. "Sooo sorry, I should have said."

"I'm kosher and Ameerah is halal," Danny added, "and I think Steve is still a vegetarian – aren't you?"

"All the more for us then, Neil," Phil grinned. "Unless you're watching your waistline…" I don't think my husband is a homophobe, but he can't resist comments like that when he sees Neil.

I went into the kitchen. Behind the closed door I breathed deeply and searched in the cupboard to see what I had. Along with some sad-looking remnants of dry goods which had been lurking around since the last century, I found a half-eaten packet of buckwheat noodles Katie had left. The sell-by date had long passed and there was scarcely a full portion but I reckoned that Lucy might have a small appetite and what she didn't know about wouldn't bother her. I also found a giant pack of pasta and a couple of jars of pesto.

My phone buzzed.

Oh God, Arthur. He'd arrived and was wondering where to park in the lane. He needs space for a pantechnicon to get his antique tiny Fiat anywhere near the kerb. Probably needs his dad to come out and do it for him.

Or it was Webster Ferris. Our old college had forwarded the letter he'd written after he saw my picture in *spool!*, its ludicrously named, uncapitalised, unnecessarily punctuated newsletter. Perhaps they had now irresponsibly given him my phone number and he was messaging to see whether I'd received the letter. Or worse, what if they'd now passed on my address and he'd decided to fly over early and was letting me know that he'd be on the doorstep with his luggage imminently? Bloody hell, what was I going to do now? Any minute he could be in our sitting room helping Phil eat through his pizza mountain – if he hadn't turned vegan during the last thirty-seven years.

The kitchen door opened. It was Neil and not a beanie-wearing son who had remembered his key for once or an uninvited old flame.

"Ron darling, I came to help before Phil force feeds me with any more slices of his Hawaiian oil slick. Hasn't anyone told him pizzas come from Italy?" He threw his arms round me and squeezed me tight. I was happy to see him too but I couldn't speak. "What's up?" he asked.

"Nothing."

"You're all jittery." Neil could smell intrigue in Oxfordshire from his house in Islington, let alone at close range. "You worried someone might work it out when he turns up?" I stayed silent.

"It's particularly noticeable in that picture. The student one you were trying to cover up with that ridiculous card from Lucy."

The water I had put on for the pasta boiled over dramatically. I busied myself turning the heat down and mopping up the flow of scalding water cascading over the hob. "Arthur looks like my Uncle Patrick."

Neil wasn't having that. "I worked it out a long time ago. You forget, I was there that day when Ferris Wheel strode into town and arranged to meet you at the Greyfriars Bobby statue. I covered for you. Remember? Something happened that evening. I knew it when you got back to the flat – and I realised what it was the first time I saw Arthur. Even as a tiny baby it was obvious. Only I know Webster Ferris was in Edinburgh. Phil doesn't. Don't worry about it." In some ways, despite this confession, it was a relief to have Neil's reassurance.

"You heard Phil – instant recall of his name. His memory is like a giant mainframe computer. He's brilliant at games like bridge where you have to remember all the cards played. If you're lucky he might play the A road game with you." Neil looked nonplussed. I was trying to change the subject. "It's something he does with his walking mates, to pass the time I suppose. You name an A road and the other person has to say where it starts and ends. I'm hopeless at it. I can only do the easy ones, like the A27. Whiteparish, Wiltshire, to Pevensey, East Sussex."

"They play a game based around major roads? And you join in?" Neil was unconvinced.

"I'm an amateur." Neil's face took on a pained expression. "They can do ridiculous ones, like the A5148. It's part of the A38 but I can't remember exactly where to and from. Somewhere near Lichfield, I think. I only know that because we broke down there once."

"My God!" he exclaimed dramatically. "If I begged them, do you think they'd let me come along and join in? It must be such fun."

I loved Neil. Why didn't I see more of him?

"Does old elephant memory ever address the elephant in the room?" Neil asked softly.

"What do you mean?"

"Well, we all laughed about it when we first saw him. The irony of it. You having a baby with Phil who looks just like Ferris. Of course, the others don't know Webster boy was in Edinburgh. Only I know that." I was speechless. "Everyone in Cambridge knew Webster Ferris; he scared the shit out of most people. They all tried to avoid him, but our group, we all knew you were seeing him."

All that time, when I thought I was being furtive and covering my tracks, keeping away from the gossips, tongues were wagging and the grapevine was passing on juicy speculation. "Did Phil know?"

"Possibly, though Phil wasn't involved until the last shows and he hadn't fired his cupid's dart at you yet."

Right on cue, Phil appeared. He looked flushed and got himself a glass of water. "What are you doing in here, you two? Neil, you haven't tried Tijuana yet. They've been very generous with the chillies. And you haven't had a single slice, Roni."

"I was just telling Roni that Simon and I are getting married," Neil explained like a school child lying to the teacher about why he had been found messing about in the cloakrooms during lesson time.

Phil wasn't sure how best to respond. "After what? Thirty odd years? Don't want to rush into these things eh, Roni?"

"It's lovely, so romantic," I added, although it was the first I had heard of it.

"The romance of tax, pensions and next-of-kin issues more like." Why Neil thought he had to explain I don't know. I wasn't even entirely sure it was true.

"I'm making some pasta pesto and I've found some gluten free noodles for Lucy." We both looked guilty.

A Feather Between the Lines

"I didn't think they'd be such fuss-pots." Phil seemed disappointed that his pizza treat had been spurned. "Everyone used to eat everything."

My phone sounded again, ringing this time. My mind was buzzing. Everyone had been laughing about the irony of it? When Arthur was just a baby? Would they be laughing when they saw him now?

"Your phone," Phil said unnecessarily. "Aren't you going to answer it?" It was on the workbench in front of me. I could barely move.

Phil picked it up and swiped answer. "You're what?…How come?…How does that involve me?…Oh I see…OK." Phil let out a long sigh. "I knew this would happen one day."

He looked angry – a new departure for the most rational man on the planet. Something or someone had disturbed the gentle understanding he had been radiating all these years. Neil and I waited for what was going to happen next.

Phil looked me straight in the face. "I told him not to let his AA membership lapse, but no, he's the only person on Earth who can own a twenty-five-year-old car and assume it's not going to break down. He hasn't even got the money for a tow truck. Dad to the bloody rescue as per."

I was so relieved. Of course it would be Arthur on the phone. And it seemed unlikely he'd return before the others had to go. I said, "Thank God!" with rather more enthusiasm than the situation warranted.

"Thank Dad more like. I'll have to go with a tow rope. He's somewhere on the A4130. Doesn't even know quite where."

"The A4130?" Neil asked, winking at me.

"Yes, He could be anywhere between Burchett's Green, Berkshire, and Rowstock, Oxfordshire. Though if he's gone that far he'll have overshot his turning. Anything is possible with that boy."

"Hardly a boy," said Neil as Phil busied about, checking his own phone, putting on his shoes and getting the car key. He went to explain why he was having to leave to the others.

"Do you think 'rushing into it' referred to our own wedding?" I asked Neil.

"No. You're paranoid. He just doesn't know what to say. I don't suppose Phil finds same-sex marriage easy to deal with. He loves you. He organised this party. All on his own."

Eventually, when Phil had left with a tow rope, some torches and several Tijuana pizzas in boxes, we made the pasta pesto and sat eating it balancing the plates on our laps, just like we had as students. Although many years had passed, it was as if we'd just had a sabbatical. A year overseas as part of our degrees, perhaps. It was strangely comforting, the big middle blob when we weren't together not affecting our relationships at all. Mandy made herself part of the group by flirtatiously cosying up between Danny and Steve, who she had quickly established were single.

As I'd anticipated, they all had to leave before Phil returned. Neil was last to go.

"I heard from Webster Ferris the other week." I tried to make it sound like a casual afterthought as he hugged me goodbye on the doorstep. "He's coming over to the UK next year. He'd seen my picture in the alumni newsletter and wrote to the college hoping they would forward his letter. Have a good journey."

Neil looked as if he'd struck gold in the water feature of his creatively landscaped courtyard garden, which he'd been showing us pictures of earlier. I could imagine him passing on the news to Simon with a mixture of relish and disbelief when he got home, a cheeky little Sancerre making the ideal accompaniment to an embellished pre-dinner anecdote.

"Whatever does he want?"

"Funnily enough he's coming to Oxford University for a week or so in May and is hoping to meet up with me and my other half." I tried to sound breezy but was unconvincing.

"Hmm. That'd be interesting. Can I come? I'll be a fly on the wall." Neil was smiling but he correctly interpreted my nervous expression as an indication that I was serious. "Roni, isn't that a hornet's nest best left undisturbed?"

"At least he assumes I have a partner and haven't ended up a bitter old maid, pining for the bastard who left me." My attempt to be jocular and unconcerned fell flat. Neil looked disbelieving. "I think I have to meet him. It's probably only fair that he should know he might be a father," I continued, vainly hoping intuitive Neil would not pick up that there might be other reasons why I would agree. In that instant I knew I would reply to the letter and that I had no intention of involving Phil in the assignation at all.

"But you realise that it's not just Ferris you'd have to tell. It's Phil. And Arthur. And your daughters and the hideous in-laws at the very least…?"

"Phil's dad is in a home. He's got dementia. He won't understand. And his mother has never thought I'm good enough for her precious son." I was ashamed of this pathetic reasoning as soon as I said it.

Before he left, Neil gave me a big kiss to go with his comments about sleeping dogs and rocking boats. "Five months to tart yourself up, then," was his parting remark. Characteristically he'd correctly identified that there might be more to this sudden wish to rid myself of the guilt I'd been carrying all these years. I wasn't entirely sure that he approved.

With the impetuous conviction of the moment, fortified by the alcohol I'd been drinking all afternoon, yet before I could review my decision, I got out a piece of paper to write a brief reply. I could acknowledge receipt of his invitation and invent a fake address or even omit my address altogether and give our apologies. I didn't have to reply at all. Ferris didn't know where I lived and wasn't to know that I'd ever received the letter. I didn't need to tell Phil anything. Just ignore it, bin the letter and we could all carry on as before. Deep down I knew this wasn't right. There were things to sort out, important issues that I couldn't keep to myself any longer.

I'd been thinking about Webster Ferris since our last meeting in 1985 and knew that I did want to see him. I wasn't entirely sure I wanted him to see me. I imagined wafting about Oxford in a Potteresque invisibility cloak so I could observe him undetected. After a wizardly wave of a wand, I'd transform into a twenty-something body-double of myself, tell him what he needed to know and disappear back into the cloak whilst I watched what happened next. A nonsensical time-waster though this daydream was, it did impress on me that I continued to view Ferris with some trepidation.

I decided to be brief, give my phone number and instructions to use WhatsApp, but not my postal address. I could always change my phone number or block him, I decided. I copied the address at Stanford University on to a creased airmail envelope which had been lurking in the desk for several years and stuck as many stamps as I had on to it, not knowing the cost of postage to the US.

Decisively I slipped coatless into the cold night air and hurried up to the post box in the lane. Sending a reply would force me to tell Phil what I should have admitted to so long ago. He did love me and he would forgive me. Perhaps he already knew and had accepted it. I wasn't sure Arthur was Ferris's child and I hadn't set out to dupe Phil deliberately. It was a silly error of judgement at the beginning of a new relationship and my mistake was not admitting it there and then. That decision had potentially far-reaching consequences, something I had failed to consider at the time.

By pushing the over-stamped envelope through the slot, I made an irreversible choice to confront the past. I put the other part of my confirmation to meet up, the longing to see Ferris again, to the back of my mind. I told myself it was a fantasy which reality would extinguish.

My, our, future was in train by the time the thirty-six-year-old boy, his twenty-five-year-old car, and several limp cardboard boxes containing congealed lumps of dough, picked off chilli garnish and cheese, seeping oil on to the passenger seat, were pulled slowly into the lane by a rope attached to the Toyota. If ever there was a moment for Phil to say, as he periodically did, "That boy is all your side of the family," this was it.

10

The following week

Ever had second thoughts?

Once the reply was in the pillar box, it was imprisoned. All Sunday I was conscious it was trapped, in view of our house but out of reach. I couldn't help but keep casting my eyes towards the tall red column in the vague hope that someone may have set fire to it or a flying saucer had sucked it up for investigation. What would Martians have made of the Earthlings' correspondence? A belated birthday card, a letter of complaint to Thames Water and a curt, matter-of-fact response to an invitation which would require a clever recipient to read carefully to extrapolate any kind of inference from the bald words themselves. A professor of English Literature perhaps?

I could have sat beside the box from early on Monday morning until it was emptied. If I hadn't expired from hypothermia in the chilly December air, I could have asked Arman for the letter back when he came with his van.

As part of a restructuring of services where Royal Mail seems to be aiming to be a real-life version of *Postman Pat*, Arman delivers our post as well as emptying the letterbox.

Postman Pat does everything in Greendale: driving the van, delivering parcels and mail, chatting up old ladies in the Post Office, emptying pillar boxes, hanging out at the sorting office, rescuing people and animals, even flying a helicopter. There is no doubt he is a one-man postal system. It's a fantastic business model for the real-life loss-making version. Think of the savings on staffing costs: just Pat, pussycat Jess (unsalaried) and Mrs Goggins in the Post Office. Arman might be in line for some aerial transport and a feline assistant, but he'll be short of colleagues at the annual work knees-up.

I was daydreaming again. I often daydream about Arman, who is very good looking and likes a chat. We have a relationship – not a romantic one (though if a billet-doux were to pop through my letterbox I can't vouch for my actions) – but one whereby he rings the bell to notify me of items of post I might want to filter out before Phil sees them. Previously this has been parking and speeding fines. It was Arman who delivered the college magazine with my drunken face on the cover and later the ensuing envelope which contained the letter from Ferris, forwarded on from my college. Now I might have to have him on alert for post with an air mail sticker – just in case the college wasn't so careful next time and blabbed about my address.

I had stayed awake for much of Saturday and Sunday nights worrying about what I had done and consequently overslept on Monday morning. When I woke it was too late. The box had been emptied; the reply, in Arman's sack in his van, was on its way to the Abingdon sorting office and onwards over the Atlantic and across the whole of the USA to Stanford University. That is if I'd stuck enough stamps on. My letter had gone but the guilt remained.

Phil had left too, taking a few days leave for a Lycra-clad stay with his bike at Granny's cottage. Regularly visiting this dump is the one tangent which veers away from the predictable orbit which forms the carefully planned and successful life he leads. His devotion to the desolate, isolated hovel that is a legacy from his family is the only glimmer of hope that one day he might do something reckless and unwise.

Long ago it had been the rural home of Phil's great-great-grandparents. It was high on a fell in the Yorkshire Dales and had been passed down through the family from father to son ever since. Presumably no one had been able to sell it, so it remained an inherited burden, a poisoned real-estate chalice, a holiday destination guaranteed to make you feel happy to return home.

Phil loves this wretched slum although it is at least two miles from any kind of other building, and, in my opinion, light years from civilisation. It has no washing machine, shower, phone or Wi-Fi signal. Indeed it has no electricity or running water. Evenings shivering by candlelight are supposed to be an attraction. Apparently it is ideally located for off-road cycling – as if riding a bike on lanes up hill and down dale isn't tedious and tiring enough. Travelling on two wheels away from tarmac adds the very real likelihood of an accident from which there is no rescue until it is too late.

We did try a family holiday there, but after just one cold and sleepless stormy night in August the kids and I repaired to Harrogate, where we gorged on huge Fat Rascal cakes from Betty's Tearoom whilst waiting for Phil to regain his senses. Truly 'away from it all', Granny's cottage is the last place on Earth anyone with a strong devotion to risk assessment and a degree in sensible decision-making would choose to spend time alone. Visits there are what prevent Phil from being consumed by his own common sense. It's his version of Arthur's bedroom. The difference is he has to catch numerous trains and cycle for miles with minimum belongings just to get there and I only have to go upstairs.

Arthur did return to that bedroom and, despite him being unlikely to choose *Harry Potter and The Chamber of Secrets* as his preferred reading matter, I wondered if I should remove the secret within it.

I hadn't been able to stop looking at that letter, sneaking into Arthur's room and extracting it from the book when Phil was at work or away with his bike. I needed to check it was still there as

A Feather Between the Lines

well as look at the handwriting and review the words, analysing them again and again in order to prise any meaning or intention I had previously missed.

I was frightened about the future, a future which I very much wanted to share with you. I recognised some years ago that, at that time, I was making impossible demands of you. If I had been more patient and looked at the situation from your point of view perhaps things might have been different.

I knew these sentences verbatim, as if they were quotations I had learned for an exam.

It's my long overdue atonement to apologise. 'The commencement of atonement is the sense of its necessity.'

I ran my fingers over the text like a small child tracing the words in a book, mouthing their sounds as if I was a novice reader.

It's taken me over thirty-seven years to feel joy not sorrow when I think about you and to have the courage to contact you.

Better hidden in plain sight, I decided. I would tell Phil about Webster Ferris's visit as soon as he came back from Granny's cottage. I needed to get it over with. Phil had seen the photograph in *spool!* and he would understand how it might have provoked Ferris into getting back in touch.

I didn't know which was more ridiculous, the new name for the college magazine or the idiot with paper umbrellas in her hair who grinned inanely out from the picture on its front cover. Phil had been at a different college to us. Other than potentially catching the loudly voiced criticism and scathing mockery that Ferris was keen to broadcast on the rare occasions he came to see a Pared-Down Players production, I doubt they had ever spoken. Phil would have been too busy adjusting his Fresnel lamps and sorting out feedback issues to lurk around the audience post-show picking up their reviews. He'd recall the foul-mouthed Yorkshireman, but he'd have a clear and sensible response.

Phil had realised how much I had enjoyed reconnecting with The Pared-Down Players on Zoom during lockdown and it had given him the idea to have the surprise party. What a kind and thoughtful person he was. How could I go behind his back like that? The world's most rational man would understand, I convinced myself. Together we could decide whether to do a DNA test. If it turned out that Webster Ferris was Arthur's biological father, Phil would even help me and our son to deal with the situation. If it turned out that Ferris was interested in the child he had conceived, Arthur could possibly meet him in May. Why hadn't I just told Phil?

I knew why.

11

Afternoon
Sunday 18th December 2022

Out of the window I could see Mandy with a bale of cloth. "Come on, Roni, it's cold." Mandy knew Phil was away. That's why she had the samples with her. The tartan transformation was in progress and my involvement was required. I don't know why she asks me because inevitably I'm rude or dismissive and no practical help, yet, for reasons never explained, she seeks my negative validation.

"Is he trekking round the coast again? So soon – is it the worsening weather that's encouraging him?"

"He's been at Granny's cottage, coming back today. He should be on the train right now," I explained.

"You'll have to fumigate him when he arrives," she said only half joking. "I hope your washing machine is empty. Get the kettle on." The deprivation of comfort and lack of colour scheming in Granny's cottage were anathema to Mandy.

She laid the cloth bale across the kitchen table for me to look at whilst she made the tea. She likes to be in charge of timing the bag's duration in the cup or pot and add her own milk. I'm inconsistent apparently. It's the one thing she and Phil agree on.

"What do you think?" A long stretch of woolly tartan cloth

covered the surface. "Imagine: Highlands and Islands, warm fires, shortbread, a nip of whisky and bagpipes."

My phone rang before I could think up any cynical response. My stomach lurched. A frisson of anticipation cascaded through my body. Webster Ferris had received my reply and was ringing me up immediately. I'd asked him to WhatsApp but I hadn't really considered what I was going to say if he chose to call. And now I was going to have to think on the spot with Mandy listening in.

"Don't mind me," she said. "Answer it."

"Mrs Spittal?" asked an unknown voice. I don't use my married name often, for obvious reasons. I told Phil it was because I'm the last McNamara in the family but given what we discovered about my grandfather's activities in Ireland after he left Gran that was clearly untrue. Phil's mates call him Gob, not something I wished to be copied by pupils in search of a nickname when I started teaching. I remain Veronica McNamara in most situations. Phil didn't say as much but I think he understood why.

It wasn't Webster Ferris at least. No relic of a Yorkshire accent or mid-Atlantic mash-up. If someone is calling me Mrs Spittal they are either from a call centre or it's something serious. He sounded official and unlikely to move into a spiel about being a representative of a phoney 'government energy commission' trying to flog me solar panels.

"I'm a first responder." I panicked. Which one was it? Arthur? Katie? Jessica? "Nothing to worry about. Your husband has been in a collision with a bus. He's been blue-lighted to the JR."

He sounded quite cheerful. I wondered if they taught them to be like that, jolly in the face of major trauma, so you felt less worried, or whether daily calls about accidents inured him to the sensitivities of their recipients. "It was a 95. Destination Culham. I'm afraid his bike is a write-off," he added helpfully, just in case I needed more information to picture the scene. "He'll be in A&E shortly."

Mandy offered to drive me to the hospital. "You'll never find a parking space." She loves a drama and a mystery. "A bus! You don't see many of those round here on a Sunday afternoon." I felt apprehension but mostly guilt as I climbed into the passenger seat and she tossed the fabric and colour charts onto the back seat.

I always feel culpable for events which are nothing to do with me. I felt remorse when there were reports of smoking in the boys' loos at school – even though I was a member of staff who gave up years ago. I almost confessed to drawing a huge and detailed phallus on the Head's study door despite it appearing the term after I left and I broke in to a hot sweat when I saw a story in *The Oxford Mail* about gnomes being stolen from gardens in a part of the city I've never visited. It's as if I live a double life where the activities of my Mr Hyde, a Sharpie wielding nicotine addict with a penchant for kitsch ornaments, are only vaguely remembered when I return to being Dr Jekyll. I suppose it's the result of carrying a real secret around for so long.

Gran would have attributed the guilt I was feeling as we drove to the JR as a sign from the Lord. A big, bus-shaped celestial finger was prodding my conscience saying, "Don't think I don't know you're deceiving your husband and having impure thoughts about another man. Look what you've done now!"

Mandy's way of taking my mind off what might await us at the hospital was to chatter non-stop about her latest plans for the wee bothy she intended to create.

It was a relief to be turned out at A&E so Mandy and her vision of heather and drystone walling with a thistle accent could go in search of the mythical parking space.

A preposterously chirpy woman was manning the desk. She'd been trained in non-judgemental listening. "Have you, dear? I can see how that must be annoying for you," she chuckled as an aggressive man with a small bandage on his thumb was detailing just how many hours he'd been waiting. She'd been specially selected, I thought, to deal with the crowded waiting room where softly muffled groans mixed with the competing voices of those convinced their accident or emergency was more important than everyone else's.

"I'm looking for Philip Spittal. He's come in by ambulance." My voice was unusually high-pitched.

"Who are you then, my lovely?" she asked ignoring my distress.

"Mrs Spittal. AL not LE."

"Okey-dokey. Unusual name that. Spittal." She spat it out as if to indicate that there was no doubt that she had made the connection with saliva. "We get all sorts here. I'll add it to our 'things to do with the body' name list. We've had Bownes, Bloods, D'eath – they say it's not pronounced Death but it obviously is. Legge, Foot… Flemm was a good one. I think he was Dutch." She lowered her voice. "We've even had a Clapp! You've got to have a laugh at work, haven't you? What did we have the other day, Maureen?"

"Vane," replied her colleague, whose sour face indicated that she at least had been on that course school secretaries and doctors' receptionists attend to teach them an unpleasant as possible interface with the public.

"Just a bit of fun," she continued, typing furiously on her computer. I suspected she was updating the list before she forgot what a gem of a name Spittal was. "He's in Resus. Just along there to the right."

Resus? He needed resuscitating? The door said 'Press buzzer for entry' so I did. Nothing happened. No one came. Perhaps they were all busy resuscitating Phil.

Eventually someone pushed through the door from the other direction. She wasn't wearing a white coat or starched dress and apron with a frilly cap. She may have been a doctor, a nurse or a ward orderly – only people wearing fancy dress at parties or participating in fantasy scenarios have identifiable medical

A Feather Between the Lines

uniform these days. "Excuse me…" but she was gone – though not before I had stuck my foot in the way as it closed again. That was when I realised I was still wearing my slippers. Beyond was a lobby leading to a room divided by blue curtains. I called out, "Phil?" A woman appeared from one of the bays.

"This way," she demanded, directing me back through the door into a cupboard-sized room off the lobby. There were two chairs and a coffee table on which was a box of tissues and some leaflets about bereavement. I've seen enough hospital TV shows to know that this was the bad news room. My throat was dry and it dawned on me that there might be some catastrophic news about Phil. I sat in the room waiting to hear it.

I thought about calling Arthur and the girls but in the rush I'd left my phone at home. What would I have said? "I'm in a windowless cupboard in my slippers and it's highly probable your dad is badly injured – or worse."

I had a flick through *Bereavement and How to Deal With It* and then *The Five Stages of Grief*, which had no words just a variety of interpretations of the Smiley ideogram. First a white one, (nonplussed), then a red one (absolutely livid) followed by orange (haggling for a carpet in Turkey), yellow (fucking miserable) and finally green. This face was grinning madly as if it had won the Lottery.

A local funeral director had thoughtfully left a brochure. It displayed twenty-first century coffin and hearse options. I decided I would travel to my funeral in a Wallace and Gromit-style coffin-shaped side car attached to a motorbike ridden by one of the pall bearers. I wondered if they had to remove their top hat to put the helmet on. Perhaps they wear a specially adapted one – irritatingly the photograph didn't show the member of staff.

Many caskets (as they referred to them) have a vinyl wrap such as you see on buses and taxis. I fancied the one with a field of lavender, although the carpet of rose petals was attractive too.

There was even one with a racing bike, speeding towards its final destination, which snapped me back into the reality of my situation. I hoped I wouldn't be ordering that any time soon.

An eternity later the door opened suddenly. "What are you doing in here?" asked a man wearing a pyjama-like matching green top and loose trousers. He could have been a patient if he hadn't had a stethoscope looped round him like a necklace. That's the only way doctors can identify themselves these days now everyone is in scrubs. I wonder how often they actually stick them in their ears, put the cold metal disc on someone's chest and ask them to huff and puff like the wolf in *The Three Little Pigs*. Stethoscopes are like the barber's red and white pole: a symbol for those whose eyesight isn't up to reading the name badge. Today it says 'six years of study and a massive student debt' rather than 'While-U-wait surgery available whilst you get your beard trimmed,' but the principle is the same. The big bad wolf in doctor's clothing ushered a shocked-looking woman into the cupboard whilst gesturing to me to come out. Mandy was behind him clutching the tartan bale.

"There you are. We wondered what had happened to you. I had to go back to the car for the fabric." Was she planning to ask the medic's opinion? Had she asked him to move in and was seeing whether it could be incorporated into a retro *Dr. Finlay's Casebook* makeover? Or was she suggesting making a shroud out of it? "Phil's fine, except he's wearing a gown that doesn't close at the back."

"You've seen him?"

"More of him than I was anticipating." She winked. "Why are you hiding in that room? We've been looking for you for half an hour."

"Your neighbour says you didn't bring any clothes, Mrs. Spittal," announced the medic crossly. "I can't discharge him wearing only socks." Surely Phil hadn't been riding back from the station like Lady Godiva? Not in December. "Nothing has shown up on the scan. No damage to his head and he doesn't even appear to be concussed." He seemed almost disappointed.

Phil was in a cubicle behind a curtain. I could see he was annoyed. He never usually gets cross or even slightly angry, but he'd clearly had his fill of Mandy and her plans to turn her former farm labourer's cottage into a Highland love nest. There was a huge stripe of gauze with white tape down one side of his face, like a no overtaking marking on a road. His hand was bandaged and he was indeed only wearing a gown and his socks.

"Where were you?" he asked irritably. "They cut off my clothes, my bike got left by the side of the road and I don't know where my rucksack is."

I explained about the cupboard and how I thought he was dead. Phil usually deals with any hysteria by ignoring it, but I could see his patience was wearing thin. "Now I've got to go home looking like an extra from *Braveheart*."

"You're lucky I had it in the car. We were in a hurry so I didn't take it back in the house. It wasn't cheap. It's 100% wool," explained Mandy as she began to drape it around Phil so he transformed into William Wallace in a kilt and shawl. The unkempt appearance of his hair and the white stripe down his face added to the effect. "You do actually look a bit like Mel Gibson. I'm quite pleased with this," Mandy admitted, "and it's going to look fab on my armchair."

Phil had calmed down by the time we got home. I made him a cup of tea as he sat at the kitchen table scratching. "Do you think you might have got fleas or bed bugs at Granny's cottage?" I asked. It was unlikely. Presumably even pests have standards.

"No, it's Mandy's tartan. It itches."

"For a horrible moment I thought you were dead or brain damaged. Maybe you were in a coma – only to wake up in sixteen years' time and find out we still haven't won the World Cup."

This was my way of saying I was glad he was alright. Normally he would have laughed but he ignored me.

"I was really pleased with that bike. We'll have to go out first thing tomorrow to see if we can find it. I bet someone will have pinched it. I've spent a week cycling it all round the Dales without any problems and then a bus comes out from nowhere when I'm riding home from the station."

My Irish Gran used to say, "If I'm hit by a bus tomorrow none of yous will care. But anyways – I'll go to my maker with a clean conscience." There was always a snigger then a pause before someone mumbled the required reply: of course we'd care. I wondered if Gran noticed.

I did care about Phil being hit by the proverbial bus. I'd never come across anyone before to whom it had actually happened. I certainly couldn't mention the letter and the visit just yet. The conversation would have to be postponed.

12

Christmas 2022

For the first time in our marriage, Phil and I were alone together on Christmas Day. A quiet time à deux where my Yuletide gift might have been an admission, slipped between an unnecessary mince pie and a mind-blanking pint of Baileys. A written confession as the joke in his cracker perhaps. 'What did Mrs Claus do under the mistletoe on Arthur's Seat in August 1985?'.

Phil had recovered more slowly than either of us had expected. One bent wheel and a twisted skeleton of the frame were all that remained of his bike, dumped unceremoniously by the side of the road. Anything salvageable had been speedily removed by scavengers who, like vultures hovering over a thirsty man in the desert, had swooped as the ambulance drew away. There was no sign of his rucksack, which, as well as his phone, contained the rest of his Lycra collection returning for a well-earned visit to the washing machine. Every cloud…

For the first time he didn't go to work but lay listlessly in bed, barely even interested in the insurance claim form which I had printed off for him to fill in. He'd removed the gauze strip to reveal a lurid red and crusting scab underneath. Violent black bruises formed on one side of his face and his top lip had swollen asymmetrically. He looked like John Hurt in *The Elephant Man* rather than Mel Gibson giving the Sassenachs a good hiding, though, with great restraint, I managed to avoid pointing that out.

Fortunately, Phil's face had made contact only with the road and not the heavy double-decker. The bus had knocked his back wheel so he had wobbled into a pothole causing him to fly off the bike several yards in front of the vehicle. It only flattened the bike without Phil on it and the driver had managed to stop before squishing him as well.

I'd intended to salve my conscience about being secretive about the letter by casually tossing it into my chatter when I was in the bedroom taking Phil the various brightly coloured tablets the doctor had prescribed – not to take advantage of his incapacity but rather by dropping it into the stream of inconsequential tittle-tattle I hoped I was amusing him with. Out of the bedroom window I could see Mandy taking what looked like a huge hairy handbag and a sword into her house. A sporran and a claymore for decorative purposes, I assumed.

"You'll never guess what…" I began, segueing it onto the end of a monologue about our youngest daughter Katie's plan to install a reed bed sewage system in her back garden. But Phil wasn't up for guessing or just being told. When I turned back from the window, he'd fallen asleep, presumably having a worrying dream about processing excrement ecologically. Too much information about hand-weeding the reeds to remove nettles had probably caused him to zone out. I didn't persist. Looking at Phil's battered face reminded me of Webster Ferris's bloody encounter in the Market Square in Cambridge. Somehow everything led me back to him.

News of the accident meant visitors. Paula, official taxi driver, brought their mother. I got the duster out in anticipation. Despite being a late octogenarian with macular degeneration, she can spot a speck of dust at fifty paces and isn't shy about identifying it out loud.

Soon after Pamela stopped driving, Phil brought back a leaflet Surrey Police had posted through the door at Meadowmead Close announcing a record reduction in road traffic accidents. I think he felt guilty about sharing this amusing piece of constabulary propaganda which he knew I would find hilarious. My relationship with his mother was tricky and went beyond complaints about what she called 'house husbandry'. It was testament to his sanguine and rational personality that things were so harmonious between us.

"Father called Mother the c word again," exclaimed Paula when they arrived, pushing past me to put her brother in the picture as soon as possible, "and I'm a strumpet and a slattern."

"Well at least it's something Shakespearian and poetic," I suggested. Paula gave me a withering look.

"I'm also a trollop."

"Your father wants you to read him Anthony Trollope?" retorted Phil's mother, who, unlike her daughter, had not heard the full extent of the descriptions her husband had been bestowing on his nearest and dearest.

"It's just words. Ignore it," said Phil, who was very good at doing just that.

"I feel sorry for the care workers, having to put up with it. I can't tell you what he said to the vicar when he came to the home to celebrate the Eucharist on Sunday." I suspected Paula, a devout Anglican, felt embarrassed rather than sorry for the staff.

"Oh, go on, yes you can!" I suggested.

"When Reverend Jason held up the jug of communion wine, Father shouted, 'Sod off you effing w…'." She stopped mid-sentence. Paula is very literal and slow to realise when I'm egging her on.

Phil's mum had noticed the nasty scabs on his face, the lopsided monster lip and his black eye, which was surrounded by a palette of green and yellow as well. "What's happened? Philip, have you seen your face? What's happened to my boy? And don't swear, Paula. It's not ladylike."

"I told you, Mother, Phil got knocked off his bike by a bus," Paula said in a loud, clear, exasperated voice. I suspected that during the journey she'd been explaining his accident on a loop rather like the M25 itself.

"It's a good job we came, then. No need to shout. I may be nearly 90 but I'm not deaf," she protested. "If Veronica is making a cup of tea, I'd be glad to have one." Mother doesn't speak to me directly: rather she sends requests out into the ether hoping I will respond. I was barely out of the room before she was asking her sixty-two-year-old son, "Is she looking after you properly, my poppet?" in the kind of voice people reserve for cute dogs and very small babies.

"Thank God they've gone," Phil announced uncharacteristically when, several pots of tea and a whole box of shortbread selection later, they finally went. "I'm glad we don't have to spend Christmas with them." I'd never heard Phil be so critical of his family. Perhaps he was turning into his father. He even told the cat to piss off.

There were some benefits to Phil's misfortune. Being off the hook for joining them on Christmas Day, a festive feast of parched turkey and sprouts which had been boiling vigorously on the stove since early November, was a Yuletide gift for which I and my children silently rejoiced.

Latterly we had all been invited to Reigate, my parents having died and Phil's being too infirm to come to us, and we had not previously had a reason to turn down the offer. The children looked for excuses not to have to show up but realised they had to put in an appearance every few years. This year we were all spared.

Arthur, still without his own transport, was accompanying his girlfriend Tania to her parents' home near Tavistock without feeling guilty about abandoning us. Arthur favours the long and lonely walk; he finds it gets his creative juices flowing. Plenty available in Devon and, I suspect, he's worked out it gets him out

A Feather Between the Lines

of having to participate in boring chores, his return frequently coinciding with all domestic tasks being completed.

Phil has an easy bonhomie which, whilst not making him the life and soul of any event, means he enjoys the company of others. He is a good audience for anecdotes and conversation, without feeling the need to steal the airwaves himself in competition. Arthur's preference for time alone, brooding and contemplative, is another sign that genetically he is likely to be the offspring of a deep and unsettled personality who finds friendships and large groups difficult.

Jessica was relieved that she would be able to be back at work in record time. With a practical rationality which can only have been inherited from her father, she was going to make the most of catching up with some complex financial documents whilst enjoying a meal as far divorced from cardboard turkey and liquidised vegetables as possible.

Christmas is always an issue for Katie and her partner Pol, plant-based vegans who worry about over-consumption in the modern world and their carbon footprint. They cycle everywhere if possible, taking the train as a reluctant alternative. A Christmas Day world which did not involve pollutants, churchgoing and trying to explain to Phil's mother why they have brought their own food was obviously preferable. Pol recites poems in Catalan at festivals where participants stay in yurts in muddy fields. This does not result in remuneration. He describes himself as spiritual and has a wand. It's not a black stick with white ends that you wave about shouting 'abracadabra' before pulling a rabbit out of a hat or a coin out of nowhere – which is a pity because a sideline as a magician might add something to their household finances. It's an eight-inch twig with bespoke crystals superglued on one end and a leaf-shaped token bound with twine on the other. He got it online from a mystic in California having first sent details of his aura and his credit card. I might get one myself – though I'm not sure how I would describe my aura. Mardy old bat who lives in her head and doesn't engage with reality?

Phil went up to bed halfway through the King's Speech. "I want the Queen back," he moaned. "I'll never get used to singing *God Save the King.*"

Even Mandy was away, ensuring that she and her old car had made it to Drumnadrochit well in time for Hogmanay. It was bleak and not the time to be dropping bombshells.

13

Wednesday 28th December 2022

In the wasteland between Christmas and New Year and when the coast was clear of incitement from their father to keep his parents and sister company, the children came to visit for an alternative celebration. Phil felt able to come downstairs, holding court from an armchair whilst they studied his facial stripe.

Jessica lives in a tidy, new-build flat in central London with a gym, a concierge and massive service charges. Her work involves something important with numbers which is very well paid. She didn't see any humour in being knocked over by a bus. It probably says dreadful things about me that I could extract some comedy from her father's misfortune.

People say, "If I get knocked over by a bus you'll be sorry…" or "Sod it! Why not? I might fall under a bus tomorrow…" but fortunately it very rarely happens. Jessica brought some facts about buses and people in the path of buses with her when she visited. They interested her father, who shares the same lust for trivia and facts.

The chance of getting knocked over by a bus is 495,000 to 1, apparently. When I asked if she was able to say how this had been calculated or whether you could take a punt on it, they both raised their eyes heavenwards so that I was in no doubt that I was being tiresome and flippant as usual.

My Dad the bookmaker accepted bets on all sorts of unlikely

events. Amongst bona fide gambles on horses, dogs and sports events, he occasionally took a view on something fanciful. I remember one of his punters confiding that his weather-predicting budgerigar had said 'snow in June' when giving a rundown of the forecast for 1975. The budgie was not known for his insight, so Dad took on the bet. However, the bird turned out to be better informed than the Met Office, and its owner got a 50 to 1 win when snowflakes fell on the 2nd of that month at a county cricket match at Buxton. It gave Dad some good publicity in the local press as well as costing him £100. 'Bookie Beaten by Budgie's Buxton Blizzard Bet,' alliterated *The Barking and Dagenham Post*.

Jessica also explained 'the bus factor'. It is used by businesses to describe the minimum number of members of a team which would need to be taken out by a 95 going to Culham to ensure that a project stalls because of the loss of shared knowledge or competence. In our house, I realised, the bus factor was one. Without Phil to take care of the mechanics of running our finances and home, things would quickly grind to a halt. I didn't tell Jessica this, though I suspect she had worked it out. In her blunt but truthful way she is dismissive of how I have left all the boring stuff to her father yet not struck out to forge a well-paid and purposeful career for myself. She thinks I'm frivolous and that I have wasted my education. She's probably right.

Katie and Pol cycled over to visit with gifts of various homeopathic remedies including some weed-like plants which had to be steeped in hot water to make a tea. I hoped they hadn't come from the reed bed. Phil drank some and then by sleight of hand I was able to pour the rest down the sink. Katie is not like her sister. They look similar but where Jessica's clothes are expensive-looking and well-tailored and mostly shades of an inoffensive colour she calls taupe, Katie 'repurposes' hers from previous textile lives. She and Pol are saving the planet – for which I am very grateful to them. He's doing it with his poems and she is

A Feather Between the Lines

an environmental climate consultant. I'm not quite sure what that is, but it doesn't involve a budgie with foresight.

Arthur made the visit by train – the car was still taking up space in the lane, unrepaired. His latest impenetrable book was due with an editor and remained unfinished. "It's about the continuum of time yet is set in a non-specific future period where time is not pertinent," he informed us.

"Looking forward to that," Phil said feigning enthusiasm unconvincingly. Arthur doesn't expect his dad to share his gift to the literary world. He knows that he only reads fiction on holiday and that his favourite author is Len Deighton. There are no spies, wars, nail-biting situations or twisty plots in Arthur's work. He expects more from me, the one with the English Literature degree, so my lies have to be more believable.

Although I call them 'the children' they are fully grown adults. Arthur is, after all, heading for forty. It's not something I readily admit as I like to preserve the fallacy that I am far too young to have offspring who might be looking to call themselves middle-aged pretty soon. I suppose if the truth got out, I could present myself as one of those Tudor children, betrothed to Phil at birth in order to preserve dynastic links and vast tracts of land. A look at my ancestral three-bed semi in Barking and Phil's parents' between-the-wars, slightly larger detached version of the same would give the game away. Preservation of what you can plentifully find in any town or city in the UK is not required by a contractual marriage of minors.

Pol brought his wand, which he waved over Phil with what he called 'energetic intention' before they served their homemade vegan cheese. We were all going to need some focused energy if we were going to eat it. Their 'artisanal' Provolone is made with coconut milk. As ever this involves a conflict. Growing the nuts locally is impossible (palm trees and hot weather being scarce in Oxfordshire) and using imported ones involves the dreaded air miles. I questioned the protection of the name. North-western Italy, home of Provolone production, is another area not known to be fringed by palm trees.

'Provolone' tastes a whole lot better than the other effort on their cheeseboard, tofu 'Feta'. I refrained from pointing out the dearth of soya bean production in Greece which might prevent calling it the f word. I was told 'Provolone' and 'Feta' are named after the taste of the cheese, not their origin – which opens up a spectrum of alternative words you could use to label them.

Jessica was less restrained, citing a plethora of facts about how the amount of energy involved in the complex production of tofu has a worse impact on climate change for the planet than any monogastric animals. Whilst we tried to look as if we knew what monogastric meant, Phil asked Arthur to make some bacon sandwiches.

As a concession, he used Katie's vegan seeded loaf. This has the weight of a house brick and the consistency of tightly packed raffia. Not only was it good for gut health (as billed – and demonstrated over several days of after-effects) but provided hours of entertainment flossing unidentifiable seeds out of our teeth. The amount of chewing involved eating the sandwiches prevented further argument or inflammatory comments between parents and siblings.

Gripes and indigestion aside, it was good to have them all at home together and any food is an improvement on the Spittal family Christmas lunch. Even Peter Spittal had successfully got himself out of that, enjoying a delicious turkey dinner with all the trimmings at the care home whilst shouting obscenities by way of compliments to the chef.

My phone pinged with the arrival of a message. With part relief and part disappointment I saw it was a text and from Angela. It detailed instructions for a read-through of *Antony and Cleopatra* in the New Year. She was pressing ahead.

A Feather Between the Lines

I calculated that it was nearly three weeks since I had sent my reply to the USA and I had received no answer. How long did the post take? Despite dreading its arrival, I'd expected an immediate WhatsApp reply but there was none. Perhaps my curt response hadn't got there – even more stamps than the huge number I'd stuck on the envelope might have been required. Maybe it was caught up in the Christmas mail. Perhaps he had had second thoughts having read my unenthusiastic and cold message. Most probably he was away from Stanford over the Christmas period. He may be spending time with his wife and family… For the first time I considered the not unlikely possibility that during the last thirty-seven years Webster Ferris had had a personal life too.

14

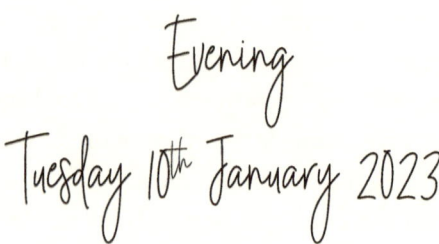
Evening
Tuesday 10th January 2023

The read-through was taking place at Angela's house. Phil was back at work – taking the car because he was yet to replace his bike, so Mandy gave me a lift. She was excited. Angela had hinted about new recruits. They would certainly be needed if Antony and Cleopatra were going to be accompanied by more than a couple of other characters.

Back south of the border, Mandy was not disseminating as many juicy details as I'd hoped about the Hogmanay ceilidh experience. The front seat of her car was taken up by a massive pair of antlers and the alarming presence of a stuffed animal head. "I don't want to damage them in case I have second thoughts and want to take them back," she explained. "Sit in the back – but not on my thistles." Close-ups with the sporran were obviously still on but she wasn't enthusing.

"I can see why you might have a rethink," I said. The beady eyes of some kind of decapitated doe stared at me from the front passenger seat. "Is it, rather was it, real?"

"Absolute bargain from a shop in the Antiques Arcade. I'm not entirely sure where I'm going to put them yet." Mandy's concerns were plainly less to do with the idea of killing beasts in the name of trophy display or interior design and more with presentation.

The creature's pitiful face looked at me knowingly, as if to say, 'You're thinking about Webster Ferris wearing that horse's head mask. Don't deny it, you foolish woman.' Of course it was right. I was remembering that trip to A&E all those years before. It was the night of the Market Place fight. I was wearing the rest of the horse costume and Webster was hiding his bleeding face from the taxi driver so he would agree to give us a lift to the hospital. The whole business of Phil's accident had reminded me of that night. It was the moment when I'd realised there was another, better side to Ferris than the unfounded rumours about him and the blunt, unpleasant aggression he presented.

Angela's house, like her footwear, is immaculate and everything looks brand new. Who buys the shade of carpet in the sample book called 'polar ice'? Angela: first in line for impractical floor coverings. If you're looking for wall-to-wall soft comfort underfoot, to my mind, it's obvious that dark tea colour is the shade to go for. Look for the one named 'just a splash of milk' or 'American tan tights'; it camouflages a multitude of misfortunes.

Hot drinks and mud are attracted to pale colours like Mandy to a single man. Angela discovered that, soon after the snow white carpet was laid, when I forgot her rule about shoes off at the door. I managed the double, soil and beverage, because I was carrying a takeaway coffee when I tripped over an ornamental stone Buddha she'd brought back from a holiday in Thailand. She forgave me, eventually, but she didn't forget. The footprints came out with scrubbing and carpet stain solution but there remains a strangely placed occasional table marking the destination of my cappuccino. The religious teacher has been moved to a position where idiots with dirty feet won't trip over him. "Buddhists believe that nothing is permanent and things are always changing," I mitigated, more to exonerate myself than justify why one part of the Arctic expanse of carpet was now more muddy field at Glastonbury. I'm not sure she was convinced.

There are thirty-four named characters in *Antony and Cleopatra* and additional officers, soldiers, messengers and attendants. That's a lot of people to fit on the stage at the Marketplace Theatre as well as into Angela's front room. The usual half a dozen, mostly female, company were sitting awkwardly on her pale-coloured sofas when Mandy and I arrived, late as usual. No one was leaning back in case they disturbed the co-ordinating plump cushions or sank so deeply into the upholstery that they would need a helping hand to get up again. Those with the most arthritic hips had made a hasty grab for the more upright chairs. It was clear Mandy and I would have to perch on a large upholstered foot stool which usually displayed books with glossy photographs of places Angela had visited on her countless long-haul holidays. I noticed they had been moved in anticipation.

"Here's our Cleo! But where is her Antony?" she teased. Everyone looked round awkwardly. Surely it wasn't going to be Vernon, one of the founder members of the Isis Mummers, who was rumoured to have been in a skiffle band on Merseyside in the 1950s with someone called Richard. People were unsure about whether this musician was Ringo Starr pre-Beatles. Was Vernon being modest or was this just another Liverpudlian called Richard? Vernon was fully aware of the mystery and did little to help solve it. He frequently mentioned old friends called John, George and Paul just to add fuel to the rumour. At 83 surely even Angela in desperation couldn't be casting him as one of the three leaders of the ancient world, a high-ranking Roman hero.

There was no doubt that the Isis Mummers was a reprise of the Pared-Down Players of my university days. The members were older but the ambition of the productions and the varied talents of their participants were similar.

"Where is everyone else?" I asked. "The friends of Caesar

A Feather Between the Lines

and the friends of Antony, not to mention the friends of Pompey. Octavius Caesar? Lepidus? Enobarbus?"

"Valerie and I are maids, but we can't agree on which one of us is going to die of the snake bite," giggled Jackie, who seemed particularly chipper after her hip replacement. Angela looked awkward. The doorbell rang. We waited in anticipation of the great hordes of new talent about to appear.

"This is Lanre," beamed Angela, "my new recruit to the Isis Mummers." There were gasps of astonishment. Lanre seemed not only to be in his thirties but very good looking. "I give you Marcus Antonius." Everyone clapped, momentarily forgetting that there were going to have to be at least another twenty unexpected knocks on the door if a full cast were to be assembled.

"Is that a big part?" Lanre asked looking alarmed. "I'm new to this kind of lark. I'm just hoping to make some new friends and have a bit of a laugh." Mandy could barely contain herself. The antlers and taxidermy might be going back after all.

"Where are you from?" she asked. The cottage might be getting an African makeover, possibly West Indian. I could see the design possibilities running through her head.

"I've moved from Birmingham. I've just changed jobs. It's kind of a fresh start after my divorce. Angela says there are lots of new members and loads of the Mummers are my kind of age and single, so I'm hoping to make some friends." Mandy practically passed out. Was it the promise of new talent under forty or the possibility of recreating the Bullring in her front room? The rest of us exchanged glances, hardly believing Angela could perjure herself quite so blatantly.

The read-through encompassed just the beginning of the first act, and it was clear that even with some doubling-up there were not even enough people present to play the parts in these first two scenes. Lanre was rather good, but it was obvious that he was expecting something less heavy which did not involve wearing a toga. He got his laugh at least when we caught each other's eye as Vernon hammed it up as Enobarbus, the oldest soldier in the Roman world.

"Angela, I've got to be frank," Lanre said as we began to leave. "I'm not sure this is what I'm looking for."

"Nonsense, you're a natural, you'll be fine," Angela replied, a look of panic on her face. She pulled me aside, "Take him to the pub and make sure he comes back next time."

"I'm not sure Shakespeare is what we ought to be doing. I've told you that before," I said.

She ignored me. "For some reason, there are several thistles stuck to the back of your cardigan."

Angela never came to the pub after rehearsals. She thought the director should maintain a distance. "Ah, the loneliness of command…" she would say when we half-heartedly felt obliged to ask her to come. She was right to stay away; it gave us the freedom to moan about her and air our grievances.

We did persuade Lanre to join us. He was quite the centre of attention. There's nothing like new blood for making people more animated. Vernon was in full flow about his skiffle-playing past, Valerie and Jackie were giggly like young schoolgirls and Mandy was the life and soul of the assembly. Together we all agreed that another play should be selected, and I was voted the one to tell Angela. Cheers.

When I got home Phil was sitting downstairs in silence. "Where were you?" he asked.

"Mummers then the pub afterwards."

"I was worried." This was most unlike Phil, who knew full well that we often went to the pub after rehearsals. In fact, we should really have made it a meet in the pub group and omitted the drama altogether. "Oh. I forgot Isis was back."

"Not like you to forget. Mandy gave me a lift. I left you some shepherd's pie."

"I didn't fancy it. I could have died you know."

"From my cooking?" Phil obviously wasn't in the mood for my flippancy.

"I've never really thought about my mortality before. It could be any day." Phil's voice was thin and shaky. He made a gesture, crossing his hands then parting them decisively. This surprised me. Phil was a man who considered everything from all angles before always drawing the conclusion that there was nothing to worry about.

"That's because your parents are still alive and you've got a sister. You haven't moved up the queue like me. I'm the next one to be pushed off the McNamara plank into the dark, unknown waters of eternity." I hammed it up like Vernon, rather pleased with my analogy. Phil was unmoved and unamused.

"There's a new man joined the group. Mandy was all over him. He's got to be fifteen years younger than her. But at least he lives a bit closer than Loch Ness." I was trying to lighten the mood.

Phil wasn't listening. "Do you ever think about a time without me?" he asked.

"No," I replied honestly. Phil was just there, like a comfort blanket. And much as I enjoyed the times he was isolated in Granny's cottage in Lycra or walking Britain's Coastal Path in Gore-Tex with his dull university mates, I hadn't considered what it would be like without him altogether. "Are you feeling OK? Do you think you should go back and see the GP?"

"I want to live to see my children settled with children of their own," he said simply. "My girls and my boy."

There it was again. The reminder that although I ought to have ignored the letter from Ferris and snapped out of the stupid fantasy that meeting up with a man I was in love with thirty-seven years ago would be in any way beneficial to anyone, I hadn't.

I could pretend I'd lost my phone and get a new one with

a different number. Ferris wouldn't be able to contact me and I wouldn't have to tell Phil that I was almost a hundred percent sure that the boy whose children he was hoping to see one day was probably not his biological son.

15

Saturday 21st January 2023

By the next rehearsal Angela had come to her senses. She had to really – given the budget and the available members of The Isis Mummers. She was saved from having to admit defeat by an initiative The Marketplace Theatre had come up with to celebrate the forthcoming coronation. A collection of short performances, one dating from each of the decades of the new King's life. Nine entertainments in total would be presented on consecutive nights during the week following the coronation. Local amateur dramatic societies were all invited to provide a contribution.

Consequently, we moved from a potential cast of well over 40 and a set encompassing the palaces of Egypt and Rome and barges on the Nile to one consisting of a station tearoom and a suggestion (offstage) of platforms and railway lines. Angela had found a short play by Noel Coward which had later been developed into the classic film *Brief Encounter*. It had seven main characters and some very small parts which she hoped could be taken by late recruits. *Still Life* had first been performed in 1936, but in the circumstances nobody volunteered to tell Angela, face saved triumphantly, that the King was born in the 1940s. The subsequent film based on the play was made at the end of the war, as I'm sure Angela would have pointed out snappily if anyone had dared to suggest it didn't fit the brief.

Mandy, who had been cast as an irritating friend who only appears in the last scene, was on another trip to Loch Ness to visit the online monster when we had our first rehearsal. Lanre had returned but the promise Angela had given him that his part was important but had minimal lines to learn was only partly fulfilled. I was instructed to soften the blow in the pub after the revelation that he was on stage for practically the whole of what was, admittedly, a short performance.

Whilst I had imagined myself to be playing Laura ('an attractive woman in her thirties'), opposite Lanre's Alec ('thirty-five, decisive, with an unhurried manner') the revelation that Angela had cast me as Myrtle ('a buxom and imposing widow') gave me my own grievance to air over a drink at The Railway Inn. At least the pub was appropriately named for the piece.

"I enter on page three and I'm barely off after that," groaned Lanre tipping a pile of peanuts from his cupped hand into his mouth and chewing forcefully.

"She thinks I'm too old," I complained unsympathetically, "but at least it's not five acts of Shakespeare. And you get to wear a Mac and not a toga. I'll help you learn the lines."

Lanre was not entirely convinced. "I've got a DVD of the film," I explained. "You should come over and we can watch it."

"Who's made a film out of that?" he laughed. "Do you still have a machine to play DVDs?"

I ignored that last comment and I didn't add that I had a video of the film too. "It's called *Brief Encounter*. I'm not talking about the 1974 remake with Richard Burton and Sophia Loren; that was a real turkey. It's the 1945 original. It's one of my favourite films. It's in black and white, obviously."

Lanre's eyes were wide with disbelief. "1945?" he echoed. "Black and white? Everyone was still wearing togas back then weren't they?" I realised that even 1974 was pre-history to Lanre, who, I feared, might be younger than Arthur.

"You're the Richard Burton part!" I chanced, hoping he'd heard of him.

A Feather Between the Lines

Lanre grinned. "You'll be a great Sophia Loren!" I wasn't that part, of course; Angela had given me the role of a comedy old bag with airs and graces behind the buffet counter. But I felt the frisson of flirtation and it made the newly sixty-year-old me feel good. "Burton was a boozer, wasn't he? I think we need another drink!" Lanre suggested, worried his jest might have been misinterpreted.

So, the following weekend, Phil, Lanre and I sat down with a take-away curry to wallow in Rachmaninov's 2nd piano concerto and black and white post-war Britain.

The stripe on Phil's face was still visible and I caught Lanre looking at it surreptitiously, presumably wondering if it was permanent and how he had come by it. Wishing to preserve an air of mystery, I chose not to explain.

At the end of the film, when Laura and Alec had parted with a last painful goodbye, he going to a new life in Africa and she back to her pipe-smoking, stuck-in-the-mud partner, both Lanre and I were in tears. Phil had long left the room to put the plates in the dishwasher and lay out his OS map on the kitchen table to study for the next segment of his Britain's Coastal Path walk. "That was brilliant," Lanre proclaimed, blowing his nose loudly. "She should have left the boring husband. She was so in love with the doctor fella."

"Coward may have been writing about 'the love that dare not speak its name' – forbidden love. The romance between two people who are already married is a symbol of homosexual love, which was illegal at the time, of course." There was a pause. I was aware I had my teacher's voice on, not one of my more admirable characteristics.

"Oh?" said Lanre. "You know a lot of things." I couldn't tell if he was being sarcastic or not. He was looking at me quizzically. I'm not sure a tutorial on Noel Coward was what he wanted with his naan and chicken dopiaza.

"Who's that in the picture on the shelf?" he asked. The

photograph of Arthur, looking awkward in his academic gown, was grinning self-consciously at us.

"Arthur, my son. Graduation photo. There are better ones of him. It's a bit out of date. That was years ago. He'll be thirty-seven in May."

"Get out!" Lanre exclaimed. "You've got a thirty-six-year-old son? He's older than me!" I was both flattered and disarmed at the same time. Did Lanre feel coming to our house was like visiting his parents? Had he come because it would seem rude to refuse? I thought we were becoming mates. Perhaps I had misread the situation. He got up to have a closer look at the ancient graduate. "Doesn't look much like either of you." Lanre was only voicing what other people must think.

"Of course, Laura in the film has two children. She's got three in *Still Life*. Leaving someone is more difficult when there's a family," I remarked, trying to divert the conversation back to the plot of the film.

"It's not easy to do, even if you don't have children." His voice was contemplative and quiet. I remembered with a jolt his divorce and felt the full force of my foot plunging through it insensitively.

"Oh, I'm sorry. I forgot."

"No worries. There's no point being with someone you've fallen out of love with. My parents just get on with it, but they can't stand each other. My mum brought us up on her own really anyway but financially it didn't make sense for me old man to be living somewhere else. He goes back to Nigeria a lot. The thing is, it's sad for all of us, in the end." There was an awkward moment whilst I considered what would be the most appropriate thing to reply. I couldn't find anything so settled on making an empathetic face, which might have been interpreted as a touch of indigestion post bhaji.

Phil reappeared with some tea and was clearly surprised by our wet tissues and the miserable atmosphere evident in the room. "I bet you're glad you came round for a jolly Saturday at the movies, Lanre," he joked. Neither of us said anything.

"We're going clockwise," Phil explained, continuing a monologue he'd begun when Lanre first arrived. "We're not doing it all in one go, obviously." Lanre's interest in slogging round the coastal paths of Britain was clearly minimal, but in the absence of further comment Phil carried on regardless. "The next leg is 137km. Somerset. Camping overnight." He put the tea on the table.

Lanre looked closely at him. I imagined he was thinking, 'Why in God's name would you want to do that at this time of year?' as well as, 'What's that peculiar stripe on your face?'

Phil had an uncanny knack of being able to read quizzical looks on people's faces. "The stripe? Didn't Roni tell you? I was almost run over by a bus." Lanre couldn't help himself laughing out loud. It was a tension breaker – but Phil looked offended.

"Why is there so much amusement about my accident?" Phil asked when Lanre had gone home.

"It's just a kind of comedy thing to happen, I suppose. Like slipping on a banana skin," I explained.

"I was inches from certain death," Phil protested in an unaccustomed dramatic foray into hyperbole and self-pity. "Your mate seemed to think it was the funniest thing he'd heard in years. You've not exactly been sympathetic yourself."

I apologised. "He thinks of himself less of a mate than a surrogate child, apparently."

"Bloody rude if you ask me."

This was new. Phil being critical? Not seeing how awkwardness can manifest itself inappropriately as laughter? He was cutting Lanre no slack, as well as suggesting, irrationally, that I didn't care about him. Most uncharacteristic. I had identified a change in him that the brush with the 95 seemed to have initiated, a sudden awareness of his own mortality. It was seven weeks since I posted my letter to California. Not that I was counting. It was looking like Ferris wasn't going to respond. Perhaps it was just as well.

"It's not on. You never take things seriously. You never have. You and your mates, finding the fact that I nearly died hilarious. The girls are sympathetic – thank goodness someone is. Arthur can't wait to mangle a tortuous description of it in his latest bloody unreadable, unpunctuated load of tosh. At least no one will know what he's on about but you're using it as an anecdote down the pub."

My phone pinged.

"If that's my son asking if I've got his car repaired yet, you can tell him, 'No. Save up and do it yourself.' "

Phil went upstairs, marching up the treads with heavy feet. He didn't even check that all the downstairs doors were locked and the milk bottles were out.

It was a WhatsApp message from an unknown number. Overseas. It started +1. I could read how it began on the screen without opening it:

Hi Roni, I'm so incredibly happy to have recei...

That bolt of electricity. There it was, streaking at high speed through my torso. I sat and looked at the screen until it went blank, hardly daring to click on it and read further. I didn't really need to look at the message in full.

All I needed to know was suggested by those few opening words.

16

Friday 4th February 2023

As promised, I helped Lanre learn his lines. We arranged to meet in The Railway Inn one Friday evening. Phil was away for the weekend, sharing fierce winds, blisters and his tent with Geoff on the North Somerset coast.

Lanre was already installed in a cosy but isolated corner of the pub. I wondered if he'd got there early so that we could sit well away from other drinkers, who, overhearing us speaking the lines, might think we were time travellers from the 1940s.

Perhaps we'd be mistaken for real-life people who live partly in the past. They participate in the modern world, but dress in period clothes and arrange their hair in fiddly wartime styles. They listen to the wireless in cold, lino-floored, unmodernised kitchens, put antimacassars on the back of armchairs and hang carpets over the washing line so they can beat coal dust out of them with something that looks like a primitive tennis racquet. I wondered if they ate Spam and a nasty, unrationed, barely palatable fish my Nan used to describe called Snoek. Do they sneak out for a McDonald's at night when their partner isn't looking or hide huge bags of Doritos in the coal shed? "Just going out for a constitutional, dearest," the man might say, putting on his mac and trilby before making his way to sit in the bus shelter and cram in a take-away pizza.

"Roni, over here!" Lanre called.

"Sorry, I was distracted thinking about people who pretend it's still the 1940s," I explained. Lanre gave me a disbelieving look.

I got myself a drink. "Get us a bag of nuts will you, daydreamer!" Lanre called in a voice loud enough to get the attention of every other person in the bar. If he had been unnoticed up until that point, it was certain all eyes were on us now. At least I knew he would be able to project to the back of the Marketplace Theatre.

I read in Laura's part as Lanre attempted to get to grips with Alec. Despite some line changes from Angela, the language seemed archaic and wasn't natural to Lanre, who had to keep his Brummie accent in check.

When he said, "It's no use running away from the truth, darling," in a perfect imitation of Trevor Howard, without warning, I began to cry. "Come on, Roni, I'm not that bad am I? That's the right line, isn't it?" he chuckled. Lanre was almost always cheerful, smiling and relaxed. He seemed to be in touch with his emotions but not ruled by them. I was envious.

This wretched play with its conflict about what is the right thing to do and its constant reminder of a solid but dull marriage didn't help. The longer I prevaricated the more awkward that conversation between Phil and me was going to be.

"Sorry. It's just this play makes me think about…" I couldn't finish the sentence.

Lanre completed it. "Look, it's none of my business but… most blokes are boring gits, you know. Some might be duller than others but unless you can't stand the sight of him, I'd say thirty whatever it is years of marriage is pretty good going. Better than a lot of people manage. He is nice to you, isn't he?" he asked cautiously.

Lanre had made a not unreasonable assumption. After all, he had seen Phil at his most tiresome, describing in unnecessary detail the coastal paths of Kent with particular reference to

A Feather Between the Lines

the Ramsgate to Camber section and the difficulties on the Whitstable to Ramsgate leg presented by access to the golf course in Kingsgate. Fortunately, the delivery of the take-away had prevented information about the progression into Sussex.

"Phil is an excellent husband," I said, "even though he now has a stripe down his face."

And then, without really thinking about it, I told him. The secrets I've been keeping for years. Parts that not even Neil knew.

Without pausing for breath, I described my turbulent relationship with the unpredictable but unique Webster Ferris. I described our last passionate meeting on Arthur's Seat at the Edinburgh Festival after I thought we were finished and I'd begun to see Phil, and how Webster had then flounced off to the USA furious that I wouldn't drop everything to go with him. I tried to explain how it was difficult to forget him because my son – ironically named Arthur at Phil's suggestion – is not only Ferris's double but has inherited his birth father's gifts with literature and his tricky personality. I told him how delighted Phil was when he found out I was pregnant with what he assumed (as I hoped at the time) was his baby, how we had got married and how I hadn't heard a word from Ferris for thirty-seven years until he saw the photograph of the college reunion in the alumni publication. And now I had received the letter from America describing his upcoming visit to Oxford (of all places), an invitation to meet up and the implied suggestion that he still thought about me too.

Lanre's mouth was wide open. "Bloody Hell, Roni," he spluttered eventually. He got up from the table, not, I realised, to leave in disgust but to process my bombshell. "Don't go away," he insisted as he went to the bar to get several types of bar snack and another drink for us both.

I wasn't intending to go anywhere. I felt strangely relieved finally to share this information. It seemed easier because I didn't know Lanre very well and because, despite spending an evening with a black and white film from seventy-seven years ago and the UK's leading authority on Kent's coastal paths, he didn't know any of the other characters involved.

I could see him thinking through the story whilst waiting at the bar. It did sound like something someone might make up – a person who was an attention-seeking pathological liar for example.

"Why didn't he contact you after he got to America? When he'd cooled off," Lanre reasoned when he came back with the drinks, as if Webster Ferris behaved according to the laws of logic. It was probably the conclusion most people would have come to. It was certainly what Phil would have done, not that he'd ever have found himself in a situation where he hadn't thought things through carefully in the first place. If Webster loved me as much as he professed, he would have swallowed his pride and called me. Why had I never heard from him? I'd often asked myself this question over the years.

Since the recent letter from America, I finally knew the reason. "He found out that I was engaged from Simeon Goldblatt, who'd been at our college and also went to study at Harvard." Lanre looked confused. "Mrs Goldblatt got her hair done at my mum's salon. Mum told her that I was engaged," I explained.

"Hang on, you've lost me here." Lanre's expression suggested that he thought I was definitely making the whole thing up.

The narrative was complicated. Further anecdotes about Barking and Simeon's involvement with my knickers being hoisted up a flagpole did little to convince him that I wasn't a fantasist enjoying fabricating an anecdote.

Lanre remained quiet, as if he was considering the £32,000 question on *Who Wants to Be a Millionaire?*. "Why were your pants flying from a flagpole?" He poured a whole pack of scampi fries into his gaping mouth. "My time at Aston was dull dull dull by comparison."

"We all got very drunk, by accident. Someone got the punch

recipe wrong. The elastic snapped and my pants came off in the boathouse loo."

Lanre laughed. "You are winding me up!" he roared. "Punch? Boathouses? You're a great storyteller. This would make a much better play than the shit Angela is proposing."

Not for the first time, I felt ashamed of my youthful behaviour. I didn't elaborate. Lanre had already decided I was fantasising without further improbable detail. It all seemed like something I had dreamt up a time long ago and which had become the truth in my confused mind.

"I wish I'd been at university in the swinging sixties. Sounds like a right laugh." Lanre clearly didn't believe a word of what I'd just told him.

"How old do you think I am? It was the 80s!" It was obvious that Lanre had slotted me into a multi-purpose old codger group in his brain labelled 'Years Older Than Me'.

1960s? 70s? 80s? – it was all prehistory to him. A far-off internet and mobile-free wilderness, a period too outdated to seem real. Like lavatories in the Middle Ages or Victorian dentistry, some things are just too archaic and unpleasant to consider realistically. I was lucky he'd come back from the bar with another glass of wine for me, not a cup of Ovaltine, a pair of slippers and a hot-water bottle.

I had finally told someone what had really happened, and it felt good to have done so. He didn't believe me or thought I was exaggerating at the least, but somehow it didn't matter. It was like a rehearsal, though I knew that when I finally confessed to the real characters in the story they wouldn't react the same way.

A monologue on the stage of the Marketplace Theatre would be one way of telling the truth to everyone. In one brutal, fell swoop, I could announce everything to an audience of Phil, his parents and sister, our children, my friends and Ferris himself. I'd finish by saying, "I didn't mean it – but one failure to tell the whole truth led to another. Everyone chooses how much they tell. I'm not the only one."

Phil's father would shout, "Sod off you bitch!" before being taken back to the care home by his embarrassed sister. His mother would ask, "What did Veronica say, Philip?" Before I could see the expression on Arthur, Phil and the girls' faces, I'd run like mad, maybe non-stop round Britain's Coastal Path. When I returned everyone would be so surprised that I'd accomplished it they'd forgive me. Or, more likely, I'd expire in the process probably on the Kent section whilst trying to find the path through North Foreland Golf Club. Lanre noticed I was distracted.

"Don't tell me there's more…" he begged, cramming a handful of cheese and onion crisps into his mouth.

I chose not to tell him about my college friend Mary and her contribution to the story. One needs a few secrets to hang on to.

Lanre's job involves going round companies looking at them with fresh eyes. He has some fancy and meaningless job title but basically he's a troubleshooter. He has a clear and incisive grasp of problems and can suggest effective solutions. He thought he'd identified that there was a kernel of truth in what he'd just heard. "If you really did get a letter from this Webber or whatever he's called, you're going to have to reply." He grinned, suggesting he was now playing along with my fantasy world. "Like it or not, you have to tell all, either by meeting him or in the letter." He chewed on some pork scratchings thoughtfully. "And then you are going to have to tell Phil and Arthur. They deserve to know."

I wanted to stay in the pub. Maybe I could encourage Lanre to tell me something about his past, about the ex-wife who he alluded to happily but never described or his childhood in Birmingham. Suddenly I didn't want to go back to an empty house and wait for Phil's goodnight phone call from his tent facing the Bristol Channel. What would I say when he asked, as he always did, what I had done that evening.

A Feather Between the Lines

"Oh, I just met that bloke Lanre from the Isis Mummers in the pub and ran through the lines with him. And I also told him how I suspect our son is actually only my son, not yours. I went up Arthur's Seat with Webster Ferris when we were at the Edinburgh Festival and we had sex in the open air."

"Did you? Not much on the telly then?"

It wasn't entirely fanciful that this would be Phil's reaction. He doesn't always listen to what I say. The enquiry about my day would be a prelude to the important stuff. What he would really be keen to discuss would be his day's walk, the weather and the meteorological prospects for the next day.

Lanre, sadly, did not fancy nestling in until closing time with a woman old enough to be his mother. "My jaw aches from laughing," he grinned. "Thanks for cheering me up. We'd better push off because we're both driving."

Poor old Lanre. The common sense of the millennial prevents him having one too many and having to leave the car at the pub and walk home or wait forever at a bus stop for a service which finished two hours earlier. He'll never know the inconvenience of having to come back the next day for his car then realising he's left the keys in the pocket of his other coat. His hair is never fully let down. His embarrassment factor is minimal by comparison to that of his parents' generation and he will never believe just how badly they behaved. He thinks they're making it up.

As we parted in the car park he said, "Don't forget to reply to him!" He broke into a solo version of *When Will I See You Again?* He had a lovely voice. Angela should have opted for a musical. He was still singing as he drove past me, fumbling for my keys in a handbag excessively large for a quick drink in a local pub. He wound his window down. "Ta-ra-a-bit," he shouted, waving. He was serenading about sharing precious moments as he turned into the road. Perhaps two pints was more than Lanre should have had before the drive home.

Despite this preposterous eruption of facts, I'd omitted to confess that I had already replied and Webster had not only received my curt and non-committal letter but revealed in his response that he had correctly read between the lines that I wanted to see him just as much as he wanted to see me.

Phil had rung whilst I was driving home from the pub. He'd left a message to say not to call back as they were turning in. The weather was windy and the temperature was lower than they had anticipated. I could have told them what sleeping under canvas in midwinter on an exposed north-facing site might be like. Even with minimal camping experience I could have given an accurate prediction as to the discomfort.

I went to bed myself. I thought of Phil shivering in his two-man tent in North Somerset. I thought of Arthur and his girlfriend in London. I didn't want to hurt either of them but it was going to happen. I thought of Webster Ferris, as I always did when I was in that comfy space between wakefulness and sleep, and how he had analysed my response. A line from *Still Life* ran through my head.

'I don't suppose being in love has ever been easy for anybody.'

17

Six months after the letter arrived
March 2023

Crown Him With Many Plays! consisted of three nights each divided into three parts representing a decade of the new monarch's life – 1948 to 2023. Our short play and its small cast were the opening performance. Rehearsals for *Still Life* were frequent because the extravaganza was now only a month away.

Angela kept schtum about the short, five-scene drama dating from 1936, hoping that no pedant would appear on the first night to disqualify us from participation. She clung to the belief that in future we might be creating the vistas of ancient Rome and Egypt rather than a refreshment room at a small railway junction in an unidentified part of Middle England. She trusted we would stand out favourably on the first night when we were billed with a three-person, gritty, glum Northern misery-fest from the 1950s and a psychedelic dance 'happening' with electronic music but no plot which was supposed to represent the 1960s. She anticipated a post-production rush of talented actors begging to join us and fulfil her Shakesperian dream.

Lanre was an excellent mid-twentieth century doctor, all trilby hat, mackintosh and clipped diction. He relished his speeches about lung conditions he was hoping to cure and soul-searching statements about the nature of the love affair he had embarked on with Laura. Angela had harboured high hopes that a resting actress from the RSC or someone back in Britain between Hollywood roles would appear to play her, but it became obvious that this wouldn't happen.

Mandy was promoted to play the part. Despite her stage fright and inability to remember the lines, she was the only one of us to look young enough to pass for thirty-something. Even under a ton of make-up and strong stage lighting, Jackie, who had excellent recall if not a huge amount of stage presence and was only slightly limping after her hip operation, did not look young enough. She was bitterly disappointed to be relegated to the part Mandy was originally playing – Dolly, the annoying friend who interrupts the lovers' parting in the final scene. She comes on, sits down immediately and doesn't budge until the final curtain. A wig and a hat, Angela hoped, would take forty years off her from a distance.

I was out for several evenings a week. Phil didn't mind but unusually he was not interested in providing technical help with sound for the show as he had in the past. Various locomotive noises were required: express trains thundering past, local chuggers gradually pulling into the station, whistles blowing and platform bells ringing. It was a pre-Beeching cornucopia of rail noises which he would normally have been meticulous about researching and recreating with a level of pedantry which may have become irritating. Angela asked me to beg but his response was surprisingly gruff. "You can tell Angela that I'm taking industrial action. The 5:43 steaming into the station will have to be provided by someone else."

Lanre was enjoying the secret he was now carrying on my behalf. He delivered several lines such as 'It's no use running away from the truth, darling – we're lovers, aren't we?' with a knowing look. When Mandy responded with 'I'm a respectable married woman with a husband, a home and three children', a line she could remember and which she repeated liberally when others eluded her, he winked encouragingly. Mandy incorrectly interpreted this as directed at her and not me. She thought it was not only a confirmation that she was doing well but also that Lanre was giving her some kind of signal on the rail track of love. The antlers and tartan were in danger of being traded in. A recreation of the Peaky Blinders gangland HQ with a portrait of Ozzy Osbourne and Black Sabbath playing noisily in the background might be on the cards. Visitors could feast on Cadbury's chocolate whilst avoiding being pushed into a replica canal water feature in the back garden. From our side of the fence, I mused, I might push a shopping trolley and some dead animals into it for authenticity.

Some kind of personality change had occurred in Phil. The bus had disturbed his rationality though not his love of cold, wet and uncomfortable activities with which to pass his spare time. I was conscious that I needed to have the conversation with him soon, but I found it harder to do so knowing that his reaction was now less likely to be measured and accepting. Laura's description of her husband – 'medium height, brown hair, kindly, unemotional and not delicate at all' – no longer described Phil fully, although Lanre was unable to resist beaming widely whenever she remembered to say that line.

One evening, when Phil and I were both home watching TV, I decided it was time. I started by talking about Arthur generally. Phil's response was curt. "It's about time he got a job and earned some money. That girl isn't going to support him forever." This wasn't an unreasonable comment about Arthur. The persona of the writer in his garret (actually a nice flat in Wandsworth bought by his girlfriend, once a fellow creative but now employed in an investment bank) whose work was valuable but unrecognised by the ignorant mainstream reader was one he curated. Positive criticism by heavyweight literary pseuds was rewarding in all ways but financial. Socialist convictions alongside a lack of contribution to society in general and living off the fat of capitalist endeavour was a paradox not explored in Arthur's turgid prose. I suspect Phil wasn't the only one thinking that, at nearly thirty-seven, he should be moving into more lucrative aspects of writing. Or perhaps in an entirely different direction.

I planned to segue into the absence of pragmatic common sense being understood by the lack of an inherited sensible gene possibly explained by Arthur's questionable parentage. Then I'd follow that up with a full-blown confession and show my love for Phil by selflessly offering to walk a leg of the Coastal Path or spend a week at Granny's cottage as penance. But the phone rang.

"There we go! What does he want now? More help from me?" Phil snarled as he got out of his chair to answer it. I knew it wasn't Arthur. He doesn't use the landline; the children don't bother with it. The only people not calling us by mobile phone are people over seventy, a few of our friends who live in areas with poor signals and a robotic woman who is obsessed with telling us that the insulation in our loft is insufficient, even though she has never had access to it.

Phil's face was serious and his responses did not immediately betray the information he was receiving. He did not look pleased. Not someone else in A&E? Not another bus? Please not a long-distance call from California – though that would act as a catalyst to my revelations.

"I'll come now. No that's fine, it's no trouble… the traffic on the M25 should be minimal at this time." I might have believed that the old Phil would be helpfully offering to pick Webster Ferris up from Gatwick Airport, uncomplaining about not having prior warning or his evening disturbed. But now?

"It's Father," he said eventually, when he had replaced the receiver. "He's dead." He was very matter-of-fact, a shade of the Phil of old. Yet there was no rational continuation about how he'd had a good life and didn't suffer. I felt a pang of relief then a flush of guilt. "He was watching the six o'clock news. When Boris Johnson was shown explaining Partygate to the Commons select committee, he shouted, 'Piss off you lying bastard, motherfucking arse-faced prick!' All the carers and some of the other residents broke into a round of applause and he just went. Out like a light."

"I haven't heard him say motherfucker before. That's a new one," I replied, immediately realising how inappropriate it was – yet still followed up with a crass, "I'm impressed he could still follow the news story." Obviously this did nothing to restore my reputation as a sympathetic and concerned daughter-in-law.

"I'm going to be with Mother and Paula. There's no need for you to bother," Phil stated before I could offer to come too. Soon he was in the car with a small overnight bag and no indication about when he'd be back, leaving me and the elephant in the room.

Phil was gone for nearly a week in the end attending to 'arrangements'. When there is administration of that nature to be done, Phil is the one you need to be doing it. Not for the first time I acknowledged that without the Phils of this world we would all be in a sorry old state. Thank God for him.

Lanre noticed Mandy was giving me a lift to rehearsals. My part as Myrtle, the manager of the station buffet, was turning out to be a good one with plentiful comic lines.

"…There are just as good fish in the sea, I said, as ever came out of it, and I packed my boxes then and there and left him."

"You haven't, have you?" Lanre joked. "You said that with conviction."

The funeral was in a soulless Surrey crematorium with a conveyor belt vibe about it. Arthur was on such strict instructions to make sure he was on time and not let his father down that he had arrived far too early and had attended the service for the previous deceased by the time the rest of us got there. I'm sure there were some confused mourners who wondered who the casually dressed, tall, dark man who'd arrived by taxi, quickly shovelling a beanie hat into his pocket, was.

There were few mourners for Phil's father; one of the penalties of very old age is that most friends and acquaintances pre-decease you. This was a fact Phil's mother was eager to point out later back at the house.

Periodically she exclaimed, "Everyone's dead," in a loud voice. "Even the Queen is dead, you know. Who'd have thought it? I'll be next."

"She was 96, much older than you." Paula was trying to lighten the mood but her mother wasn't to be diverted.

"They have all the best doctors, but she's still dead. And so's her mother," Pamela added, failing to acknowledge that the Queen Mother would have been 122 had she still been under the care of the top physicians in the land and not the overworked Reigate GP who'd had Phil's father on his list.

An ancient distant cousin was enjoying seeing our children in the flesh and comparing them to the glowing testimony Phil's mother had been giving them over the years. "The older girl looks like that asthmatic uncle we had from Hartlepool," she was telling Pamela, "and the younger one, who's wearing those bright clothes, she's the look of your grandmother, only scrawnier."

"They're both dead of course," Pamela informed her, "like everyone else."

"The boy, though, he's not like anyone. Has he got a proper job yet?"

Pamela's stage whisper was noisier than her normal speech. "He doesn't work. He's an author. His books are well received in literary circles."

"So you said," continued the cousin, "but I haven't seen any of them in the mobile library. I love reading. I'm happy as Larry when I've got an audio book of Dorothy L Sayers or Agatha Christie on.

A Feather Between the Lines

I'm partial to Lord Peter Wimsey and Miss Marple, but I can't be doing with that Poirot."

"Well they've all been dead for years." Pamela's catalogue of the deceased was growing. "Arthur's not from our side. He's got the Irish in him." She cast me a disdainful look across the room.

"I'm not dead. I'm alive and my hearing is in full working order," I replied, knowing she wouldn't hear me.

"What did Veronica say, Philip?"

"She said I nearly died when I came off my bike," Phil broadcast at maximum volume. Pamela had clearly forgotten the collision with the 95, despite the remnants of the scar on Phil's face.

"You want to be more careful. Don't show off riding with your hands off the handlebars. I've told you that countless times." Pamela still thought Phil was ten, zooming up and down their cul-de-sac on his orange Raleigh Chopper with his mates after school.

We were quiet in the car coming back afterwards. I didn't think Phil would want to listen to me prattling on. Not surprisingly he was contemplative. My phone buzzed.

"Who's that?"

"Katie. Their train is cancelled. They're still at the station."

"I fail to see how getting a lift with us is contributing to their carbon footprint. We are travelling anyway." Phil had a point, but I was lying. The WhatsApp was from Webster Ferris.

> Flying to London 7th May, up to the northwest 8th, Oxford 9th. Please let me know where and when we can meet – I'm free pretty much all the time before the lectures begin on the 17th. 'With mirth and laughter let old wrinkles come'.

Only Ferris could casually drop a quotation from *The Merchant of Venice* into a WhatsApp concerning arrangements. Free for ten days? He'd got various bits of the country covered too. No leeway for wriggling out because it was too far or because I had something on. If I was going to turn down a meeting, I'd have to be honest about not wanting to see him. I typed my reply.

> Oft expectation fails and most oft there where most it promises.

He responded quickly,

> Ah! *All's Well That Ends Well*. The title is hopeful at least...

Impulsively I replied,

> We were small and thought we knew nothing / Worth knowing. We thought words travelled the wires / In the shiny pouches of raindrops, / Each one seeded full with the light / Of the sky, the gleam of the lines, and ourselves / So infinitesimally scaled / We could stream through the eye of a needle.

It took me a while; I can't type on a phone as quickly as my children. A frisson of excitement shot through me. Webster Ferris was arriving, with unintentional irony, on Arthur's birthday.

What on earth was I doing? Returning from my father-in-law's funeral not only had I told a lie which was bound to be easily exposed but I was flirting in messages by quotation right next to my husband. There was a short pause before I saw the words 'typing' under the phone number at the top of the message. It stayed there for a long while until a reply pinged through.

> The nobel prize-winning Irish poet? It's about telegraph lines near a railway if I remember correctly. Such beautiful words, Miss McNamara. I must look it up. Trust you to have it within grasp. I think you knew more about the world than me. I was

A Feather Between the Lines

the child who couldn't understand. I revert to Shakespeare. 'The miserable have no other medicine but only hope'.

I didn't dare carry on. I started to sob.

"I'm finding it difficult to cry," Phil admitted, looking straight ahead through the windscreen but passing me a tissue from his conveniently located supply in the door pocket. "I know I should, and it would make me feel better. But I can't. I never have been able to." I stayed silent. "I envy you and your connection with your emotions. I hoped it might rub off on me over the years, but I don't think it has."

I messaged Katie. They'd caught the train easily and were about to retrieve their bikes from the rack at the station and 'be home in no time'.

Ahead the 40mph signs were flashing on the gantry and the traffic slowed dramatically.

"I'm coming off at junction 13 and going to get on the A 308," announced Phil, adding "Robin Hood Gate, Richmond Park, to Bisham, Berkshire," just in case I might have morphed into one of his walking chums and be about to announce this information before him.

18

April 20th 2023

Neil was on the edge of his seat, leaning forwards at the kitchen table, his elbows resting on its surface and his hands locked together. If it hadn't been for the wide-eyed look on his face, one might have assumed he was praying.

We had confided our innermost secrets to each other at university, so it wasn't strange that he was probing the depths of my current situation. He was now, of course, acutely aware that previous sharing had been unequal, particularly in the world of romance and lust. Neil had been brutally honest, frankly often in greater detail than I had wished for, but I hadn't traded fairly. I had kept my affairs of the heart to myself, and he was now relishing the opportunity to catch up.

Since my surprise party we'd communicated updates on the big reveal by phone calls and cryptic messages. Now a convenient out-of-town work meeting brought him near Oxford and he wasn't going to miss the opportunity to pin me down in person.

"When is Gob back from work?" he asked, calculating how long he had to interrogate me. "I can't wait to catch up with the bus-flattened, personality-changed version." Although I had explained the catalogue of reasons why I hadn't quite got round to my confession, Neil was unconvinced. "I don't think you really want to tell him."

"Of course I don't. I just know I should. It's been a burden carrying this knowledge. I feel deceitful. But now he's lost his own father it makes it worse – taking his son away as well. And what about Arthur – shouldn't he know?"

"Don't be so dramatic. Does it really matter? You're not even sure yourself." Neil pulled a face which confirmed what he and I both knew; it was almost certainly true. "There are hundreds and thousands of people who think their father is someone other than the person who provided the sperm at conception. Are they unhappy? Probably not. They might be if they found out. There's a case for just leaving things be. Ignorance is bliss." Did he imagine I hadn't been over this a thousand times myself? "Just playing devil's advocate," he added.

"It's called lying by omission in the Catholic faith. It's a sin."

"Lordy, look who's coming over all pious and devout. Little Miss Agnostic having a wobbly. Sorry I mentioned the devil."

The bell rang. Mandy in all probability. Despite my telling her Neil was gay and had been living very happily with Simon for almost thirty years, a glimpse of him entering our house was guaranteed to have her dinging the bell and finding some excuse to come in.

"That'll be Mandy. I'll get rid of her," I promised, despite knowing that was almost impossible.

But it wasn't her standing on the doorstep.

"I know I should have contacted you first, but I was nearby and thought I'd just try in case you were in."

Neil came into the hall eager to witness me trying to prevent Mandy getting a foot in the door. "Mary Featherstone! – isn't it? My God, how are you?"

Indeed, it was Mary, the friend from college with whom I had recently reconnected at the forty-year reunion and whose secret I was now harbouring along with my own. Soon she was sitting round the kitchen table too and the kettle was on for more tea.

"I haven't seen you since that last summer at the Edinburgh

Festival," enthused Neil. "Tell me, how have the last thirty-seven years been?"

Mary was apologetic about arriving unannounced and when I already had another visitor, but she showed no sign of pushing off in a hurry so that Neil could carry on playing the nosey psychoanalyst with me.

"Do you remember Bomber?" Mary asked Neil. "He practically shared a room with Roni in our first year."

"Some gossip I don't know?" Neil's eyes twinkled with the promise of some information for his special subject.

"Definitely not! He flew on noisy 'missions' thrice daily with a girl called Binka who I had to share with after my room was flooded," I explained to Neil. "You and I weren't friends in the first year, were we." Neil looked quizzical, as if he didn't really believe me.

"Well," Mary continued, "last summer I was looking round a castle in Scotland and there was his photograph in a frame in the drawing room!" This seemed a rather tame revelation for a special and uninvited detour to our house. "It was his home! He's the Duke now. There he was, wearing a kilt and bald as a coot. He's got eight children and a scary-looking wife."

"Was she the Binka woman?" Neil was looking for a sniff of interest in this lame tale.

"No." Mary looked awkward. There was clearly something else she wanted to tell me which had necessitated the unannounced visit. She'd have to tell Neil as well now. Or just go home.

"I've been visiting my son in Oxford. He's at the university. I expect Roni told you," she explained.

"No, my dear," scoffed Neil. "Roni doesn't tell me anything." He shot me a knowing look. "What's he reading?" Neil clearly assumed Mary was an older mother and had a student son.

"He's a professor of English Literature. The youngest professorial appointment the Faculty has ever made. He's just about to publish his new book, *The Townley Mystery Cycle: who was the Wakefield Master?* I thought Roni might have said."

"A guaranteed best-seller!" Neil exclaimed. "Roni has kept all this to herself. She is a keeper of secrets, the soul of discretion." He was loving this. "How old is he then, if you don't mind me asking?"

Mary blushed. "Luke's just had his thirty-seventh birthday." Neil looked confused. Mental maths was never one of his strong suits but even he could calculate that it was about thirty-seven years and ten months or so since we had graduated. He took a large swig from his teacup to avoid saying something he'd regret later. "I've told Roni, and I may as well tell you. It's not a secret, I just hadn't admitted it before." Neil's eyes widened: more intrigue! He kept the large volume of tea in his mouth fearing swallowing might cause him to miss something. "Luke's father is Webster Ferris. You will remember him. Everyone does."

A fountain of tea shot from Neil's mouth, dousing some shortbread biscuits I had just put on a plate. He tried to swallow what was left in his mouth, but it made him choke and gag. I slapped him on the back, rather harder than was strictly necessary to prevent inhalation.

Mary laughed. "I know. He provoked that reaction in a lot of people at the time, but he was much misunderstood."

Neil belched.

"Looking back, our union was an aberration on my part. It happened just once, on the day of our graduation, but I must stress our coupling was at my instigation. I'd never had a boyfriend and I wanted to try it out. Webster was very unhappy, and men often express their emotions through sex, don't they?" she continued in a matter-of-fact, unemotional way. "In fact, I'm a lesbian but I hadn't recognised it at that time."

I thought Neil was going to pass out at this further admission. He had to excuse himself to the bathroom to recover.

"Perhaps I shouldn't have mentioned it. Was I too factual?"

Mary sighed when he was out of the room. "I'm surprised he's bothered. You took it much better when I told you."

"Oh, you know Neil, always the drama queen!" I was glad that my pretence of an understated, non-committal response had been successful that morning in Cambridge when my head was spinning and my heart was thumping. That unforgettable moment last September when Mary's surprise admission prodded my conscience and started the cascade of emotion and turmoil that I had been suffering ever since.

"I saw a leaflet in Oxford this afternoon, when I was with Luke. It's why I called in. There's a lecture series in May. Shakespeare. Luke is attending obviously." She scrabbled in her pocket and pulled out a flyer which she put on the table. It read:

> "Letting 'I dare not' wait upon 'I would' – cowardice, inaction and suppression of desire in Shakespeare's plays."
> The 2023 biennial Shakespeare lecture series will be given by distinguished author and critic,
> Professor Webster Ferris, MA (Cantab), PhD (Harvard) from Stanford University, California.

"I've decided I'm going to tell Ferris. He may wish to meet Luke. I thought I ought to let you know. Perhaps we could attend the lectures together. Or is that a silly idea?"

I could have trumped her. 'You don't know the half of it. I'm already in touch with Ferris and by the way, he impregnated me too, in the open air on Arthur's Seat.' But I just stood there, mute. I was inhabiting a real-life version of the uncountable number of pupils' stories I had marked over my career, those where the resolution of a convoluted plot had spiralled out of any realistic hope of sensible conclusion and where the exasperated author could only write, 'and then I woke up and it was all a dream,' just to finish the bloody thing.

A Feather Between the Lines

A key turned in the lock and I could hear Phil removing his shoes in the hall before he joined us in the kitchen.

"Well I never! Mary Featherstone. I didn't know you were coming too. Roni never tells me anything." Phil grabbed a lump of shortbread from the plate and shoved the whole thing into his mouth. "Pre-dunked biscuits, that's a new one. Did you use the leaky pot, Ron?" Mary and I hesitated about whether to tell him how the enrobement of 'jus de thé' had occurred. "Actually, I kind of like it. It might catch on." Phil poked another into his mouth before I could try to remove the plate. His mouth was still full of soft dough. It coated his lips and dribbled from his mouth.

"Well hello, Gob!" exclaimed Neil, who had returned speedily from the bathroom in case he missed any more nuggets of gossip gold. "Brought any pizzas with you?"

"Neil, there you are. I was expecting you and found Mary. Been powdering your nose in anticipation of my arrival?"

"What's happened to your face?" Mary was transfixed by the stripe, which was showing little sign of fading.

"Run over by a bus. I could have died." Phil shoved yet another shortbread into his mouth as Mary stifled a giggle and Neil peered in for a better look.

"Do you remember Webster Ferris?" Mary asked, eager to change the subject in case her question had been too personal and her response too disrespectful.

"Do I? That aggressive bastard. The stereotype Yorkshireman with no manners?" Phil moved to the sink to wash his hands. In his eagerness to experience the soggy biscuit he had forgotten his obsession with pre-eating hand hygiene. Because his back was to us, he missed Neil's look of surprise at this sudden departure in the conversation. Mary calculated that this was not the time to share news of her liaison with Ferris with Phil, correctly assuming that I hadn't shared the information with him.

"I picked up this leaflet about some lectures he's giving next month. I guess you don't want to go."

Phil grabbed the flyer. "What's he doing here? I thought he pissed off to America to be rude to the Yanks years ago." Phil's memory was accurate as usual.

"I think we should get a group booking. It'd be fun!" Neil suggested mischievously. "Your son can come too, Mary."

"A son? I didn't know," Phil said accusingly.

Fortunately, before there was a necessity for me to divert Mary from sharing any details about Luke and his father, the doorbell rang again. "Who the bloody hell is that?" Phil's short temper and his irritated stomp to find out was a surprise to Mary.

"Oh dear, Phil seems to be a bit tetchy," Mary observed.

"It's all go here," Neil grinned. "I feel like I'm in a Brian Rix farce. What fun! Who's that knocking at the door?" He began to imitate Paul McCartney singing *Let 'em in*. Above the singing we could hear some commotion in the hall.

Phil returned. "If we are talking sons, here's mine." He pushed Arthur into the room, snatching the beanie from his head as he did so. There was a collective silence.

"I'm coming home for a bit, Mum," Arthur said, aware of the awkward atmosphere but not understanding why it was there. "I hope that's OK. Tania and I have decided to chill out for a while. I would have rung but my phone was out of battery. I got a mate to give me a lift in his van."

"She chucked you out more like. There's a huge pile of his stuff in the hall." Phil sounded angry.

I was paralysed, unable to decide how to play this situation. Neil was inspecting Arthur closely. He wasn't a carbon copy of Luke Featherstone, but he looked very much like the photograph Mary had shown me of him at her house last September. In turn they were both variations on the theme of Webster Ferris. The likeness was uncanny. Mary was transfixed by this doppelgänger. Only her mouth moved, opening and shutting silently like a goldfish monotonously making its way round a bowl.

"He'll be thirty-seven next month and he's boomeranging back to live with mum and dad." Phil's face reddened and the stripe became more noticeable, as if it were a warning light on the dashboard of a car which was about to overheat.

The 'pile of stuff' cluttering up the hall was an irritation to Phil, who still prized order and neatness despite his transformation courtesy of the Oxford Bus Company. He had spent the whole of our marriage trying to minimise my belongings and corral them into a sensible, easily accessible collection of essentials and had been infinitely patient about the impossibility of doing so. He went into the hall and grabbed a couple of boxes and some plastic bags overflowing with clothes. Arthur didn't seem to own a suitcase.

"Christ these are heavy!" Phil shouted. "You can carry some of it upstairs. I'm not doing it all on my own."

"Books," Arthur explained. He scooped up the soggy remains of the tea-soaked shortbread from the plate and posted it into his mouth before going to help his father ferry his belongings upstairs. "New kind of cake Mum? Looks delicious. I'm starving."

Neil found it hard to hide his disgust. "Who ate the rest?"

"Phil. Some things are best left unsaid."

Our eyes met in a brief but intense moment. "Ab-so-lute-ly."

Even Neil, lover of intrigue and purveyor of gossip of the most unverified kind, felt too uncomfortable to hang around and see what was going to happen next. "I'm going to love you and leave you," he said, blowing a kiss as he sped to the front door and out into the lane.

Mary remained silent but the look on her face told me a quick calculation about Arthur's age and appearance had prompted a realisation she had yet to find the words to express. I put the cups and plate into the sink and looked out into the back garden at the blossom on the trees. For the first time I considered that I too might be chucked out of my home because Phil had had enough and couldn't accept the deception which I had perpetrated over the entirety of our marriage. New Phil was not rational and understanding, he was displaying previously absent emotions like anger and impatience.

Arthur and I might have to lodge with Mandy for a while, crammed into her spare room. We'd have to share a bed not only with each other but with all the remnants of previous makeovers, the bagpipes, some shabby-chic window shutters and a huge headache-inducing canvas of primary coloured squares, with just a Provencal tablecloth as a blanket to cover us. Even in this difficult situation I was still daydreaming. I felt ashamed.

Eventually Mary broke the silence. "That young man cannot be Phil's son. He's nothing like him. He could be Luke's brother. Why didn't you tell me last time we met?" I couldn't speak. I remained looking out of the window. "I'm right, aren't I? Or is this just a huge co-incidence. Arthur should be older than Luke, that's the only thing. Or did you see Webster again, after we left?"

I exhaled, long and deeply, which coincided with a sudden flurry of a breeze outside. As if I possessed some supernatural power, blossom was gently shaken from the tree so there was a confetti-like shower of pink-tinged petals making a slow journey down to the lawn.

"Does Phil know?" I shook my head. I couldn't look her in the face. How could Phil not know? Everyone else seemed to make the connection.

"Does Phil know what?" He was back in the room.

"I'm afraid," explained Mary cautiously as my heart began to thump, "Roni and I have something to tell you."

"What now? Who else is dropping in uninvited?"

"Those biscuits you liked. I'm afraid Neil spat tea all over them. It was too late to tell you before you ate them."

I sighed; Mary's quick thinking had saved the day. Or perhaps it hadn't. That might have been the opportunity to get the whole sorry business out in the open.

"Why did he do that? How disgusting. You could have stopped me, you daft cow." Phil looked as if he was going to be sick.

"I'll get out of your way." Mary had taken offence on more than one count. She headed for the door. I followed but she wasn't interested in goodbyes.

"She's turned into a sour old bag," Phil called at a volume which could be heard all over the Thames Valley. "The years have taken their toll."

I grabbed the car keys. "I'd better go to the shops to get some more food if Arthur is here for supper too." I hoped I might catch up with Mary outside and apologise.

"Don't bother. Let the bastard starve."

Phil was getting worse. Was he becoming like his father? He was certainly swearing more than ever before. Mary had driven off before I could reach her.

On the way to the shop I called in at the GP where the evening surgery was in full flow. I waited in a line at the desk to ask for an urgent appointment.

"You have to ring at 8am for an on-the-day appointment." The receptionist chanted the familiar mantra as if she was a recorded announcement reminding tube travellers to mind the gap between the train and the platform.

"But you don't answer the phone."

"I do answer the phone. You are obviously always too far down the queue to come to the top of it before the end of the allocated booking period."

"Can I book an advance appointment then? It's for my husband, Philip Spittal. He had an accident and a blow to the head. He hasn't been quite right since. I'm very worried about him."

She tapped almost all the buttons on her keyboard. She could well have been practising a piano concerto. "There might be one four weeks on Friday with a locum. But you'll have to call the surgery to book it."

"I'm in the surgery now, surely…"

She looked impatient and craned her neck past me to signal to the next person in the queue that it was now their turn to receive a dose of her desk-side manner. I didn't budge. I got out my mobile phone and dialled the surgery number. First there was a recorded message about staff not tolerating abuse and an instruction about not ringing for test results other than between 1 and 1:10 on a Tuesday, and then her phone rang. Grumpily, looking somewhat surprised, the receptionist answered it. "Yes. Doctors' surgery."

"I'd like to book an advance appointment."

She tapped the keyboard for an extended period again. "Name?"

"Philip Spittal. AL not LE."

"As it's for your husband, you'll have to ask him to call himself, Mrs Spittal," she replied, aggressively returning the receiver, a look of satisfaction creeping across her face. "Next."

19

The next day

The following morning I discovered it was true. Tania had asked Arthur to leave so they could assess 'things' from a distance whilst apart. They had been together since university, but Arthur hadn't realised there was anything wrong. "She never said anything," he complained, though I doubted she would have agreed with that. I suspected she would have had to spell out anything worrying her in very direct words for him to get the gist. For someone who purported to make a living from writing about the foibles and life experiences of others, he had little empathy for the emotions of those directly around him.

From what I could make out it seemed that Tania had woken up to the ticking of her body clock and realised that my lovely son did not promise the security, responsibility and reliability required to be a parent.

He didn't explain how he felt about fatherhood – the definition of which could encompass anything from anonymous sperm donor to full-on house husband. I didn't ask. I'm sure he, unlike her, hadn't thought beyond his own narrow world of words to a life which included dependants. As he approached his thirty-seventh birthday, he probably should have considered it at the very least.

There would be no grandchildren, then, even accidental ones, from that relationship. Tania was far too sensible.

In a way which indicated that she had probably read the runes correctly, he seemed affected by this change of status only in terms of his own situation. Nearer to forty than thirty, not in a relationship, owner of a car he couldn't afford to mend until his agent secured his next advance (not guaranteed) and living with his parents. I was more sympathetic than Phil, who previously could have been relied upon to come up with some rational solution and appropriate words. He'd gone off to work chuntering about boomerangs and kids never being off the payroll.

"Dad seems a bit weird," Arthur observed. "It can't be a midlife crisis, he's way too old for that." Arthur had a knack of reminding us, unintentionally I hoped, that we were way past an age where we were considered viable and that a trip to Dignitas was a tempting possibility we probably should be considering.

"There are no signs of him getting a sports car or a motorbike or wearing jewellery and clothes that are too tight for him. He hasn't swapped his anorak for a leather jacket," I reported. "I don't think he went white-water rafting or free-fall parachuting last time he was at Granny's cottage either."

"He's not on Tinder is he? Or Grindr?" Arthur shared my ability to get carried away with fanciful scenarios.

"He's been unsettled since the accident," I explained, "and then with Grandad dying…"

With a sudden horror I realised Arthur was reading the lecture leaflet which was still on the table. I panicked. Should I seize the moment with a blow to the jugular?

'Actually, there's no need to worry. Everyone is pretty convinced that Phil is not your dad anyway, biologically that is. In all probability, I conceived you in the open air on a volcanic outcrop in Edinburgh with the man giving these lectures whilst I was in a relationship with your father. I have told neither of them about this.' I could have done it with this no holds barred summary. Harsh but reasonably succinct.

A Feather Between the Lines

As usual I stayed mute.

"You going to any of these? Can anyone go? I must look this geezer up."

I managed to squeak that it was unlikely that I would and attempted to change the subject. "The Isis Mummers have a production coming up. I'm probably going to be tied up with that."

Arthur laughed heartily. "What crap are you doing this time? I can't wait."

"Angela wanted to do *Anthony and Cleopatra*," I began.

" 'The triple pillar of the world transformed / Into a strumpet's fool'." Arthur could barely contain his glee. Like Webster Ferris he could immediately pluck a quotation from the air. "Don't tell me, you're Cleo. The oldest strumpet in Egypt!" Arthur laughed loudly. "Surely that old codger who pretends he was best mates with The Beatles isn't going to be Antony!"

"She's had second thoughts, but not because of my age I'll have you know. We're doing a Coward. And a short, one-act, small cast, one-set wonder at that. We're representing the 1940s in a smorgasbord of entertainment for the coronation."

Arthur looked sceptical. "She'd better go to one of these lectures if she's thinking of moving into Shakespeare. Might pick up some tips." I thought I'd diverted the conversation but I clearly had not.

His recharged phone was now back in its usual place, attached to him by an invisible yet unbreakable thread, ready for checking and consultation in a nanosecond. "Professor Webster Ferris. There's an American name for you!" He began googling. I was anxious that the availability of instant information might just tell him more than he wanted to know. Was there a photograph I'd missed?

"Hmm. This dude is pretty heavyweight academically. Oh, first degree at Cambridge funnily enough – but it looks like he's been in the States ever since. Perhaps he came over here to study initially. Oh no. Born Rotherham. He's a Yorkshireman – with a name like that!" Had he noticed we were a similar age? Was he going to ask if I had come across him at university? Or if Phil had? What would I say?

Arthur was disappearing down an internet wormhole. "And that's interesting. Actually, I think I have read something by him. Yeah, he doesn't just write academic texts, he's published several novels under a pen name." This was something that my own entry-level stalking hadn't revealed. I tried hard not to look interested. "It's deep stuff: heavy duty, dark novels about loss and redemption and not being able to find love. R.V. Ironside, that's the name he writes fiction under. It says here he had a drink problem for years. That doesn't surprise me. Nothing like being miserable as fuck to get your creative juices going." Arthur looked at me. "What's wrong, Mum?"

"Don't try it," I said. "Not the booze. The breakup will be enough – won't it?" I could feel my face flushing.

R.V. Ironside – his penname came from that monster cactus, the one he named after a Rotherham United goalkeeper, which he kept in his room. The cactus he bequeathed to me as he left Cambridge. The one I'd kept. The only plant I'd never managed to kill. The one I left behind by accident when we moved house. R for Roy, the goalie, or for Roni? V for Veronica? It was entirely possible he had spent the last thirty-seven years writing reams of heavy duty misery under a penname which reminded him of me.

And he is, or had been, an alcoholic. How naive I was, I realised. Why did I assume that Webster Ferris would just be a slightly aged and probably improved version of his former self? Lightened by the positive optimism and accepting classless meritocracy of the Americans, tanned by the Californian sun, energised by the healthy outdoor lifestyle, he might even do Tantric yoga and eat a plant-based diet. Or maybe not.

A Feather Between the Lines

Of course, he would certainly have a history from those missing years and I hadn't considered that. His agonising issues with liquor – or worse – may have led him to spend most of his salary on counselling and drying-out clinics. He could well have lost all his hair and be inflated to 4XL size by addiction to hamburgers and huge portions of fries and never walking anywhere except around the supermarket to pile his trolley with overprocessed foods like Cheez Whiz, Twinkies and Froot Loops with Marshmallows. Or he might be cadaverous and wrinkled, raddled by the years of drink and dried out by lack of vitamins. What gave me the ridiculous idea that he would return as he had been when I last saw him in 1985?

I hadn't thought a reunion would be easy, but it would undoubtedly be harder than I'd imagined. Dispassionately I tried to assess the necessity of and motive behind meeting up with Ferris. I should give him the chance to be contrite about his parting with me, as his letter had suggested he wished to be. And the question about his possible son? We could maturely discuss the way forward regarding Arthur. If Ferris was not interested, I would leave things be regarding everyone else. After all, I didn't know for sure myself. Perhaps Neil was right about sleeping dogs.

I couldn't acknowledge the truth; the real reason I wanted to see this man who I had been thinking and dreaming about for so long.

"You should go, Mum. I'll come along if I'm still here," Arthur enthused. He examined the flyer closely again. If only he knew. Not for the first time, I wanted to rewind and start all over again.

20

Friday 5th May 2023

How despicable am I? Later that day, after introducing me to R. V. Ironside, Arthur had decided to go out to sit by the river and consider revisions to the text of his own latest work. As soon as he had gone, I'd got my laptop out for some deeper level investigation. Now I had the heads up on Ferris's pseudonym, I might discover more about the man himself.

I'd previously discovered that the Stanford website had no photographs of Professor Ferris. Where he was listed under 'People' in Department of English there was a photograph of an ancient library where most of the others had mugshots, and clicking on 'profile' just showed an outline of a fir tree instead of a photograph appearing above his stellar CV. Searching the combination of pen name and images disappointingly revealed nothing.

There were some internet reviews of R.V. Ironside's canon. 'A raw truth, interestingly developed.' 'Turgid and depressing but I was unable to put it down.' 'A long haul through the misery of the protagonist's situation where there was no hope of redemption.' One reviewer even suggested that reading such an upsetting tale had caused her a total breakdown which she described as cathartic. Webster Ferris, therapist to the depressed. There was a thought.

All his fiction was out of print and very few books by R.V. Ironside were listed on Amazon in the 'other, used and collectable'

A Feather Between the Lines

section. Reluctantly, I picked *The Falling Shadow*, which was described as 'one man's descent into depression, his attempts to reconnect with his past and confront his demons'. This seemed the most cheerful on offer to add to my basket. I was both fascinated and apprehensive about what I would discover.

That letter he had sent me, now concealed in Arthur's copy of *Harry Potter and The Chamber of Secrets,* contained the sentence: 'I have been writing to you and about you indirectly for many years'. Did he mean that as R.V. Ironside had he been writing about me and our relationship? It was unbearable.

The book took an agonisingly long time to arrive but did so very late in the evening on the day before the coronation. Phil took the parcel in. "Another book? Haven't you got enough yet?" Phil thinks that there is a finite number of books which any one person should own, a saturation point beyond which the ability to read or enjoy them becomes redundant. Plainly he was thinking that if I had not reached it already, I was pretty close.

I was itching to start reading but couldn't open the parcel there and then. Suppose Arthur asked why I'd sent for it, or mentioned it was Ferris's pen name on the cover? When I went upstairs to bed, I opened the carton in the bathroom. The cover showed a man standing under an arch at night-time, his shadow enlarged by a nearby streetlight. It could have passed as a detective novel. I contemplated taking it to bed to start reading.

Even I had the sense to acknowledge that might not be appropriate. Getting stuck into an outpouring of painful regret and longing, possibly based on a relationship I had had with the author, whilst propped up in bed next to my husband was insensitive at best. I slid the book between some sheets in the airing cupboard to avoid discovery.

I dreamed about the falling shadow of the man on the cover, lonely and desperate to be reconnected with his former lover. In the way in which fanciful dreams surreally involve mundane things which have occurred during the day, he was pursued by a woman in coronation robes eating cupcakes and shouting about wanting a baby.

21

Coronation Day
Saturday 6th May 2023

The cupcake: my coronation nemesis. Whilst Phil and Arthur were watching carriages and ceremonial clothing on TV, I had to be busy in the kitchen. Unwillingly I had been persuaded to contribute to the celebratory 'big picnic' in our village.

The Duke of Norfolk had been landed with making arrangements for the royal ceremony and dignitaries at Westminster Abbey. We had Lavinia in charge. She lives in the biggest house in the village, built on the site of a medieval manor house. Two hundred years ago the original building was immured inside a Georgian construction whose symmetry and perfection is the envy of every wealthy house-hunter bent on an exodus from London and the adoption of a country lifestyle.

Together with the title deeds of this dwelling comes an assumed feudal obligation to corral everyone else in the village into purposeful activity. Without Lavinia there is no doubt that there would be no communal events in our neighbourhood, and this earns her a grudging respect. However, a thinly disguised loathing for her bossiness and jealousy of her ability to get things done follows in her wake.

I despise her for a different reason. Like Angela, she can wear white trousers. They accompany her during a day spent near small children eating chocolate, blackcurrants and gravy, sitting on an uncountable selection of grubby outdoor furniture and taking two excitable Labradors for a walk over the fields. I know that up in her boudoir at the big house, with its wall-to-wall albino shag pile, when she slips them off at night they are entirely stain free.

Lavinia had taken it upon herself to organise everyone into a rota of picnic food production, the abundance of which would have fed all of those who had been sat waiting in Westminster Abbey since the early morning. I had sympathy for those amongst them who were elderly as well as for the weak-bladdered. Initially chuffed to make the invite list, they were now surely fixated on release from their water-closet free prison rather than the ancient rite itself. I was glad to be unimportant and at home within reach of facilities.

Non-stop access to the goings-on on TV was a flaw in Lavinia's masterplan; for a picnic the following day, cooking was required in advance, possibly during the coronation itself.

I had been given what I considered to be the short straw. 'Cupcakes with a national theme', she had decreed in a way that suggested allocation of the production of such a thing was doing me a kind of favour. Lavinia has a way of making you feel she's letting you off something more taxing because, when all is said and done, she doesn't really consider you're up to anything more complex.

She was probably right, but I was irritated not to be part of coronation chicken production or recreating a quiche recipe which we had been encouraged to believe Charles and Camilla had knocked up themselves in the kitchen at Highgrove. Those considered unlikely to mess it up had been entrusted with the right royal recipe by Lavinia. News about my prowess in the culinary sphere had clearly got out.

A Feather Between the Lines

Hence, between celebrity spotting and laughing at ridiculous hats in the congregation, I was heavily involved in the production of dense sponge lumps with varying degrees of burnt tops which I then had to disguise with thick red, white and blue buttercream icing. Fortunately, this kind of delicacy is no longer called a fairy cake.

My focus was not on Westminster Abbey, the first coronation in my lifetime, or the state of our kitchen and the unattractive, garish, leaden ordnance whose production had caused the mess. I could only think about the airing cupboard, another chamber of secrets, and the mysterious volume lurking under a pile of sheets on the shelf.

When King Charles and Queen Camilla were bumping back along The Mall in the golden carriage, topped with precarious heavy crowns like participants in the book-balancing race at the village fête, I noticed Phil had fallen asleep.

Arthur had been reading a book and scrolling through his phone whilst watching the ceremony. Who says men can't multi-task? He was sitting on the sofa, his long legs curled around each other, his scruffy black curls – badly in need of a shearing – forming a helmet-like halo around his face. Those well-defined cheekbones were in sharp contrast to Phil's more rounded features, which were framed by his fairish, dead-straight hair, now thinning somewhat.

I grasped my opportunity. I sped upstairs, opened the airing cupboard door and retrieved the book, then locked myself in the bathroom. I felt nervous.

This wasn't the first time that I recognised that I would never have been able to parachute into occupied wartime France with an SOE wireless and a secret code. If the fright engendered by jumping from a small plane into a hostile night sky hadn't killed me, the possibility of being discovered by some nasty looking members of the SS with monocles and full-length leather overcoats would have finished me off long before I had attempted to transmit a single word. I was hyper-ventilating and having palpitations just holding what looked like a detective novel in my own bathroom in Oxfordshire.

I opened the book and began to read.

> The fading of the light was always the beginning. Dying shafts of sunlight hitting an uncompromising hard surface were like the bolts of pain that racked his torso. Though constant and unforgiving, he relished their jolts because they reminded him that he was still sentient, still human, not the anaesthetised corpse that he feared he had become. She was there in those powerful streaks of reality, elusive, just out of reach but ever present. So long as he could sense her and imagine her existing somewhere, even if it was far away across the seas, he knew that he could survive. But survival was all it was. It was not a life he enjoyed. The fading of the day's light was the prelude to a night of misery and self-loathing from which he regularly hoped he would not return.

Bloody hell. That wasn't going to be a hit with holidaymakers at the Terminal Two bookshop looking for a bit of pleasant distraction on a sun lounger. In any other circumstance, I would have been laughing raucously, desperate to share the misery with Phil or anyone else who'd enjoy chuckling at the pretentious imagery. But I felt a burden of sadness and guilt which was impossible to shake off. I could hear the muffled sounds of cheering crowds coming from the TV downstairs. I understood the word heartache in a visceral sense as never before.

22

The Big Lunch
Sunday 7th May 2023

We trooped over to the recreation ground the following day, armed with the heavyweight but patriotic mini cannonballs. Some coronation Big Lunch events had proper royals in attendance but not ours. In recompense, Lavinia had taken it upon herself to behave royally and waft about with a sense of bearing suggesting her blood ran blue.

A neighbour whose culinary prowess had been deemed even worse than mine had been allocated 'decorations'. She had half-heartedly strung some plastic Union Jack bunting between a few trees and positioned a life-sized cardboard cutout of the royal couple at the entrance to remind us why we were there. Mandy was tutting about what she called 'the poor design concept' – with some justification. She would have been the ideal person to recreate Buckingham Palace or Windsor Castle on the village recreation ground. Instead, she'd been allocated 'crisps and potato snacks', which indicated how bad Lavinia considered her cooking to be.

Phil had been busy cleaning our deckchair collection of the spider web and bird dropping robes it was wearing after overwintering in the garden store. He'd also got a folding table from the garage and I'd managed to find a tablecloth. Surprisingly, the weather was holding up. It was also Arthur's birthday and Phil's mother and sister had been asked to come along as well as our daughters.

Mandy announced that Scots Nationalist Iain and his republican tendencies were stopping north of the border with no intention of celebrating the crowning of the monarch. I was piqued, not because I thought he should show allegiance to the throne but because it meant that I was not going to meet him. Mandy had invited Lanre to come and join us in his place. She introduced him to Pamela, who had been enthroned in the best and most stable deckchair. "This is Lanre, who is one of the stars of our latest production, *Still Life*." Mother eyed him curiously.

"He's still what?"

"It's a play, Granny. It was the forerunner of that famous film, *Brief Encounter*." Jessica was patient explaining but couldn't resist her usual rider of interesting facts. "The British Film Institute ranked it as the second-best British film of all time and it got three Academy Award nominations."

Pamela had alighted on *Brief Encounter* as something she recognised. "My mother went to the pictures to see that, just after the war when I was a girl. I remember when she came back her handkerchief was wet through – she'd cried that much. Father said, 'You're not having money to go to the flicks if you're going to cry about it.' I'm not sure she ever went again. Ah, happy days." There was no trace of irony in her voice. "It used to be on television all the time, but they don't bother with black and white these days," she continued. "Who are you playing, Larry?"

"I'm Alec," Lanre explained.

"She said his name was Larry," Pamela insisted. No one took on the challenge of explanation.

"He's the Trevor Howard part," Paula declared at full volume.

"He doesn't look anything like him. Or Stanley Holloway

A Feather Between the Lines

for that matter." Pamela looked poised to make an inappropriate comment.

Jessica managed to interrupt her. "Trevor Howard had a drink problem in later life. He was a big star, but it ended rather sadly for him."

"She should have left the boring husband and gone off with the doctor I think," Mother continued, obviously retaining full recollection of the plot, "but divorce was a dirty word in those days. You made your choice and you had to stick with it."

Lanre and Mandy looked awkward underneath plastic Union Jack bowler hats. As participants arrived, Lavinia had crowned them with festive headpieces together with the implication that refusal to keep them on might mean imprisonment in the Tower. For reasons undisclosed, I'd been chosen to wear a cardboard cone with red, white and blue foil strips coming out of the top secured by a piece of elastic under the chin which almost garrotted me. My pointy hat made me look like a Poundland Disney Lady of Shallot; it was an example of medieval millinery certainly never worn in real life. Perhaps it was a culinary dunce's hat.

Mother was in full flow with her opinions about relationships, oblivious to the sensitivities of her audience. "Have you got yourself a young man yet, Jessica? It's about time, isn't it? It's all very well having a big salary and your own home but you'll leave it too late for kiddies. Look at Paula."

No one did look at Paula. We exchanged glances with each other but avoided her obvious embarrassment. "Katie has Pol Pot, or whatever his name is, and even Arthur has that Tina woman. Where is she by the way? Not coming? I don't know why you all can't get married. I'd like to be a great grandmother but I expect I'll die first." There was a silence and a tacit but collective decision not to challenge or respond to any of this. Just when we thought the subject was exhausted, she asked, "Are you married, Alec?"

"I'm divorced," Lanre admitted.

"At least you had a go." Mother spoke as if he'd failed a driving test but had the promise of infinite repeats. "Even the King is divorced. That Diana was too young for him. I expect she wanted to go to discotheques, and he just likes shooting birds and gardening."

"Where is Arthur? Birthday boy," Katie asked, trying to change the subject. She and Pol had brought their own contributions to the event. Naturally, he'd written a poem in Catalan which he promised he would be reading out later and she began handing out home-sprouted alfalfa seed and mung bean sandwiches, made with their own organic chia and quinoa bread. The journey over in the cycle pannier had left them a little misshapen but fortunately the density of the bread kept the stringy fillings from showering out like wind-blown seeds. I seized the opportunity to return to the house to ferret out her brother.

There was no one home. I couldn't resist retrieving R.V. Ironside's book from under its protective pile of sheets in the airing cupboard and began to read. I was only about ten pages in, immersed in a graphic description of a mining disaster in South Yorkshire, when Phil suddenly appeared. I slammed the book shut like a child caught looking up dirty words in the big dictionary at the library.

"Typical you, skulking in here with your nose in a book." I had no answer. "The search is off, he's reappeared. He'd been for a long walk. He's mooning about because Tania hasn't sent him a birthday text or something."

Back at the picnic table, Arthur had a face like a perished hot-water bottle and Paula was looking concerned. "Mother has just announced that she is going to move. Sell the house. It's the first I've heard of it," she stated incredulously.

Phil's eyes lit up. Far from regretting losing another part of his childhood, I knew he was salivating at the prospect of months of trips to the dump, carefully categorising and recycling over sixty

A Feather Between the Lines

years' worth of accumulated possessions from the family home.

"My friend Joyce lives in something called a sheltered flat. It's ideal and she's got herself a gentleman friend to go with it." Pamela looked strangely animated. "I think it's time for me to move on. Have a new beginning before it's too late. There's another one available apparently." No one was quite sure whether this referred to living accommodation or late-life romantic partners, or possibly both. Paula's face softened as she sensed a future being let off the hook.

Pol announced he felt the moment was right to perform his verse to the assembled crowd. "La corona que va violar la terra," he began.

Lanre looked shocked. "I speak Spanish not Catalan, but I'm pretty sure the title is about a crown raping the earth." I reassured him that none of us ever understood Pol's poems and that Granny couldn't hear it anyway.

As the Isis Mummers' production was nearly upon us, Lanre, Mandy and I had made a secret agreement to try and slip off to run our lines when we'd had enough coronation quiche and merriment. It seemed a good moment to sneak away as Pol began to recite.

"Come and read in the other parts," I whispered to Arthur. "We want to go through the lines." So, as my cupcakes, the butter cream turning oily in the sunshine, were passed politely but uneaten from table to table, Arthur, Lanre, Mandy and I skulked into the field next to the rec. and, lying in the grass, looking up at the sky, ran through the entire script of *Still Life*.

With not a cloud in sight, I watched a plane high in the air, it's contrail leaving a gradually fading streak across the blue. Up in the stratosphere, Webster Ferris, homeward bound, was flying back to Blighty. He could be in the UK right now. I imagined the jet skywriting me a message: He's back!

23

Monday 8th May 2023

On the following day, a bank holiday, Phil suddenly announced he was taking the rest of the week off and going to Granny's cottage. This was a surprise to me – but perhaps I should have seen it coming.

He had come back from Oxford with a replacement bike the week before. It was unusual for him to make such a purchase without months of research on comparison websites and cyclists' forums. Old Phil rarely did anything spontaneously, certainly not when making a decision about an item which would have such importance to him. I wondered if he had been planning it and just hadn't told me – but it seemed not. New Phil was a spur of the moment kind of guy.

"I just called in the shop and this one sang to me," he explained as if kismet and the stars always dictated the direction of his life. Next he'd be telling me that Pol's wand had been involved, like a divining stick indicating the source of some kind of cycling karma.

I don't know much about cycling but the thin-wheeled, narrow-saddled, luminously painted version that he'd brought home looked just as uncomfortable and uninviting as that every other Lycra-clad exercise-crazed man in the area tortured himself with. Research not necessary – just feel the vibe.

"What about the trains on a bank holiday? There might be a bus replacement service – what about the bike?" Some of Phil had rubbed off onto me after nearly thirty-eight years of marriage. The idea that he hadn't minutely planned his route with reference to alternative arrangements (known variously as plans B, C and sometimes even D) was incomprehensible.

"If that's the case, I have the advantage over any passenger who can only walk or sit on a bus. Have bike, will cycle."

"You haven't ridden since the accident. Shouldn't you start back gently?" But Phil was gone, pedalling off down the lane without a hi-vis vest or a goodbye. He hadn't even shut the back door or told the cat to make sure I didn't get up to anything – a repetitive quip which he generally made every time he left the house.

There was an afternoon rehearsal of *Still Life*, full costume and on the real stage, planned. The performance was later that week and an obvious but unacknowledged panic was building. I decided to spend the morning with the R.V. Ironside book, languishing tantalisingly, smothered in sheets, back in the airing cupboard. It might take my mind off the scenario developing in my head: a return to the hospital and another trip to the bad news cupboard, the tissues and the bereavement leaflets.

I rejoined the narrative where I'd been interrupted previously. A man was searching for light in a dim basement whilst an incredibly noisy wake for the victims of the pit disaster I'd read about the day before was taking place in the room above.

Arthur's sudden appearance downstairs made me snap the book shut. "Not enjoying that?" he asked. I turned the book over so he couldn't see the title or author. The intercession was a not unwelcome break from the misery. "I've been looking through my bookshelf. I've found something lurking there," he explained, a wide-eyed look of surprise on his face.

Oh shit. Harry Potter and the Mysterious Letter. This was it. Explanation time. At least we were alone in the house.

"Look what I found!" He shoved a book towards me.

It wasn't *The Chamber of Secrets* as I had expected. The cover showed the ghostly outline of a woman disappearing through an open door, and the title, *The Apparition of Love*.

"It was on my shelf, and I'd forgotten all about it. I knew I'd read something by R.V. Ironside. It was a few years ago. I can't remember what happens, other than it was relentlessly grim. I might reread it."

He looked at the flyleaf and laughed. "Get this. *'R.V. Ironside has lived in the US for many years having left the UK in the 1980s. Despite writing about his homeland and his life there, he has never had the courage to return.'* I wonder what happened when he was here!"

It had been there all along, hidden in plain sight. A book written by Webster Ferris had been in my house, right under my nose. It had been in the very room where I had sought solace and spent many a solitary and happy hour with my thoughts and daydreams. He had been there too, with his thinly disguised pen name and painfully sad prose. If I was the vanishing woman, then we had been there together. With an aura and energy worthy of Pol's wand, it struck me as symbolic of the way in which Webster had occupied my mind all these years – present but unseen.

"What's up, Mum?" Arthur asked. "Is something wrong?" My expression must have taken a turn for the worse.

"No. I am worried about you though. Don't read that book. It might make you feel more miserable."

"It's OK. I'm cool about the Tania thing."

"Do you love her?"

Arthur looked awkward. What son wants to discuss that kind of thing with his mum? "Probably," he admitted sheepishly.

"Don't let her get away then."

Arthur left me the book and went into the hall speedily before I could ask him any more personal questions. "Just going out," he called as the door slammed. He was unlikely to have remembered a key.

A Feather Between the Lines

Before the doorbell could ring to announce his return, I shot upstairs and into his room. The curtains were only half pulled but in the dim light, picking my way through discarded clothing, abandoned plates and half-drunk cups of coffee, I managed to navigate my way to the Harry Potter collection and retrieve the letter. An ability to live in an ordered and hygienic way had not come with the 'Happy 37th Birthday' cards Arman had delivered for the big day. No wonder Tania had cut her losses.

Where to conceal it next? Now Arthur was home, books were a no-go area. There were very few other parts of the house where Phil was unlikely to be. He did his share of the cleaning and laundry, he did all of the DIY and home maintenance, he tended the garden, and he even cooked. The last was probably more about self-preservation than the distribution of labour, but it suited me.

It was not lost on me that I should not have been keeping anything hidden from a man who was not only my husband but also the ideal cohabitee.

If they ever decide to produce a programme called 'Partner Off' in the style of 'Bake Off' or 'Pot Off' (that show where the male judge bursts into tears at the beauty of a freshly fired conical vase created on the wheel of a blue-haired potter with a limited sense of practicality), he's a shoo-in. Twelve aspiring 'perfect other halves'. One goes home each week until the remaining winner is crowned Ideal Partner.

Phil would breeze through the practical round: hoovering, dishwasher emptying, sorting recycling and getting the bins out on the right day. He would impress the judges with his speed at oiling hinges as soon as they start squeaking and mysterious and unique ability to stop a loo seat from sliding to one side when you sit on it.

He'd ace the technical round: finding the best utility and internet providers, claiming tax refunds, analysing insurance quotes and remembering passwords for websites.

And the showstopper? The round where he'd have to surpass all the other contestants by 'going over and above'? Each week, Phil would emerge victorious as the most obliging and easy to live with person – not by bouquets of flowers and surprise mini-breaks to European cities, but by constant, rational and sensible support and understanding.

Phil's performance in the final would make him outright winner. By showing compassion and common sense in the face of his partner's foolish and unreasonable behaviour over many years, he would rise above his competitors. Faced with being shown the letter, he would not only be understanding about its contents being divulged some months after its arrival, but he would forgive his wife's further communication with the sender and her jaw-dropping revelation that their son had probably been fathered by its author. He'd win the prize, a tasteless wall plaque with 'Forgive and Forget, I love you whatever' written on it in cursive, neon-lit script, and we would live happily ever after with no arguments about where such a tawdry trophy should be displayed.

I was daydreaming again. This was unlikely to be New Phil's reaction, now he had become as fallible as everyone else courtesy of a 95 bus on its way to Culham and an unrepaired pothole. I pushed the letter inside a sock in my drawer. Even with his new mysticism and lack of caution, Phil wouldn't be wearing my socks.

Predictably, the dress rehearsal was a disaster. The costumes varied from Mandy's carefully researched ensemble with hat to Vernon's sharp suit and thin tie from his skiffle band days (which was accompanied by an anecdote about how it had once been worn by a George of his acquaintance). He'd made a badge saying 'Ticket Inspector' just in case anyone was in any doubt.

The cast's nightmare was being trapped in an eternal performance: a story that never ended because Mandy kept repeating, 'I'm a respectable married woman with a husband and a home and three children,' as a response to anything another character said. Lanre, having learned every single line in the entire piece, was able to rescue us from the horrific prospect of never proceeding to the final scene by adapting her lines to say himself. 'Aren't you thinking that you can't go on any longer, that other things matter like decency and self-respect?' to which Mandy would just have to reply, 'Yes.'

I heard nothing from Phil that evening. Customarily, when he arrived at Granny's signal-free cottage, he would cycle over the fells to the misnamed Sun Inn. This bleak hostelry is two miles from the nearest shop or petrol station, high up and blessed with eternal strong winds and frequent power cuts. There, from what is probably the last working call box in Britain, he'd ring me to say he was about to enjoy a pub meal and a pint or two of ale. Even Phil couldn't face the Calor gas stove on the first night. But there was no call.

I decided to abandon the first Ironside novel and try the one that had been living incognito in our house for so long. I stayed up reading *The Apparition of Love*. The protagonist moved from one miserable scenario to the next, each time failing to communicate his feelings as yet another person in his life slipped away. As he sank into a spiral of despondency, only ameliorated by huge alcoholic binges and resorting to narcotic substances, I felt thoroughly miserable. I decided to go to bed and surrender to the relentless wretchedness. No wonder this and Ironside's other novels were no longer in print.

I lay there in the early hours of the morning, worrying about how autobiographical the book was and what had happened to Phil. I tried to convince myself that lack of contact was because high winds had torn down the phone lines. Perhaps Trading Standards had forced the Sun Inn to shut its doors, demanding closure because its name was a misrepresentation to customers.

Sleep eluded me as my mind turned over. I had never thought of myself as unhappy. Few people are ecstatic all the time, only idiots who can't confront reality. That was right, wasn't it? We all have ups and downs, that's normal. Even even-keel Phil was now finding moments when his mood dipped.

I was aware that the room was getting lighter. Dawn was approaching and with it the recognition that I felt lonely. Not just in our bed, Phil's absence noticeable by the area I could colonise on his side as I tossed and turned, but also in my day-to-day life. The doubt about Arthur's parentage, the guilt about not telling everything to Phil: I'd temporarily got those problems off my chest by telling Lanre – but he was just a dispassionate sounding-board. I'd confided in Neil – he at least knew the parties involved. But I was still harbouring, alone, the biggest confession of all.

24

Tuesday 9th May 2023

I was woken by my phone ringing. Who was it? The hospital telling me Phil had been flattened by a lorry whilst cycling the wrong way up the A34 shouting "Winchester, Hampshire to – Oh Christ I can't remember where it stops!"? Webster Ferris demanding my address so he could come round and give me an in-depth critique of his book? Arthur telling me he'd been trapped outside the front door all night, not only without a key but also the common sense to go round and see if the back was open?

It was Angela. She was at the Marketplace Theatre overseeing the final details of the set and collating of props. "Can you come?" she asked. "I can't get Mandy out of Greggs."

It was not impossible that a devastatingly handsome assistant wearing a T-shirt announcing 'I'm single and looking for love' had started working in the bakers. Mandy had certainly been calling in to the shop regularly when we had evening rehearsals at the venue the previous week. She'd be the last customer as it closed at 7pm, leaving with a bag of hot sausage rolls and large sugary doughnuts which she was unwilling to share with the rest of us.

Fortunately, because the car was at home, I was able to drive into the town and investigate.

The bakery was situated just along from the theatre building in the market square. Mandy was sitting alone with a large latte and a half-eaten pastry at a table near the counter. She looked anxious.

"Angela made me take a day off work to rehearse my lines but there are no sausage rolls!" The link wasn't immediately obvious. "Can you believe it? I've got a sausage savoury bake, but it won't do. Too runny. It's mid-morning. How can they have run out?"

"We've got a delivery malfunction roll-wise. They never came in," explained a large lad in a Gregg's baseball cap and apron who was standing behind the counter. "In terms of our sausage-based range, as well as the sausage, bean and cheese melt, we can offer sausage breakfast roll, sausage and omelette breakfast roll, bacon and sausage breakfast roll, sausage breakfast baguette, bacon and sausage breakfast baguette, and sausage and omelette breakfast baguette."

"Spam, Spam, Spam, sausage, Spam, Spam and Spam," I quipped. Both Mandy and the lad looked blank. "You know, Monty Python." There was no response.

"What's Spam?" the lad asked suspiciously. "Python meat?" He was clearly worried that I may have serious food issues that had not been covered in his brief training in dealing with unhinged customers. He might not have any knowledge of popular culture fifty years ago, but he had clearly been spared the tinned nightmare of my early years. There are some things that the youth of today can be grateful for.

"I want a sausage roll!" demanded Mandy, like a toddler Eve told she can eat anything in the Gregg's garden she desires – except just one item. "I need the pastry: the soggy warmth of the bottom and the flaky texture of the top," she drooled. "I can't remember the words without one."

Mandy's stage fright was manifesting itself in many surprising ways. She had clearly developed an addiction as a crutch to support her in her abject terror. Only the greasy, pappy texture of a hot sausage roll melting on her tongue could quell the horror of being on stage without a clue what to say next. It was only with

A Feather Between the Lines

the promise we'd return later in the morning and a large pack of doughnuts to take away that I could persuade her to leave.

Angela was delighted that I had managed to get her out and that I would now be able to take over helping her to practise her lines. As a form of compromise, Mandy and I spent the rest of the morning doing just that on a bench in the market square keeping an eye out for the Gregg's delivery van.

To be fair she knew many of the lines. Her problem was saying the right one at the right time. "I can't do this. I should never have said yes," she groaned, angrily biting a large chunk off a doughnut. Thick, blood-like raspberry jam oozed out and down onto her lap. Mandy, like me, was a person unable to contemplate the white trouser.

We sat on the bench until it was afternoon. Mandy was almost word perfect yet unnerved because there was no sign of the delivery van. As we returned to the theatre to give Angela the partial good news and view the set, its refreshment room counter poised for being stocked with sausage rolls, my phone pinged. A message: Phil safely enjoying the discomfort of Granny's cottage?

> I've arrived. Installed in a college room, strangely familiar yet more luxurious than forty years ago. I can travel from tomorrow if you are free. Let me know when and where. 'I like this place and willingly could waste my time in it.'

Ferris – typically plucking an appropriate Shakespeare quotation to end his message. Who else did I know who would do that? I remembered some lines from the rest of the scene in *As You Like It*:

'But if thy love were ever like to mine / As sure I think did never man love so / How many actions most ridiculous / Hast thou been drawn to by thy fantasy?' Was he thinking of these words too? Both of us drawn into ridiculous actions by a fantasy? I replied:

> 'Presume not that I am the thing I was'

Henry IV banishing Falstaff might deflect the romantic association, if one was intended.

Almost immediately, I could see Ferris was typing. I was never going to win at this game. He could always out-Shakespeare me. Despite numerous years at the chalkface trying to persuade schoolkids that the Bard might offer some words of wisdom, I knew I could never match his recall.

> 'If you pardon we will mend.' I acknowledge I have some explaining to do at long last.

I had some explaining to do too, I reminded myself. This was the purpose of the reunion. Check out Ferris's interest in finding out he might have a son he didn't know about and then proceed with Phil, Arthur and all the others accordingly. Simple eh? I needed to choose a neutral, easy-to-locate venue in central Oxford from which I could escape easily if his reaction was characteristically explosive and potentially violent. I needed to get my confession over with.

> I can do late morning tomorrow, if that suits you. Bar of the Beaumont Hotel in Oxford at 11?

> Oxford? Very convenient for me. I'll be there. In plenty of time. 'Better three hours too soon than a minute too late.'

This was a reference to my poor timekeeping and not his longing to see me. I hoped. I shot back:

> 'A friend should bear his friend's infirmities.'

A Feather Between the Lines

I needed to stop this. I recognised it was not just a game of finding appropriate quotations, but a kind of flirtation. I felt anxious and excited at the same time.

> 'Can one desire too much of a good thing?'

As You Like It again. I wondered how many other women he messaged in this way. It was just as ridiculous as Phil and his mates' A roads game. More nuanced and relying on apt selection and not just recall of facts, but nerdy nonetheless. Were there Californian beach babes trying to out-quote him between riding huge surf waves and consulting crystals about which 'erbs they needed to blast in their NutriBullets to ensure long life? Did his super intellectual wife and he exchange messages in Shakespearian English about what time he'd be back for dinner or if they were going to catch a movie before engaging in an academic debate about whether the first folio contains reliable texts of the plays printed in quarto editions?

A shock, like a strike of lightning being grounded by a conductor on a tall building, traced down my spine. I suspected, indeed hoped, that Rotherham FC-supporting, bird-watching Webster Ferris had no wife and no bikini-clad lovelies to play 'trade-a-quote' with. It was a game we had played together (face to face) nearly forty years ago, just us and no one since. Our game. I replied:

> 'The devil can cite scripture for his purpose.' Got to go now.

I turned off my phone decisively. I wasn't going to let him win by having the last message.

"Can't you see how wrong it is? How dreadfully wrong!" Mandy was trying to project to the back of the auditorium. Along with the line about being respectable and married with three children, this was a multi-purpose and pertinent response she gave to any cues she was unsure of. I felt sick. Angela was looking desperate.

"Will you go back and see if there's been a delivery? She's eaten all the doughnuts."

25

Wednesday 10th May 2023

The last point of no return. I felt uneasy standing at the reception desk of the Beaumont Hotel. The reality had seemed so far off last October, as if a meeting were still part of the fantasy, but the day had arrived. The date and place chosen by me, an over made-up, sixty-year-old woman wearing a pair of jeans a size too small which wouldn't do up. Not only was I late but the place had got pretentious ideas since my last visit. A liveried doorman had watched me in – I could add venue choice to my list of regrets about the whole experience.

I leaned up against the desk while I tried, surreptitiously, to pull up my zip. "I'm looking for the bar." My voice was strangulated, giving the impression I had recently been punched by Mike Tyson.

"We have four bars. Which one do you mean?" The receptionist was wearing a tightly fitting navy-blue suit and made up like an assistant on a beauty counter. She had one of those sleek flight attendant-like buns, from which, despite spending the journey from LAX to LHR sprinting up and down the cabin, no single hair escapes.

Her tone indicated that she was fully aware that I was not a resident, nor likely to be able to afford to be one. It also expressed the correct assumption that I hadn't been inside since an interior designer had slapped expensive paper and unusual coloured paint onto the walls of this once slightly faded, creaky-floorboarded, typically British hotel.

"You can sip champagne in the quintessentially English drawing room, have speciality drinks or tea and coffee in the wood-panelled Morse Bar, or, if it's intimacy you're looking for," she paused briefly and raised an eyebrow as if this was most unlikely, "I might recommend The Snug. Or you could visit the Wonderland-inspired cocktail experience."

"Wonderland?" I asked, curious about the inspiration behind this cocktail-drinking experience.

"The Alice Bar. As in 'Alice in…'" she gave me a look which indicated patronising further explanation might be required. "There once was a famous writer who lived in Oxford who wrote a book called *Alice in Wonderland*. Have you heard of Lewis Carrol?"

"Of course I have. And I've heard of C.S. Lewis, an Oxford don, author of over thirty books including the Narnia series and several about Christianity. Got a bar named after him?" I didn't want to appear a simpleton, despite sounding and looking like one. My high-pitched mad-woman voice sounded threatening.

The receptionist was unimpressed. I wondered if she was fumbling for a panic button hidden on her side of the counter to summon security. I could feel myself overheating. As my voice had risen, my zip had lowered again. I needed to calm down.

"Perhaps the Morse bar then?" she suggested. "Seen Morse on TV? It was filmed in Oxford." She pointed behind me.

I turned round and through the open doors could see what, without question, was Webster Ferris, sitting in an armchair by a fireplace under a huge photograph of John Thaw's Inspector Morse. They were both looking straight at me.

A cocktail of fear and excitement overwhelmed me, an experience The Alice Bar was unlikely to serve in a glass. As I contemplated how to make my entrance, a flotilla of Japanese tourists passed through the lobby between me and the bar. An endless stream poured down the spectacular grand staircase, trooping past me, out through the door and onto a coach which had arrived outside. I lost sight of Ferris.

When, after a considerable amount of time, I could see back into the room, I noticed that he had stood up, as if he thought I might be swept along too for a trip to Blenheim Palace or Bicester shopping village. We locked eyes. Now he had seen me, he would be watching as I walked the length of the room to greet him. I put one hand below my waist to steady the zip and began my approach.

I was unsure which expression to adopt on my sashay down the catwalk. How do you convey a casual, "Hi, good to see you!" whilst feeling terrified at the prospect and unsure what to say when you reach the end of the room? The journey was long enough to establish several things about him. I had forgotten how tall he was and how long his legs were. He was still the same slim shape and had retained most of his hair although the unbrushed black curls were now flecked with grey. He looked remarkably healthy given what I had gleaned from Arthur's googling about his struggles. He wasn't smiling. He was motionless, his dark penetrating eyes staring from above those familiar high cheekbones.

What was going to happen when I eventually got to him? A handshake? A kiss? Not on the lips surely, perhaps comically awkward, going for different sides then colliding in the middle. A huge one-handed hug, the other still gripping the jeans? Maybe nothing, just silence?

"I knew there were no chance you'd be here at eleven," he announced when I was within earshot. "What were you arguing with that receptionist about?" Typical Ferris. I should have anticipated his blunt delivery and lack of social niceties.

"She accused me of not knowing who Lewis Carrol was," I explained. "I told her I thought they should have named a bar after C.S. Lewis instead. Better *The Lion, the Witch and the Wardrobe* and *Screwtape* rather than someone who wrote nonsense poems and took photographs of young girls in the nude."

Webster Ferris did not look confused by this opinion. He was obviously still capable of working out what I was drivelling on about. "C.S. Lewis defected to Cambridge eventually and his brother was an alcoholic. Perhaps they didn't think it suitable," he replied. He could be very literal, I remembered. "This ought to be the Sergeant Lewis bar in that case," he added, a surprising hint of a grin appearing, "if you wanted to continue the theme."

"Do you get *Morse* in the US then, or have you read the books?" I couldn't imagine Ferris wasting time watching TV or getting stuck into a crime novel when there were scholarly texts to be re-interpreted.

"Of course. It's on PBS. There are thirteen books, I believe, but over thirty TV episodes. Colin Dexter was like Hitchcock; he appears in almost all of them. You can spot him in the background if you look." I couldn't because I'd no idea what Colin Dexter looked like.

Although I'd only been speaking to Webster Ferris for a couple of minutes, here he was already showing off his superior knowledge. Not only that, but it also seemed to have expanded from literature into popular culture.

"The Morse Bar. It's a bit tacky, though, isn't it?" I suggested.

"Give over," he continued. "Morse is a very cultured man, and he were fond of a drink. I reckon he'd be right chuffed." Inspector Morse looked down smugly at me from his portrait, as if to say, 'That's you told.'

"Any road, have you seen the price of the drinks in this place? I suppose you'll be wanting one." Amazingly Ferris had retained his Yorkshire accent along with his figure and spiky personality.

"Ooo, you can take a man out of Yorkshire, but you can't take Yorkshire out of..." I began. Why did I say that? What a boring, predictable, unfunny comment. Webster made no reply.

A Feather Between the Lines

He went over to the bar. There was another armchair beside the fireplace, next to a small table on which there were two empty coffee cups and some sugar. Was Ferris with a partner and where was she? I sat down on one chair and my zip descended with unprecedented speed. I pulled my sweater down to cover the soft bulge of middle-aged spread that had outed itself.

At least he hadn't chosen to sit on the sofa opposite the chairs and the fireplace. There would have been decisions about how close we sat to each other and about exactly how often we would turn towards each other as we talked. Perhaps the three of us would have sat in a row, his other half too looking straight ahead at John Thaw's face. Where was she? In the ladies?

While he was up at the bar ordering my drink, I was able to assess him. I would have recognised him even from behind. It was hard to credit that such a long time had passed since I had seen that back disappearing at high speed down Arthur's Seat. I'd pursued him for as long as I could, gradually becoming further and further away from him until he disappeared altogether. That day was the last time I had seen him. The beginning of all those days thinking about him with that curious mixture of hatred and love.

Neither of us spoke when he sat back down. After an awkward pause, the bartender plonked down a tall glass in which a slice of lemon, some ice and a cocktail stirrer bobbed about in what looked suspiciously like a gin and tonic. I was expecting coffee or preferably a cup of tea. I don't drink much alcohol these days, certainly not before noon.

"Aren't you having one?" Shit. Not the best thing to say to a recovering alcoholic who hasn't actually told you yet that he can't touch booze. Nor to someone pretending not to be an alcoholic who hopes you didn't notice him downing a sneaky short whilst he was up at the bar.

"Not at these prices." Given how things were going, I was going to have to drink it.

"And, before you start telling me I'm proper tight-fisted and don't like spaffin' me cash, I got you a double. Don't be tellin' me I've got short arms and long pockets, you mardy lass." He'd assumed exaggerated Yorkshire overdrive to emphasise his point.

"If you talk like that in America, does anyone understand what you say?" I asked.

"No one has understood me since 1985," he said enigmatically.

This certainly was an odd conversation to be having so early on with someone you've only just met up with after a nearly thirty-eight year gap. One unwise quip from me and any early promising connection had ground to a halt, as if we had been suddenly unplugged from a giant generator of bonhomie. We sat in silence again for a bit. He was still an awkward and unpredictable bastard.

"You've come on your own then," he stated eventually, as I took a polite sip of what tasted like neat alcohol from the glass.

"Phil is at work; he sends his apologies." I didn't know why I said that – it sounded (and was) untrue.

"Still married to him, then. Goldblatt told me you ended up with the tech," he scoffed.

An atmosphere was brewing, blown in by a silly comment from me. Webster applied no filter to his comments and was impulsive, which often meant he got things wrong. He took things personally and plainly still had a volatile and unpredictable character.

At Cambridge he used his fists to show his displeasure or to right wrongs. Not ever on me, but on people who annoyed him. Perhaps I was no longer immune – he might deck me with a right hook, here in the Morse bar. Now he'd been in America for so long, he probably carried a firearm and would shoot me for my lack of courtesy and poor wit. It could be a Morse episode: *A Joke Too Far* – though with John Thaw dead, both in real life and in the Morse series, production would be a bit tricky.

Daydreaming again. I took a big swig of the drink whilst trying to think of something to say to fill the silence. Perhaps this was the moment to get it over with. 'We've got three children. One of them is probably yours, though, but I don't have to tell him or Phil if you're not interested.' The gin had already started making my head spin and the combination of that and the gaping trousers would make running away quickly difficult if he got his gun out or made a fist at me at this disclosure.

"Did you come over on your own?" I asked eventually. Shit, it sounded like I was enquiring about his availability.

"Do you think the university pay for more than one person?" He wasn't giving anything away but it seemed there was no one about to make a surprise appearance in the bar, at least.

"I recognised you immediately," I told him, downing another great gulp of my drink. I thought I'd try to sweeten the atmosphere with some flattery. "'When forty winters shall besiege thy brow, To me, fair friend, you never can be old'." A bit of Shakespeare thrown in, just to get us back on an even keel.

Ferris lifted his head slightly. "That's two different sonnets," he stated accusingly. "Do you remember the next lines of them?" I couldn't, not immediately. Why did I start this? I took another slurp. " 'When forty winters shall besiege thy brow, / Thy youth's proud livery so gazed on now, / Will be a tattered weed of small worth held'." He looked straight at me, smiled a little, exhaled quietly and then looked down. "I'm afraid that's me."

I had no response. That surge of current, that curious mixture of excitement and fear that only he could ignite, was running through me again. It had done so for the last God knows how many years, ever since I first saw him in Dr Bennett's study and every time I thought of him since. I tried to fish the lemon slice out of the glass with the cocktail stirrer to give myself something to do to stop me crying.

He looked up. "And the second one? That's you. 'To me, fair friend, you never can be old, / For as you were when first your eye

I eyed, / Such seems your beauty still'." His face was motionless but his dark eyes penetrated mine, even though I tried to busy myself downing the remains of Oxford's most expensive gin and tonic.

"Roni, what are you doing here?" called a familiar voice. It was Angela, immaculately dressed as usual and heading straight for us. "Are you going to the Cretan exhibition at the Ashmolean? You didn't say. I'm meeting Joy here in the bar. We could go together."

Joy is also a former colleague. If ever some parents had been disappointed that the optimistic hope the choice of name they had given their baby had not been fulfilled, it was hers. She had the ability to lower the mood of a room just by entering it, her presence a magnetic drain on any joie de vivre bubbling about before her appearance. She was fiercely academic and always disappointed by the intellectual curiosity of the pupils and, indeed, the staff. Only Angela had enough rigour to satisfy her standards. Joy would not want me tagging along.

"Actually, the exhibition is about the Labyrinth myth," Angela corrected, addressing this comment to Webster Ferris, whom she had been eyeing curiously whilst talking to me, "and the excavation at Knossos. Have you been?"

"In a Labyrinth to fight a minotaur, half man, half beast? No," Ferris replied forcefully, "and I haven't been to Knossos and I don't want to go to the exhibition."

"It's just across the road," Angela explained, somewhat unnerved by his directness. "I'm Angela. I don't believe we've met." She thrust out her hand expectantly.

"This is my cousin, from America," I said impulsively, in a slight panic, before Ferris could tell her anything I'd rather she didn't know.

"And staying at this luxurious hotel." She retracted her unshaken hand. "What's it like? I've only ever been in this bar. It's a convenient place to meet. Did you come over for the coronation, or have you come to see the performance? Maybe both!" Angela trilled flirtatiously. Thank God Mandy wasn't with her.

"He's staying at a college as he's here to give some lectures," I explained. I wanted to be in charge of the narrative and I didn't want Webster Ferris finding out about the Isis Mummers.

"Lectures?" Angela was curious. I should have expected that. Soon we'd have Joy tipping up and they'd be arranging another outing to go along and listen. "About what?"

"Shakespeare," Ferris said curtly but Angela didn't notice his irritation.

"Not the *"Letting 'I dare not' wait upon 'I would'* series, is it? Well I never! Wait until Joy gets here! We've got tickets already and we're very much looking forward to it. Roni, I can't believe you didn't tell me you had such a well-respected academic as a relative. So exciting. Which university do you teach at? Remind me."

Ferris ignored her. "Cowardice, inaction and suppressing desire; that's the theme." His voice was blunt and he was looking straight at me.

"Well, our little show's theme is just the opposite, isn't it, Roni? You'll be able to compare the difference. Coward with cowardice." Angela laughed in case anyone thought this was a serious suggestion.

I needed to leave. Immediately. Before Joy showed up. Before we were frog-marched across the road into the Ashmolean, then along to the lecture theatre and back to the Marketplace Theatre, trailing a thread like a modern-day Theseus. I needed to escape from my own labyrinth of lies, indiscretions and half-truths.

"Gosh, the time!" I said without looking at any clock or watch, standing up and hoping Ferris would follow. "Webster has to be somewhere and we're late already. Sorry."

"Your cousin Roni will steal the show at the Marketplace Theatre." Angela touched Ferris's arm as he rose. "You'll see tomorrow. And if we don't speak then, I'll catch you at the first lecture."

By the time we sped past the reception desk and out down the steps outside, I was moving so fast that my zip was fully down.

"Who the fook was that?" Webster asked loudly as we passed Joy on her way in.

26

Webster followed me, hurrying the short distance to the end of Beaumont Street. At the junction, although I was holding my sweater down with one hand, I managed to grab him with the other as he raced ahead into the traffic.

"You got a death wish?" I asked as a taxi and several bicycles swerved to avoid him. I pulled my hand away from his arm, aware that this was the first time we had touched. "Sorry, but you weren't looking."

"Haven't got used to crossing the road here yet. I'm used to looking the other way."

The huge pre-noon goblet of gin and sudden burst of energy were making my head spin. When the lights changed, we crossed over and I had to sit down on the steps of the Martyrs' memorial. A group of language students were eating some sandwiches there, chattering madly in Italian. They eyed me suspiciously and one offered me a bottle of water. Webster stood watching.

"You OK? You were moving in an odd way," he commented eventually.

"I've got an arthritic toe."

"But you're holding your stomach."

This was not the moment to confess about the zip. "I'm not used to drinking so much, so quickly, so early in the day."

Webster looked up at the monument, as if mention of drink might lead to a topic of conversation he wanted to avoid. "Latymer, Ridley and Sir Thomas Cranmer. The sixteenth century Oxford martyrs. An American poet, a woman, wrote a poem about them. 'Such natural debts of love…' it begins. Do you know it?"

I didn't and I wanted to avoid anything leading to discussion about devotion and obligation. The students looked expectant. Were they thinking he was going to recite or that I was about to throw up? I hoped neither would happen.

"Can we go for a walk? To get some air?" The reminder that I was close to where people had been burned at the stake wasn't helping my stomach.

We set off at a more leisurely pace, past St John's College, northwards towards where St Giles divides into the Banbury and Woodstock Roads. When he stopped to look across the street, I managed to zip up again, hoping that by steady movement and careful breaths I could will the thing to stay at the top.

"Hey, The Eagle and Child. Isn't that where C.S. Lewis and the Inklings used to hang out?" Even with acquired American idiom, Ferris's huge, fact-filled brain and immediate recall was scanning, making connections and disseminating information like a one-man, energy-guzzling supercomputer.

"It's closed. Didn't reopen after the pandemic." My contributions were less impressive.

"You must live in Oxford," he observed. "You seem to be familiar with it." I told him I lived nearby, careful not to reveal much detail. My Potter-like invisibility cloak, the one I wished I could assume to view him from afar, was wearing off. Thanks to Angela and her unfortunately timed rendezvous in the hotel bar, he already had more intel on me than I had hoped I would have to reveal.

We walked in silence for a while until, as we turned into Keble Road, he explained that he'd also nearly been mown down by traffic crossing the road in Wigan on the bank holiday. How bizarre for this Yorkshireman to fly from San Francisco to London then travel to Oxford via Greater Manchester. He came from Rotherham, his parents had both been dead for years, he had no siblings and no family left. I knew that for a fact. Who was there?

"Last game of the season for the Millers. Nil-all." He assumed that I would have worked this out. It would be obvious that, after over thirty-seven years overseas, the first thing he would do on return was to watch a Championship football match, not even at his team's home ground, which ended in a dull and predictable draw. "It were good to see the Latics go down! And we were already safe, near the bottom but alright."

When I had got to know the brightest student in the English faculty at Cambridge, I'd admired the eclectic mix that comprised his complex and somewhat surprising interests. He wasn't predictable and dull; he constantly surprised and excited me then and I could see that this aspect of his personality remained. It had attracted me to him and, alarmingly, I recognised that the spark of chemistry which had ignited our relationship and which I had hoped, like Wigan Athletic, had been relegated to daydreams and fantasy was still present.

We crossed over at the end of the road and went through the gate to The Parks. I needed something to eat. There was an ice cream kiosk just inside the entrance. "Sit here," I said bossily, indicating a small table with two chairs. "I'll get you a 99."

I wasn't entirely sure that a cone of soft, swirled, white ice-cream with its chimney of chocolate flake was the thing to soak up the gallon of gin sloshing around in my stomach. It might make things worse.

"You'll notice I got you a double," I showed him as I presented the treat which had not one but two flakes planted in its crown. "No expense spared on my part either."

For the first time, Webster Ferris grinned widely. "This is grand," he beamed. "I've not had one of these for years."

Everyone has his own method, devised in childhood, for devouring these treats. We concentrated silently on consumption for a while. I licked round where the cone met the ice cream, Webster was using one flake as an implement to shovel ice cream into his mouth.

He looked at me directly. "He doesn't know you're here, does he?"

"Who?"

"Why did you want to get away from that woman so quickly? Why did you say I was your cousin?" He fired questions at me as if I was one of his students whom he suspected hadn't read the text of the week.

"She's a bit of a pain in the arse. We used to teach together. I thought you'd rather be scoffing a Mr Whippy than stuck in a dark room with some shards of Minoan pottery and a crackpot theory about discovering the home of the Minotaur." I tried to look unperturbed, licking my ice cream in a nonchalant kind of way. Ferris gave me a wise look. He was making assumptions about my behaviour.

"Teacher, then. I was wondering. I'm sure you're very good at it. High School?"

"I'm not working at the moment." I was keeping information to a minimum, like a secret agent, trying not to blow my cover.

"Still acting though…" He smirked. He'd never thought any student productions I'd participated in were worthwhile. "So, Noel Coward now. Is it a shortened Roland-type version or the whole thing?" Trust Ferris to have complete recollection of the master of the Pared-Down Players and his abridged versions of playwrights' works.

"Actually, Roland is dead," I said sharply and unnecessarily, bringing this line of enquiry to a firm halt.

Extruded ice cream, chocolate and gin did not make happy companions in my poor stomach. It was already developing knots at the prospect of what I was intending to tell Ferris. I suggested we go for a walk so I could casually drop my bombshell in an open-air location where the effects of the resulting blast might be mitigated. Incredibly, although I had known this might be coming for several months, I hadn't really thought about what I was going to say.

A Feather Between the Lines

"Have you got a family?" I began.

"Do you mean children? Not me. I wouldn't have made a good father." I pulled a questioning face. "I've had enough problems looking after meself. It's not summat I ever wanted."

"I've got three kids," I continued. I thought I'd go for a gentle introduction before I slammed in with 'Well you've got one anyway and he's all grown up, so you don't need to do much fathering!' "Two girls and…"

"Look, swifts!" He pointed way up into the sky where some small birds were flying at high speed. "A sign of summer coming." They looked like most of the other birds I generally ignored. I remembered Ferris's bird table and feeding station. Another unusual accessory for a student. "Did you see them? Did you hear them scream? You have to be quick."

I don't know much about birds. They have feathers, some are bigger than others, they lay eggs and most of them fly. That's enough, isn't it? Webster Ferris sensed I needed some instruction.

"They're not easy to identify – swept back wings like a boomerang with a short, forked tail. Easy to confuse with swallows, which are bigger with longer tails, or house martins, which are smaller but with straighter wings. Swifts are the fastest flyers of all birds." He was certainly more excited about this than hearing about my children. " 'They've made it again, / Which means the globe's still working, the Creation's / Still working refreshed, our summer's / Still all to come'. Poet?" he demanded.

I didn't know. " 'True hope is swift, and flies with swallow's wings'." I tried to counter with Shakespeare.

"Ted Hughes," he chastised, unimpressed with my offering, which only featured a similar bird with a more pronounced tail. He was an extraordinary man, and it was suddenly plain to me that it would be impossible to judge how to tell him that, sitting in our house, was a thirty-seven-year-old doppelgänger whom I believed to be his son.

"Swifts spend most of their time in the air. They migrate, thousands of miles, but they always come back. Back to their mate. Just one. A lifetime partner." He wasn't looking at me but gazing way up into the sky. Searching for more birds or not wanting to see my reaction? "A swift symbolises travel, change and communication," he added. This was turning a bit Californian – an analogous confession with added crystals and aura wands to which I would never have the spoken words to respond.

"Hello, Miss." A teenage girl and her friend were on the path in front of us. I recognised them both from my last year 9 set. I'd had little success sharing the rich tapestry of English Literature with either. "What are you doing here?" There is a large portion of the student body who think that teachers exist only within the realm of the school, dying at the final lesson's bell until resurrected by the dawn of a new teaching day.

"I thought you'd gone!" stated her mate witlessly. It was worse. She supposed all retiring teachers go immediately to their grave.

"School can't be over yet," I said.

"We're on study leave." She sounded convincing although I doubted either of them would have leap-frogged to the year above and be mid GCSEs. Fortunately, it wasn't my problem anymore.

"That your husband, Miss?" asked the friend, managing to combine a sense that not only was it miraculous that I should have a partner but also that said man was in some way a poor choice.

"No, it's not," interjected the first. "Her husband did them lights for the school play." They both guffawed, as if Phil's freely given expertise with lanterns, balancing precariously on a stepladder, uncomfortably contravening health and safety regulations, was in some way a joke without parallel. "He's called Mr Spit!" she laughed, demonstrating saliva on her tongue to show she knew what the word meant.

Phil. Where was he? Marooned on the fells? Stranded on the platform of a railway station waiting for a train that wasn't running?

A Feather Between the Lines

Lying on a hospital trolley unable to recall where any A road begins or ends? What was I doing? My focus and priority should be with my husband. Why was I standing in a park in Oxford with Webster Ferris, not my cousin or anyone to whom I was related? Did it matter that Arthur may genetically be his son when he had been loved and nurtured by Phil from the moment of his birth?

"I've got to go. My parking ticket is about to expire." For once this was true.

I ran as far as my arthritic toe would allow, which was only far enough to get me to the entrance of the Parks. My zip was unfastened, my unfettered stomach wobbling in time with my steps, as I continued at a slower pace, back down St Giles and past the hotel to the car park. I felt as if I had run a marathon. Drops of sweat ran down my face mingling with the salty tears that had been falling rapidly.

It was too late. A square, cellophane envelope stuck to my windscreen showed that a zealous parking attendant had slapped a fine on my car only minutes previously.

When I reached home, Arthur was sitting in Phil's armchair looking blankly into the distance.

"Is everything alright?" I had a sudden feeling of dread.

"There was a phone call. It's bad news. Dad…" Arthur looked like he had been crying too. So this was it. Divine retribution for my stupidity. "Dad… I haven't spoken to him but…"

Who had made the call? My mouth was dry, my heart was thumping, but it sounded like Phil was alive. Perhaps he was clinging to life in a coma only to discover upon awakening the crushing news that his new bike too was a write off.

"Tania and I are over for good. Finito."

I let out a sigh of relief which I hoped Arthur would interpret as disappointment or possibly compassion.

"I'm going to have to come home permanently. I don't think Dad is going to like it."

"It's OK. He'll be fine. He's had a difficult few months, I told you. The accident, then Grandad. Even when someone is old and ill and not really themselves anymore, it's still a shock when they die."

This, like many of the homilies I dished out, was made up. I didn't know if it was true.

I kidded myself that I was pleased my parents had died when they were still compos mentis and that they hadn't had a prolonged exit, lasting to very old age, irritable, incontinent and insensible. Dad was still in his 60s, felled out of the blue by a heart attack, only half a dozen years older than I am now. Would it have been easier if I'd had them around longer, shadows of their past about whom I might have said, "It was a blessing, in the circumstances," relieved when the time finally came?

My Irish Grandmother, always on about her 'particular judgement' – the time when the boss upstairs would scrutinise her behaviour with a fine-toothed comb – died in her 90s. Miserable but sentient, she outlived both her sons and her daughter-in-law. "I made my bed and the Good Lord has ensured I must lie on it for a long time." Gran saw herself as a miscreant pupil or recalcitrant staff member called to the Headteacher's office but made to wait outside. The Head, finishing a crossword at his desk, was making her stew, standing awkwardly outside the door waiting for admission. Gran had lied with good reason, but I had already committed worse sins.

"Are you OK, Mum? What are you thinking about?" Arthur had turned to look at me. "Have you got a black eye? And your face is all stripy."

In the mirror I could see what sweat and tears had done to the masque of make-up I'd thought necessary to disguise sixty years and several sleepless nights. I looked like a child's painting of a panda, accidentally left too near the sink in the art room so that streaks of water had ruined its crude attempt at beauty.

A Feather Between the Lines

"And your jeans are undone. I can see your stomach." Arthur could barely hide his revulsion. "I'm going to have to borrow the car to collect the rest of my stuff," he announced. "Will *you* ask Dad? Please?"

"I'm a bit worried about him. I haven't heard anything since he left on Monday."

"Oh, he rang yesterday. Didn't I mention it?"

I went to the downstairs loo. I wanted to be alone, but my phone buzzed almost as soon as I had locked the door. Phil – wondering where I'd been when he called, or why I hadn't sent him a message to pick up when he next had a signal?

> "Hope" is the thing with feathers / That perches in the soul / And sings the tune without the words / And never stops – at all.
> (Emily Dickinson)

WhatsApp, of course. And not Phil. He'd never send a poem or verse. He didn't see the point of poetry; it failed to move him.

I turned the phone off. I didn't want any more communication from anyone. I washed my face and as I looked back at myself in the mirror I had to confront the truth. I hadn't been crying because I was worried about my husband, because I felt duplicitous about arranging secret meetings, or guilty because I had failed to own up to an indiscretion way back in the past.

The little feathery bird fluttering within my soul was singing a tune about Webster Ferris. It had not stopped since 1985 and was unlikely to do so now. I didn't have Gran's belief in the Good Lord, but I recognised that if I faced a particular judgement there would be some explaining to do.

The Show must go on
Thursday 11th May 2023

*C*rown Him With Many Plays. Just who at the Marketplace Theatre had thought up that play-on-a-hymn title for the coronation extravaganza?

"It's *Crown him with many crowns.*" I explained to my 'children' when they queried the title. I sang the first verse including soaring melody in the middle, "*Awake, my soul, and sing/ of him who died for thee…*" They looked at me pitifully, unimpressed.

No one knows any hymns these days. It's a problem at weddings. As the organist strikes up the opening notes, most of the congregation can only mumble into the order of service. Just the few oldies who started their school day singing from a well-thumbed *Hymns A & M* covered in an offcut of wallpaper advertising their parents' decorative choices can belt out the tune to keep the show on the road.

I've got a favourite hymns list for my funeral but realistically, unless my grieving relatives choose *The Animals Went in Two by Two* or *Who Put the Colours in the Rainbow?*, it'll be a quiet old affair.

Still Life, representing the 1940s (or thereabouts), was kicking off the proceedings. I was grateful. Get it over with and go home. I was already working out how I could avoid watching the second

A Feather Between the Lines

and third parts of 'our' evening when I gave Arthur, Katie and Pol their tickets when they arrived at the theatre. I had no idea what time Phil (still not back from the time-warp cottage) would arrive, so I left his to be collected on the door.

Nerves had been building during rehearsals and the atmosphere in the dressing room when I arrived on the Thursday night was palpable.

Lanre had been wearing his mac and trilby since he arrived straight from work. He was pacing about the cramped room reciting his and Mandy's lines. She was clearly suffering from a sugar rush, peaking too early by starting the doughnut stash at about three o'clock.

"The boys never showed nerves," Vernon was telling the assembled company, "but I knew they had them. Not John, of course; he had nerves of steel."

My hair was piled up on my head in what I thought approximated a 1940s style. I wore a floral apron over a frilly-necked blouse and had pendulous earrings of the kind I'd noticed Joyce Carey wearing in the film. I'd realised at the dress rehearsal that these were possibly a mistake. They swung when I moved my head and then, like the balls of a Newton's Cradle, carried on in motion for a lot longer. When I delivered a cue to Vernon's Albert, the ticket inspector, he was transfixed, his head moving from side to side in time with them until they stopped and freed him to say his line.

Angela was out front, on the stage, stocking the refreshment bar with sausage rolls and more doughnuts so that Mandy's addiction could be satisfied at a moment's notice. She had to time it well: before the audience started to arrive but not so early that the sausage rolls went cold and lost their comforting warmth. If the pastry hit was the wrong temperature, it didn't satisfy the craving.

A few lines had had to be altered because of Mandy's cravings. Beryl, my assistant in the tearoom, played as a young girl in the film but morphed into a woman of indeterminate age played by Val (who is older than me), had to remember to switch mentions of rock cakes and Bath buns to doughnuts.

It was more confusing for the audience during the actual performance. Mandy, already terrified after her first brief but wordless appearance on the stage, had to come on again almost immediately with a handkerchief and a smut in her eye. Instead of asking for a glass of water to bathe it with, she demanded a hot sausage roll. I suppose it made sense when I subsequently had to ask her, 'Better?' and she replied (as per the script) 'I'm afraid not.'

We got through it. The two main characters met by chance, fell in love, stopped their affair and parted to return to their spouses, prevented from saying a proper goodbye by an irritating friend. Mandy reminded everyone she was 'a respectable married woman with a husband and a home and three children' rather more often than scripted. My character flirted with the ticket inspector and got a pleasing number of laughs with lines such as, 'Now look at me Banburys. They're all over the floor,' even though there was clearly nothing but sausage rolls and doughnuts in stock at the counter.

Mandy, frequently silent, was taking great bites out of doughnuts whilst Lanre extemporised. He even ran together a whole page of lines making a medical monologue describing his work trying to prevent pneumoconiosis. During this tedious speech you couldn't blame the audience for being more amused by the continuous drip of jam from Mandy's chin.

Lanre was fantastic holding everything together. Laura and Alec progressed from their accidental first meeting through five scenes and nearly a year of subsequent liaisons until Jackie, as Dolly the annoying friend, interrupted their final goodbye and the last sausage roll.

I was glad it was over. During a short interval the refreshment room was transformed to a dingy 1950s flat. The counter was replaced by an ironing board, and some stockings, resembling emaciated severed limbs, were suspended around the set to look as if they'd been hung up to dry. Presently, two men and a woman were on stage shouting at each other in accents which were taking a wild and unpredictable tour of the north of England. Back in the dressing room, I gave up my mirror and seat to one of the long-haired hippies getting ready for the third part of the programme.

Angela was happy at least. She bustled in from the side door, grinning and enthusing, eager for the return of compliments. "Roni: a triumph," she gushed. I wasn't sure if this referred to me or her but took the praise for myself greedily. "He's in the foyer," she announced. "I saw him on my way through. I'm so glad he made it. He's waiting for you there."

So Phil had arrived, by the skin of his teeth, and watched our offering. He'd decided he couldn't face watching the other two performances and was lurking in the foyer. I couldn't blame him, not really his thing. We could sit them out together until Arthur, Katie and Pol emerged.

I took off the apron but decided to keep on the rest of the costume, including the hypnotising earrings. I went out of the side door, into the alley and along to the front of the building to the foyer.

The management of The Marketplace Theatre like to pretend that they are in charge of a large West End venue, striding around with a sense of importance unnecessary in a converted multi-use building in a very small provincial town. Several of the audience, who'd taken too long with their interval drinks, had been told officiously to wait for a 'suitable break in proceedings' before they could re-enter the auditorium. To the side of them stood Webster Ferris.

"What the bloody hell are you doing here?" I spoke in a loud whisper whilst I scanned the waiting miscreant playgoers to see if Phil was amongst them.

"I came to see the play. Condensed Coward. Just like the old days."

"How did you know where to come?"

"Your pain-in-the-arse woman. She mentioned it yesterday. I looked up where it was and here I am. She's very pleased I'm here. She told me it was an honour. There's not many people say that."

I had to get away from the building, out of the reach of anyone who might see us together, beyond Angela's misinformed meddling and clear of a potential entrance, stage left, from Phil. I hustled Ferris out of the front door, across the market square to The Old Post Office. It no longer cashes pensions or doles out stamps having been transformed into a wine bar some years ago. A seat at one of its al fresco tables gives a panoramic view of both entrances to the theatre as well as of people approaching by foot, bus or bicycle – or those leaving it and heading straight towards you across the marketplace. An SAS sharpshooter would have been satisfied with my vantage point, yet I felt ill at ease.

"She were right about you stealing the show. You had some cracking lines," he began, "but why was that Laura stuffing her face with food all through? I don't remember Celia Johnson eating sausage rolls in the film. Perhaps David Lean cut that out."

I was relieved that I hadn't known Webster Ferris was in the audience during the performance. I couldn't respond to his back-handed compliment and silly jibe. I was too cross. How could he be so insensitive as to think he could just show up without telling me? We sat there in silence, my eyes fixed on the theatre doors.

"Why did you run off yesterday?" he said eventually.

"I'm surprised you ask that. You're the expert at running away. You always ran off at the slightest suggestion of things not going how you wanted them to. Particularly the last time. It's getting on for thirty-eight years since you ran away from me on Arthur's Seat."

"I know," he said quietly. "Do you think I haven't thought about that since?"

A Feather Between the Lines

"I can't do this, Webster. I'm married."

"A respectable married woman with a husband and a home and three children?" Unlike Mandy, Webster was word perfect.

I started to shiver. I felt rather stupid in my 1940s clothes, odd hairstyle and dangling earrings. It's a rare May evening at The Old Post Office when you can pretend you're in continental Europe and sit at an outside table without a coat.

"Here, have my jacket," Webster offered.

I refused. There is something very intimate about being offered a jacket and accepting its pre-warmed outsize protection being placed over your shoulders.

I've noticed men aren't so forthcoming when you get older. They can't wait to take over your shivering when you're twenty-one and freezing to death in strapless evening wear. At my age you are expected to dress for the climate. If you haven't – then that's your fault and they're not going to get cold themselves on your behalf. No jackets for the mature woman.

Wearing Webster's jacket and accepting his protection would be a statement and, just then, I wasn't prepared to make it.

"I'm not asking anything of you, Roni." He sounded hurt. "I'm not expecting anything. I just wanted to see you. I want to explain." He paused. "You didn't answer my message yesterday. I thought maybe the only way I'd see you again was to come along tonight."

"All that stuff about swifts only having one mate and feathers in souls. It's too much."

Like a bird in flight, he swerved that comment. "I just want to talk to you. I've had some help to try and sort myself out, but I still don't always get it right."

Here we go. Time to bear his soul. Not a singing bird but a full-blown confession and painful examination of his ghastly life thus far. I still wasn't looking at him.

"I started drinking heavily after I got to Harvard. It numbs your feelings, keeps them at bay." He paused. "I should have got in touch with you as soon as I got there – but I was too proud. Then Goldblatt told me you'd got married and I thought, 'Sod you'."

That was a bit blunt. I made no comment. My gaze was fixed over the square at the theatre. I couldn't look at him and he in turn was staring down at his feet. He didn't want to look at me either.

"It weren't your fault I didn't get in touch with you. I don't mean that. I were incapable of understanding how you might have felt or how unreasonable I were being, demanding you come with me." He paused. He'd said this much in his letter. And it was certainly true.

"The drink was under control – or I thought it was. It creeps up on you. I functioned pretty well for a number of years. Got my PhD, got an academic appointment, published, but then…" Then what? What had happened? "It took me twenty-five years to get some help. I had to go away somewhere, leave Boston and just stop everything for a while." He was vague, understandably so. I wasn't going to find out exactly what brought it to a head. Not that night. Perhaps not ever. "I stopped. It wasn't easy. I haven't had a drink since 25th October 2010."

"Well done," I said. It seemed inappropriate, as if he had just told me he'd come top in a spelling test or swum his first length at the swimming baths. I thought of him in that hot summer of 1984 and how I'd come across him at the open-air pool in Cambridge. How I'd taught him to do a width of doggy paddle and how those encounters had been the pivot from which our embryonic attraction to each other had started to mature.

He smiled. "Me agent were furious. I'd got a nice little line in writing fiction and he were taking his fifteen percent, thank you very much. When I stopped drinking, I couldn't write any more. It just wouldn't come."

A Feather Between the Lines

'I know all about that, R.V. Ironside,' I wanted to say. His books may be mired in gloom, but they'd clearly been lucrative.

"I got lucky, a professorship at Stanford – so I moved right across the country into the sun. I've had a lot of help since I've been there. And finally, I've been able to come back home."

"Is this the first time you've been back to Britain?"

"Yes!" He seemed surprised himself. He was looking at me now.

"Weird. Is it like being a prisoner released after a long sentence?" I giggled. "Everything has moved on whilst you've been doing your time and, when you come out of gaol, you don't recognise anything and can't make any modern things work."

"I can see the freed prisoner analogy on one level," he reprimanded, like a supervisor picking me up on a stupid comment I'd made in an essay, "but I have been participating in the world, you know. And we have British TV in the US to keep me up to date with home. It's hard to remember what it was like here in 1985. It seems so long ago in some ways…"

"And like yesterday in others," I added. He smiled.

"I came on the bus from Oxford. They haven't changed! I sat upstairs for the novelty of it. It's fooking slow and right uncomfortable. It's not something I do in Stanford but things over here aren't all that different to California. Apart from the shit weather and lousy plumbing."

I'd calmed down a little, although I was still anxious that at any moment a crowd of family, former colleagues from school, pupils, people from the village and the entire membership of the Isis Mummers could appear and ask some awkward questions about my companion at the table. 'This is Arthur's dad, everyone. Enjoy the rest of the show.'

"Therapy has helped me to understand my behaviour and given me the ability to address it."

Was this Webster Ferris speaking? He sounded like someone on an advert.

You had to hand it to the American shrinks. They could take a hard old boot, this working-class Yorkshireman, who frightened the entire student body at Cambridge University and most of the staff, who appalled those of a sensitive nature, who took on scabs in the miners' strike and settled his differences with his fists before becoming a full-blown transatlantic alcoholic, and enable him to come to terms with his personality and his past. Had they waved a mystic wand at his aura and damaged psyche? They must have earned every cent of the thousands of dollars it must have cost.

I chose my words carefully when I spoke next. In truth I did not find baring my emotions any easier than the pre-counselled Ferris had.

"It took me a very long time to deal with you abandoning me like that," I admitted.

"Not that fooking long!" he replied angrily. "You were married to Cambridge's dullest man only four months later."

Original Ferris was back! Here was my cue. I mustn't screw it up like Mandy. "There was a reas…"

Across the square, the doors of the theatre opened. Another interval. The kitchen sink drama had become a decade of the past and, after a swift drink, the psychedelic sixties were about to begin.

Through the aperture I could see the reason: tall, dark, curly haired and the image of his genetic inheritance. He had emerged from the auditorium for an interval drink. That meant Phil, Katie and Pol wouldn't be far behind. If I could see them, they may well be able to see me. And Angela. She'd be there, parading around the foyer in search of compliments and looking for my erudite cousin. I couldn't do it. I couldn't tell him.

"I have to go," I said. "There's a taxi rank just over there. Get in one. Please don't hang about."

Lanre was in the foyer eating a doughnut. "Bloody lovely these. This is the last one. Do you want some?" He'd taken the mac and trilby off but looked incongruous in his suit and tie.

A Feather Between the Lines

Arthur came over to us. "Mum, I'll take a picture." He held up his phone and Lanre (sugar coated lips) and I (sweating through a face of stage make-up) grinned.

The image will be preserved for just as long as Arthur can avoid losing his phone, or until he gets a new one and thousands of selfies and snippets of the very recent past will be abandoned with his old device. The photograph album is mostly a thing of the past. Those poorly framed, slightly out of focus snaps will no longer be a witness to people you'd have forgotten otherwise and an attractive, youthful self that you can barely remember.

There was no Phil. The bell rang and the audience downed their drinks and went back for a deafening concoction of electronic sound and consciousness-expanding light.

"The prodigal son," Lanre said when we were the last ones in the foyer, being told by the management that there was no way we should even contemplate reclaiming our seats now the third part of the show had started. "They certainly look alike." I said nothing.

"I reckoned that was him – the fella who was standing here earlier, talking to Angela. Did he enjoy the show?" You couldn't get much past Lanre – he and Angela could both have helped Thames Valley CID bang up all the felons in Oxfordshire. "I thought you were making it up, Roni, but it's true, isn't it?" What could I say? "I was looking for you," he added. "Mandy is being sick in the loo. A queue is forming."

I had to drive Mandy's car home, her green face poised over a Sainsbury's carrier bag all the way back. At least it got me out of having to suffer the '60s happening.

I could see there were lights on at our house. In the hall were Phil's panniers and his cycling shoes were neatly placed in the shoe rack. I found him upstairs, fast asleep and snoring gently in bed.

28

Friday 12th May 2023

When I woke up, Phil was already downstairs. He was reading the paper and drinking tea. It looked like he had guzzled his way through most of a pack of bacon, several eggs and half a loaf of bread. The frying pan was washed up and on the draining board. The washing machine was on. I could see fluorescent Lycra tumbling round in the drum. Perhaps Phil was returning to his old self.

"You must have been hungry!" He grinned but chose not to respond. "I wondered what had happened to you. You didn't turn up at the theatre last night and you didn't call." I tried not to sound accusing.

"It was such a lovely day. I decided to stay a bit longer and get a later train. Why not?" This was not classic Phil behaviour. He usually had trains identified and booked weeks in advance. I'd assumed this trip would be the same.

"I had a ticket for you on the door. It was the coronation extravaganza, *Crown Him with Many Plays*. Did you forget? Arthur, Katie and Pol came."

"You had some support in the audience then. That's good. Hope it went well."

"You usually call to let me know when to expect you," I replied, trying to word my worry in a way that implied I was concerned rather than cross.

"Ah," he said, "well, if I'm going to be able to contact you, you need to have your phone turned on. I called the landline, but no one answered."

I had turned my phone off after Webster's message on Wednesday night in a bid to be undiscoverable. I realised I'd forgotten to turn it back on again. Where was it now? It wasn't immediately obvious on the kitchen table or workbenches.

Had I left it behind at the theatre? I'd made a very speedy exit when I ran to collect Mandy's car as the 1950s cast were crossing their legs impatiently outside the one loo backstage. I'd hovered outside the theatre, engine revving, still in costume, as Lanre persuaded his puking co-star into the passenger seat.

Had it been lurking in the kitchen when Phil came home? Could he have found it and read my WhatsApp messages? He was certainly smart enough to work out my easy passcode to turn the phone on – though moral enough to have decided that this might be an invasion of my privacy. I hoped.

"You parked the car badly," he commented, showing a glimpse of his former self.

"I got a lift in and back with Mandy. Arthur drove it." Instantly I regretted not taking the rap for this parking faux pas. Now wouldn't be the moment to say Arthur wanted to use it to collect more possessions from Tania's before moving back permanently. I changed tack. "What shall we do today?"

"You can do whatever you like," he said generously. "What do you want to do? I think people should do whatever they want." This seemed uncharacteristically unplanned. Perhaps there were things to celebrate with New Phil.

"What about going out for a pub lunch?"

"Good idea. You could certainly do that. I've got to get ready." He got up from the table, "I'm meeting Malcolm and Geoff. Britain's Coastal Path beckons."

"Are you away for the weekend then? You didn't say. It's not on the planner." Every movement in Phil's life is announced in advance in tiny but neat pencil jottings on this super-sized calendar which hangs on the kitchen wall. Or they used to be.

"Must have forgotten. I'm making the most of my week's leave. I'm taking a leaf out of your book. There's a lot to be said for the spontaneous decision and last-minute arrangements. Ask Mandy if she fancies a pub lunch," he suggested as he left the room.

I thought it unlikely that Mandy would be wanting to eat anything at all, perhaps ever again.

I was feeling guilty about Ferris. He had apologised for his behaviour or at least tried to explain it. It can't have been easy for him to do that. Perhaps I'd read more into his comments about birds and his messaging of quotations from poems than was intended. I wasn't dealing with a normal personality. No amount of counselling, psychobabble or aura connecting could possibly make Webster Ferris follow the general rules of engagement with other members of the human race.

Arthur came into the kitchen to make coffee. For someone who shows little interest in domesticity he is very particular about this ritual. A specific roast of bean is required, a precise amount of which must be ground and put into his cafetière. The process of preparation of this thick, black ambrosia conforms to a rigid structure. It's a coffee symphony. The only parts in which I'm allowed to participate are the first sonata (purchase of the expensive beans from a speciality shop) and the final movement. That's the one where the disposal of grounds, washing of the many elements of the creation vessel and putting away of the grinder and equipment are not the responsibility of the barista and consumer. The two movements in the middle, the preparation and the drinking, are exclusively Arthur's. You could argue that we should just leave it to this thirty-seven-year-old, but the scattered debris field drives Phil wild.

"Want to go for a pub lunch, Arthur?"

"With you?" He looked slightly horrified. "What about Dad? I'm busy. They've given me a deadline." It looked like the publishers as well as his girlfriend had got the measure of my son.

Next door, Mandy's car was still outside – she must have called in sick at work. I looked through the window to see if my phone was on the dashboard or seat, but it wasn't obviously in view. I decided not to knock on the door carrying a tray of doughnuts and hot sausage rolls to ask for the key.

The end of *Still Life*, although I had welcomed it, was an anticlimax. I didn't want to read any more R.V. Ironside and the newspaper was full of grim stories. Phil was busy packing up OS maps and his walking boots, Arthur was working and Mandy was best left alone. I went for a walk and thought about Ferris and those last two years at university when I had known him. How could two years out of sixty have such an influence on my life?

Phil was getting ready to cycle to the station when I returned. "Geoff is bringing the tent. Two night's camping and I'll be back on Sunday evening. Is that enough information or do you want it in writing?" He switched very quickly between laid-back, laissez-faire Phil, tetchy, unreasonable Phil and his old self.

I'd finally got him to agree to see the GP. It was getting on for five months since the accident and I was hoping that a consultation might throw up some answers about his personality change. "Your phone is in the downstairs loo by the way," he called as he pedalled off out into the lane. Had he been looking at it? I doubted it, but as with so much else, I couldn't be sure.

When I turned it on it pinged into life. Five WhatsApp messages: a reminder from the vet to get flea treatment for the cat and four messages from Ferris.

Yesterday

I'm sorry. I shouldn't have come.

22:45

Lectures are on 17th, 18th, 22nd and 23rd. Please come. I should like to have you there.

23:55

Today
Please don't run away from me. Come and see me. I'm in a guest room at the college. Porter's Lodge on Broad Street.

02:58

'Not to understand a treasure's worth till time has stole away the slighted good, is cause of half the poverty we feel, and makes the world the wilderness it is.' William Cowper

10:31

The parting quotation was from a depressed eighteenth-century poet with documented mental health issues. No prizes for working out why that struck a chord with you-know-who. And who was the treasure? Me? Or was it Ferris's admonishment reminding me that I had let him slip through the net?

There was also a text, left by Neil the day before.

> Well. What is going on? Desperate to know. Got a meeting near you tomorrow, High Wycombe. Call me.

So I did. It was too late for a pub lunch, but he reckoned he'd be finished about 4pm so we arranged to meet for tea. I drove down the M40 to a shopping mall just off the motorway. There, in a department store café, we indulged in a cream tea for two.

"Sorry this is a bit ordinaire, darling, but I couldn't think of anywhere else," Neil apologised.

He was in his element, eager to hear 'developments', and I was glad to have someone to discuss them with. I told him the lot, from the Beaumont onwards. I could rely on Neil for some waspish comments but ultimately to have some astute analysis. He was clearly thinking as he carefully apportioned the remaining cream and jam between us to coat our final scone.

"I'm still not convinced that you should tell Ferris about Arthur. Have you thought it through – the implications? I don't really think there's much doubt, but there's no DNA evidence – is there?"

"Perhaps you're right. I feel I should – but maybe I'm just looking to clear my conscience."

"Ferris admitted to you that he hadn't really wished to be a father. It's not like you're giving him something he's had a great longing for." Neil chuckled, a mischievous glint in his eye. "If only he knew there are two of the little darlings for him to distribute his estate between."

Luke Featherstone, the secret half sibling, another problem. Should Arthur know about him? Would Mary tell him first?

"You need to go and see him, regardless." Neil poked the remains of his scone into his mouth and decisively refilled our cups with the last of the tea. He was right, as ever. I had dismissed Ferris rudely and he deserved a bit more sympathy after his honesty. "You've got something to tell him."

"I thought you weren't convinced it was a good idea?"

"Roni, you need to tell him that you are still in love with him." I opened my mouth to deny it, but no words came out. I tried to look appalled. "It's quite obvious."

"I love Phil," I managed to say, eventually.

"Yes, it's the eighth wonder of the world, sweetheart, but I'm sure you do. You're also in love with Webster Ferris. Still. After all these years. It's not a finite resource you know; you can give and feel as much love as you wish. Mind you, there's no accounting for taste. Something between the two of them might be more desirable…"

We parted in the car park. "Phil likes sleeping outdoors,

unsanitary conditions, cycling, tramping round paths which are perilously likely to landslide into the sea and he functions well in appalling weather. You hate all those things. Fundamentally, you have nothing in common." This was blunt but it was mostly true.

We did have the children in common (even if they weren't biologically in the same gang) and we'd banked approaching forty years of marriage and companionship. He had supported me when my parents died and during the ups and downs of boring domestic life. I wasn't sure Webster Ferris would have done that. He might have found an apposite quotation but that was all.

"Do you still get a tingle of excitement when you're with Simon?" I asked.

"Bien sûr!" Neil winked. "Thirty years on, my tingles are just as exciting as they ever were. But I am going to be in trouble if I don't get back soon. We've got people over for dinner. If you want to get things off your chest, you need to be up front with dear old Webster and go from there with the rest of it."

"I don't want to leave Phil," I said.

"I'm not suggesting you do. I just think you should be honest about your own feelings. Tell the prof. It may not be what he wants to hear, so then, well…" He got into his car and wound down the window. "Keep me posted!" Deep down I had more than an inkling that the professor was looking for just such an admission.

So in a 'do or die' kind of way I drove to Oxford and went straight to the college – before I could change my mind. I marched decisively through the ancient gateway.

"Where do you think you're going?" an accusatory voice called out. "There is no admission to the college or grounds during the examination season." A porter in a short-sleeved white shirt and uniform-type trousers and with a stance reminiscent of a sergeant major about to bully some squaddies on the parade ground was looking directly at me.

A Feather Between the Lines

"Surely no exams are going on right now? It's too late in the day," I replied.

"Are you a member of the college, Miss?" his tone implied he already knew the answer to this question. "Or a member of the university?"

"No."

"Then I repeat, there is no admission to the general public at this time of year." His body language was aggressive. Veins were sticking out on his neck.

"It's forbidden," chimed in his colleague, a woman wearing identical clothing and the self-satisfied grin of a prison officer who has the only key to your cell. Perhaps she thought that, as I didn't have an Oxford education, I might need some simplified translation of his words.

"I've come to visit someone. I'm not sightseeing."

"Do you have an appointment?" He raised his eyebrows. "Does the person or persons in question know you are coming?" He was wearing an earpiece. He was probably miked up and able to instruct a marksman high up on a roof: 'Fire!'

"No."

"Not here for the Viscount Grey dinner, then." This was a statement rather than a question. "Because if you were, I would have to inform you that jeans, such as you are wearing, are not permitted at high table on a formal occasion."

"You'd have to have a change of clothing on your person or go home and re-clothe," the apprentice Cerberus chimed in, relishing participation in the hypothetical scenario.

"Could you tell Professor Ferris I'm here then? He is a visiting professor."

"I am aware of that fact, on account of being the Head Porter," he gloated. His assistant grinned sycophantically. "The gentleman in question is here from Stanford University."

"That's in America," she chipped in helpfully.

"California, to be precise." The Head Porter was determined to keep the upper hand in the dissemination of information. "I could contact the Professor to tell him that you are here. Indeed, I would," he added generously. "However, I am unable to inform Professor Ferris you are here, because he is not here himself."

"Do you know when he's coming back?"

"We are unable to give out that kind of personal information," the woman announced boldly.

The Head Porter obviously didn't like her being in charge of directing the narrative. "All I can say is what he told me when he left earlier this afternoon," he confided, speaking more quietly. "He informed me, unofficially," he spoke this last word slowly, stressing it was clear that he had broken no protocols, "that he would be spending the weekend with Mrs Ferris."

"Mrs Ferris?" I wasn't expecting that. "Mrs Ferris? Who's that?"

"I expect that's his wife, don't you?" The woman looked triumphant. More explanations for the simple-minded.

Why shouldn't he have a wife? I'd asked about family, and he'd said he had no children. You had to be very precise when talking to Webster Ferris. If I'd asked him if he was married he would have told me. Perhaps meeting her was the undisclosed event which had started sobriety.

He was, no doubt at that very moment, meeting up with her in some classy London hotel. They'd spend the weekend catching up with whatever the RSC was performing and enjoying some heavy-duty, alternatively interpreted Shakespeare at fringe venues for comparative discussion later. At this very minute, although in the same room, they would be communicating by WhatsApp, out-quoting each other before pre-show cocktails (non-alcoholic for him) and a post-performance dinner at an expensive restaurant. She'd pay, of course, the generosity of a wealthy American heiress being the answer to every Yorkshireman's dream.

A Feather Between the Lines

Thank God he couldn't see me, red-faced and feeling slightly nauseous after too much cream and strawberry jam. Thank God I hadn't declared my feelings only to face ridicule or refusal or worse, a scenario which involved proposed adultery and more shame.

29

20th May 2023

Phil's mother's 90th birthday. Unlike Christmas, there was no getting out of that for anyone. We all trooped over to Reigate for the occasion.

I sat in the back of the car with Katie and Pol. They bore the guilt of travelling in a petrol-fuelled car which would be stuck in traffic on the M25 even without them on board. Apparently, the temperature in the seas might rise by at least two degrees because of our journey.

We contemplated this whilst jammed behind a car transporter whose cargo threatened to slip off, and in front of a left-hand drive HGV whose driver's attention was on his phone rather than our Toyota. To our side a coach announced TOURISTENFAHRT in large letters. I pointed it out to try and jolly things along but predictably it was not well received by my more sophisticated companions.

Arthur's long legs and sharp elbows were in the front with Phil. A collective sigh of relief accompanied our exit at junction 8 together with a groan at the predictable announcement: "A217 Fulham, London, to Gatwick, West Sussex."

Jessica, whose job involves flying all over Europe and even between UK airports, smugly claimed the moral high ground by arriving from London by train.

It was a shock to see the For Sale board planted in the front

A Feather Between the Lines

garden of the house, even though we knew it was going to be there. I wondered how Phil was feeling, or the children for that matter. The house had always been there, a permanent fixture in the background for their whole lives.

Indeed, it was part of the Phil package for me too, ever since I had first been taken home to 'meet the parents'. I recalled going inside for the first time, pregnant and anxious about the reception I might meet. Mr and Mrs Spittal (as I called them in the early days) had been welcoming and certainly delighted that they were going to be grandparents.

I had been well received by Paula too, delighted to be relegated to the position of reserve grandchild provider, a post which she continued to hold until round about her 40th birthday. Since then, she has been demoted with regularity: from 'past childbearing' to 'unmarried and likely to remain so' and now to her present position, 'first port of call for Mother and previously Father'. This was inevitable once she'd made the rookie's error of staying in Reigate when she moved to a place of her own. The family house was a backdrop to all the events of their lives, unchanged and permanent. Now it would become someone else's.

"The estate agent is a very nice young man. He told me that there will be no bother selling a lovely house like mine. He has people queuing up for a property like this. They regularly write letters to the agency begging to be told when this kind of thing comes on to the market."

Pamela had, as most of us do, given her business to the liar with the best sales patter and most over-inflated valuation. We knew that after a few weeks he would be clamouring to reduce the asking price, claiming Phil's mum had 'put it on for way too much' in the first place.

It wasn't Phil's mother's house, we learned. Only half was hers. The terms of Peter Spittal's will revealed that he had left his half of the house to Phil and Paula. This, I'm sure, softened the blow of its potential sale for them both. Paula could look at upgrading or even moving out of immediate reach now Pamela was hell bent on the sheltered flat with its promise of companions and assisted living – and, if we had read between the lines correctly, possibly something more…

"You kiddies can have anything you want from the house. I'm having all new in my apartment at Weald Court," Pamela announced to her grandchildren. I hoped she hadn't noticed the lack of enthusiasm for beige coloured Dralon covered furniture and a mixture of plain and tastefully patterned but nondescript curtains.

If you assembled a 'mood board' for the decoration of 39 Meadowmead Close (as interior designers do) you'd just have to stick a selection of biscuits onto a sheet of cardboard. Shortbread carpets, Rich Tea walls, Malted Milk curtains, Nice biscuit cabinet doors in the kitchen with a Ginger Nut roller blind and a digestive sofa with a cheeky Jammie Dodger cushion – a surprising spot of red alleviating the tedium. Then you could eat it when the monotony got too much.

The colour palette was Jessica's mix of inoffensive taupe but nothing like the eclectic riot of organic hue and texture with which Katie and Pol decorated their home. This offer of furniture and accessories was a challenge for them, always promoting recycling and repurposing, buying from charity shops and upcycling things people had left out for the refuse collection. There wasn't much in the Spittal's Reigate homage to Middle England which would interest them, however much it was chopped about and painted zany colours. The contents of the unsold house promised a future conundrum.

Paula had had a hand in the preparation of the birthday lunch, which was something to be grateful for. She's a worse cook than me so all the food had been bought in from a classy pre-prepared frozen food shop on the High Street in Reigate. She had

A Feather Between the Lines

been perpetuating the ruse of passing off their products as her own creations for several years. I was in on it, having caught her unmoulding a frozen boeuf bourguignon into one of her mother's casseroles on a previous visit. It was a handy tip she'd passed to me and there was a conspiracy of silence between us.

"She can make a very nice shepherd's pie, I'll say that for her," Mother confessed in a rare compliment to her daughter, as Paula, looking slightly awkward, put a large Pyrex dish containing one onto the dining table. Unsurprisingly, as she had got older, and once her husband had gone to live at the nursing home, Pamela's enthusiasm for catering for numbers had diminished. It was a relief to everyone but lovers of overcooked meat and waterlogged vegetables.

Paula had even bought a vegan meal for Katie and Pol. As a thank-you Katie had brought a contribution to the feast, a birthday cake which was presented for pudding. "It's a vegetable and bean cake. No eggs, butter or sugar," Katie explained as she inserted some short and previously used candles into its green surface. "I hope you like it, Granny." Pol began a poem he had written for the occasion whilst the rest of us took a deep breath and asked for a small slice.

"I'm going on a cruise as a birthday treat," Pamela announced suddenly, "with Joyce and her gentleman friend. I'm having a separate room, on my own, which I'm not very happy about because you have to pay a supplement."

"You could share with Paula," I suggested mischievously, trying to rid myself of the image of a geriatric threesome which had popped into my head.

"I'm not invited," Paula responded, sounding surprisingly disappointed.

"Joyce says cruises are popular with single travellers. Gentlemen who might be widowers. Or bachelors." No one knew quite how to respond. "Joyce has been on several. There's never a dull moment on board. She got up to all sorts of things."

"Like what?" Phil was embarrassed but curious.

"Well, she had a go at carving a horse out of ice. And she did things with flowers. She got a prize for being creative with chrysanthemums. It was the talk of E deck apparently."

"Why go on a ship to do that?" Jessica asked, with unnecessary but justifiable logic.

"What did Jessica say, Philip?"

"She said, 'where is the ship sailing?'" Phil replied, giving his literal daughter a frown.

"On the sea of course."

Before we could find out more about Joyce and her exploits afloat, Phil stood up and raised his glass. "Congratulations, Mother, for reaching 90." We toasted this achievement, inwardly marvelling at the new lease of life which had come over her. "And I've some news which will interest you," Phil continued.

Was he going to confess that he'd been nosing through the messages on my phone in the downstairs loo? Had he been keeping his discoveries for maximum exposure to the gathered audience? Miss Marple explaining all to the lunch party at Meadowmead in a postprandial reveal? Would he disclose everyone's coming and goings over the last few weeks, finally exposing me as the one to have had assignations of a nefarious nature which would seriously undermine our marriage?

"I've made a decision," he continued. "I'm retiring in June. I'm stopping work to do the things I really want to do."

"What's stopped working?" Pamela asked.

Why didn't Phil tell me about his plans beforehand? I tried to hide my annoyance when we got in the car to go home. To make the journey back even more unpleasant, we were having to share the footwell in the back with Pedro.

Pedro is a very tall and long straw donkey who wears a hat with pom poms on its brim and has two large panniers on either

A Feather Between the Lines

side of his saddle. Phil had chosen him as a souvenir on a family holiday to Spain in the early 1970s. Because the airline refused to put it in the hold, his indulgent father Peter sat squashed and immobile all the way home with Pedro across his lap in the cabin. These days security would be surrounding it with sniffer dogs or banning it for health and safety reasons. It's certainly highly flammable and HM Customs would have a field day searching for insects in residence likely to contaminate British soil.

Pamela had been trying to palm Pedro off on us for years because he took up a lot of room in Phil's old bedroom. We'd always been able to think up an excuse before, but now it was impossible to leave him there. The estate agent said he had to go because house viewers needed to see the full size of the room and Pedro was interrupting something he called 'the flow'.

Paula, still bearing a fifty-year grievance because she had only been allowed a pair of small wooden castanets in the gift shop, had suggested burning him. Phil wasn't having that. I was hoping Pol might find an affinity with a fellow countryman, possibly repurposing his panniers into a poetry book display stand. He wasn't jumping at the opportunity. Perhaps Mandy would meet a Spaniard so I could shove the beast her way to feature in her front room when she re-did her interior as a finca or cortijo.

"Pedro is coming back with us," Phil insisted. "He is part of the family. As the fifth P in the Spittal pod, he is not travelling in the boot." Conclusive proof, I feared, that the rationality which had characterised my husband's previous persona was all but lost.

Much as I had tried to push him out of my mind, Webster Ferris, like Pedro staking his territory on the Custard Cream-coloured tufted twist in Phil's bedroom, wasn't going anywhere. A flow of WhatsApp messages reminding me about the two lectures he was giving that week, follow-ups saying how disappointed he was I hadn't attended, along with entreaties to meet elsewhere had pinged daily on my phone. I'd ignored them all.

There was no message that day, Saturday. Another cosy weekend with the wife perhaps? I could have blocked him but that would show I cared about the fact that he was married. Where was Mrs Ferris now? Ensconced at the Beaumont Hotel at his suggestion? Enjoying the beauty of its gothic splendour, up to her eyes in William Morris wallpaper and custom-weave carpet in a boudoir themed on the works of Oxford's JRR Tolkien? Only because I'd introduced him to the place would she be luxuriating in the 'Lord of the Wedding Rings' suite.

They'd probably had a delicious lunch in the Wonderland Restaurant and were finishing off with coffee in the Morse Bar. I expected she'd been all around the Ashmolean Museum, lapping up every floor not just the Knossos special exhibition. She might even have promised to donate thousands of dollars and be in line for getting a gallery named after her. The Cindy Ferris gallery would display things you hadn't thought existed although it was bloody obvious that they might.

It was not only Phil who was becoming irrational.

30

Sunday 21st May 2023

The loan of the car for the next day had been secured by Arthur at the end of the journey back from Reigate. Volunteering to carry Pedro from the car, he'd swiftly secured the vehicle with a statement beginning, "Mum said it would be OK if…" Arthur had niftily teed up the apportioning of blame to me when, inevitably, we would be late for the *Still Life* post-production party that evening.

Now he was a curmudgeon, unwilling to spend time doing things he might not enjoy, Phil was not enthusiastic about going. We both had to acknowledge the very real possibility that Angela would be serving up a fait accompli for The Mummers' next extravaganza with supper. She could be very persuasive. Phil's going home bag might easily contain a toga and the script for a five-act play in which he would be playing most of the sixteen named friends of the Roman triumvirs and many of the other non-speaking officers and attendants. The likelihood of the car not being back at 6 o'clock as instructed, Phil repeating, "Where on Earth is he?" every five minutes from five-thirty and me ending the evening with the promise of a nylon Cleopatra wig, a rubber asp and the opportunity to ham up death by snakebite, was a wager my dad would have welcomed at McNamara Bros Bookmakers.

When Arthur finally turned up at 8 o'clock, the interior of

the car was crammed with more junk than I could believe he had accumulated. "Accident on the M4," he announced breezily.

Arthur must be the most jinxed traveller on the planet. He's only got to take to the road and pile-ups, lorries shedding their loads, one-way contraflows with ten mile per hour restrictions and all kinds of traffic misfortunes happen spontaneously in a combination which, fortunately for other drivers, is extremely rare.

He half-heartedly brought some items into the house but there wasn't time to unpack the boot or remove most of the boxes taking up the back seat. I'd already rung Angela to let her know we'd be late before we got into the car.

"You can rely on him not to think of anyone but himself," Phil began as he drove down the lane. He had a point. "He should get his own car repaired. Am I supposed to pay for that too?"

About half a mile from Angela's house the engine started to splutter and cough. The car shot forward with an alarming lurch before backfiring loudly and coming to a complete halt. There was silence for a while. "Typical," Phil said quietly, exasperated as much by his own uncharacteristic failure to check the petrol gauge before we left as by the inevitability that Arthur would not have thought to fill the tank on his way back home.

Phil kept an empty jerry can in the boot for just such a situation. Naturally he had never used it before. Had Arthur jettisoned it to make room for the important cargo now crammed into the space? After rummaging through the library of books, the loose items of clothing and the large number of boxes of papers which had been crammed inside, eventually Phil held the can aloft. He was triumphant, as if he'd won the last prize in a lucky dip. There was something to be thankful for, I pointed out.

"You'd better walk from here. We're really late. I'll find the nearest garage and get some petrol." It was comforting to see Phil was still able to plan decisively in a crisis.

A Feather Between the Lines

I could hear conversation punctuated with polite laughter when I rang Angela's bell. "We started without you," she explained, ushering me into her hall.

"Phil will be along in a bit. The car ran out of petrol and he's gone to the nearest garage with a can." Angela looked shocked at this revelation. She'd already been warned about the useless son and his inability to return the car home in time, but the useless father…? Who would expect Phil to be running on E for empty?

"Come through. Come and say hello," Angela enthused. She went ahead of me into the dining room, "Ta Da!" She put out her arm, like a magician's assistant drawing attention to a body which had been sawn in half. "We thought we'd surprise you!"

Sitting at the table, tucking in to a plate of delicious-looking food was not a severed torso but Webster Ferris. I was speechless. He looked up at me, smiling but unsure of what kind of reaction he might find.

"Your cousin has been entertaining us magnificently," Angela twinkled. Could this possibly get any worse? Undoubtedly. When Phil arrived.

Most of the cast of *Still Life* were present in Angela's tastefully decorated dining room. "You look a bit miffed. I hope you don't mind me muscling in," said Joy, who, with customary sullen face, was also a surprise guest at the table. "I know it's supposed to be an Isis Mummers get together, but the professor's lectures were so interesting that I begged Angela to include me. Who would have thought you'd have such an academic cousin?"

"We didn't see you in the lecture hall. Did you shoot off at the end?" Angela continued. "You probably had a reserved seat. Actually, that made it easier to give you this little surprise." She looked pleased with herself. A meal with a twist. Little did she know what might be about to happen when Phil was reunited with my relative from America.

Mandy was sitting next to Ferris. She looked at me crossly.

"Where have you been hiding this cousin of yours?" she hissed. "He says he been staying in a guest room in a college. You might have told me when you visited. I'd like to have come for a nose." I suspected Mandy's interest might lie beyond the room itself. Potentially Angela might be in on some kind of irresponsible matchmaking – Palo Alto CA being even further away than Drumnadrochit. "It's a good job I came straight from my friend's," she added, "and wasn't relying on you a for a lift. I'd have missed half the evening."

Angela indicated a seat next to Lanre. He was concentrating hard on buttering a perfectly shaped home-made bread roll in order not to look at me. I couldn't tell if he was sniggering or sharing my burden.

"Poor Jackie, her hip is playing up," Valerie squeaked from the other end of the table. "She'll be sorry to have missed Professor Ferris telling us all about Stanford and California."

This was a cue for Vernon to contribute an anecdote he'd been constructing. "The lads played in San Francisco in '64, '65 and '66." He looked at Ferris. "I expect you've been to Cow Palace and Candlestick Park, Webster," he added, in an over-familiar way, emphasising his Liverpudlian accent in case the professor failed to make the connection. "Their last ever paid live performance, Candlestick Park." Webster looked unimpressed. He was staring at me in a disconcerting way. "It's hard to get your head round the fact that they actually split up a very long time ago. Yet remarkably their music has kept them alive. Now we've lost John and George they'll never be back together again." Vernon was overdoing it this time. He didn't actually name The Beatles but he'd thrown in enough hints to ensure there was no doubt who he was going on about. Val smiled weakly because she was nicer than everyone else. He was either a fantasist or we had been foolishly missing out on some excellent first-hand anecdotes all this time.

Angela placed a plate of food in front of me which she had

thoughtfully kept warm on a hostess trolley at the side of the room. Other than Pamela Spittal, Angela is the only person I know who still has and uses one. I doubted the electric food warmer would make it to the sheltered flat, so Angela would soon be unique. I didn't feel hungry.

"I've been telling the professor about my ambitions to explore Shakespeare with the Isis Mummers," she confessed coyly. "Your cousin agrees with me that you'd make a very good Cleopatra." She spoke coquettishly, as if there had been intimate conversations between them, pillow talk even. "He says you'd make a perfect temptress of the Nile." Angela giggled like a sixteen-year-old saying risqué things in front of her aged maiden aunt. It was unbearable.

Webster looked straight at me, but his expression was blank. " 'Age cannot wither her, nor custom stale her infinite variety'," he quoted.

"Absolutely," gushed Angela. "I've been telling her that all along. I'm determined to do it." Lanre looked alarmed and Mandy paled, visions of barges full of hot sausage rolls and doughnuts floating towards her down the Nile turning her stomach. "Roni has amazing recall. She is unbelievably good at learning and remembering lines," Angela added, unintentionally making it worse for Mandy. "Just like you, Professor! It must run in the family."

"Exactly how are you related?" Lanre asked with a cheeky grin. "You don't need to draw a family tree or anything." Whose side was he on for God's sake?

"It's not just Shakespeare," Webster interjected. "Roni has an amazing recall of poetry, particularly Yeats. It must be the Irish side of the family."

Angela sighed. "Poetry does not have the importance it should have in the school curriculum today." Joy shook her head vigorously. There was nothing more bonding for them than discussion of falling standards in education.

"I love poems," Mandy declared, gazing up at Ferris. "Do say one for us. Pleeeease." She clapped her hands like a seal asking for fish at the zoo. I had an image of her cottage styled as a vision of San Francisco, her hall representing the entrance to the Golden Gate leading into a sitting room recreated as the interior of a cable car.

" 'When you are old and grey and full of sleep, / And nodding by the fire, take down this book, / And slowly read, and dream of the soft look / Your eyes had once, and of their shadows deep...'" Webster was directing this straight at me. "How's the rest of it go, Roni? I've forgotten."

"I can't remember," I replied, avoiding his gaze and pushing the food around my plate.

"Of course you can!" Angela was forceful. "Roni had an appallingly difficult year 10 boy recite that poem in assembly once. I remember it well. There wasn't a dry eye in the house at the end. Don't be shy, Roni." This kind of quasi-intellectual cabaret was what Angela hoped for at all her dinner parties.

" 'How many loved your moments of glad grace, / And loved your beauty with love false or true, / But one man loved the pilgrim soul in you, / And loved the sorrows of your changing face.' "

I tried to make my voice as dull and monotonous as possible. I had to stop for a moment before continuing the last verse, louder and more pointed.

" 'And bending down beside the glowing bars, / Murmur, a little sadly, how Love fled / And paced upon the mountains overhead / And hid his face amid a crowd of stars.' "

For a short while there was a silent moment of contemplation, before Vernon spoke. "Eh, I have to hand it to you. This is top grub this is, Angela."

I could feel my face reddening and my throat became dry. I left the room and went out of the back door in Angela's kitchen into the garden. I thought I was going to be sick, faint and burst

A Feather Between the Lines

into tears all at the same time. Presently Angela appeared at the door.

"Don't you feel well or is it a hot flush?" she asked.

I sat on her garden bench. "I'll be OK in a minute."

"Do you mind if I serve the tiramisu?" She disappeared.

I tried to breathe deeply to control the turmoil threatening to erupt all over Angela's herbaceous border.

Presently I heard movement behind me. I thought it was her with a bowl of creamy goo I couldn't eat. But it was Webster. He sat on the bench beside me. "Why did you make me do that?" I asked.

"I wanted to hear your voice reciting it. Not some crappy double-entendres in a sub-standard Coward, but beautiful words."

"What the fuck are you doing here, Webster? You've got to stop turning up out of the blue."

"I didn't have any choice. Angela can be very persuasive." This was a joke, I thought, but I wasn't going to laugh. His voice became more serious. "You didn't reply to my messages. You read them – I could see the blue ticks. You didn't come to my lectures. I thought I'd never see you again."

I breathed out deeply. "Actually, I did come and see you. I came to the college – but you'd gone away for the weekend. The Head Porter was not very welcoming. He told me you'd gone to see Mrs Ferris."

"Aye, he's a jumped-up bastard that one." He paused. "If I'm honest, it were an unsettling trip."

Had they rowed? Perhaps they'd disagreed about the RSCs interpretation of whichever Shakespeare they'd been to see.

"It were familiar but like I'd never been there. Like a dream but not like the dreams I have about it. I do dream about Rotherham. Not everyone's idea of a good night's sleep."

He'd taken her to Rotherham! That would have been an eye-opener for a tanned, matcha drinking, poké bowl eating lovely from San Jose.

"I wanted to see the New York stadium. There weren't a match on, of course. It's right smart but it's not the same. And I went back to Millmoor. It's still there – a ghostly collection of half-altered terraces and stands. It's just been abandoned. I looked through the fence remembering all those matches I'd watched. It's almost as if you can hear them echoing round its windswept terraces. I tried to remember my dad taking me – but I couldn't. To be honest, I can't really remember him at all. It upsets me, that. I were only four when…" He couldn't finish the sentence and the sadness in his voice was noticeable. He wouldn't have been great company reliving all his yesterdays. "I went to Arthur Street, Rawmarsh. Our house looked so much smaller than I remembered. It weren't big to begin wi', just a two-up, two-down but…" I'd never known his address; he'd always kept it to himself. Worried perhaps that I might suddenly turn up out of the blue? Like him. How ironic that it was Arthur Street.

His voice had become more northern as he spoke about his town and his home. "The wors' thing were that when I got to the cemetery I couldn't find the grave. I thought I knew… but it weren't there. There were a man in a building who gave me the plot number and helped me find it. It were all overgrown. I don't know what I were expecting. He said, 'Tha wants to clean that headstone, lad.' Telling me off like. He called me 'lad'. I'm going to be 62 in August. It were like he knew it were me parents down there."

Of course. Mrs Ferris, his mother. The woman who had become so unwell with MS that he had been allowed to take a year out of university to care for her before she died. The reason he had reappeared at college demoted to my own year. He'd been away through misfortune and not because of the bad behaviour, violent misconduct and criminal activity that the student body preferred to ascribe to his absence.

Mrs Ferris, his mother. Overgrown since 1983, reunited with

her husband after the pit accident seventeen years before and waiting, since 1985, for her only child to come back and pay his respects.

Mrs Ferris, his mother, the person who, he had told me once, was the only woman he had ever loved apart from me.

I wanted to hold his hand and tell him I was sorry but with legendary timing Angela reappeared at the back door. "Phil's made it," she announced. "I kept a plate warm for him. He's catching up. I'd better go and check Vernon hasn't eaten all the tiramisu. I've never seen a man wolf down so much."

I stood up to go inside. "Roni, promise me you will come and see me. I'm free tomorrow. I'll be in my room. I'm just doing preparation for this week's lectures."

"OK," I said. "I promise." I tried to calm myself before going back inside.

Angela was in the kitchen busying about. "I think it's very touching how he cares about you." Did she mean Phil, worried about my sudden indisposition? "I wish I had a relative like that. Such a shame he lives so far away and you don't see each other very often."

Phil was eating at high speed when I returned to the dining room. "What's up? Are you feeling ill?" he asked.

Angela brought him in a bowl for some tiramisu. "There's a surprise guest to go with your pudding, Phil," she announced. "He's in the bathroom at the moment." She placed the dish beside him, getting very close to his face as she did so in order to examine it through her bifocals. Val and Joy had also been shooting surreptitious glances at Phil whilst his attention was on the plate. They too were getting their first view of the fascinating facial stripe, still visible after nearly five months. Vernon's eyes were fixed only on the huge bowl of cream and coffee liqueur-soaked sponge. He wanted to be the first to offer to gobble it up if Phil didn't feel like it.

It seemed an eternity before Ferris returned to the room.

"Here he is! Of course, you know each other anyway," Angela gushed. Ferris didn't look the least bit worried.

Phil looked confused at first and then defensive. "Well, well, well, the American professor. Didn't expect to see you," he said eventually.

Lanre's eyes were wide open. This was the kind of cabaret he preferred. A good old domestic drama, not a recitation of a sentimental poem, but Angela was oblivious to any subplot running concurrently to her perceived script.

She prattled on, telling Phil how she had approached the professor after the lecture to secure him as top guest at her soirée, how she was truly honoured that he'd given up his evening to come to the Marketplace Theatre and watch our performance and how sorry she was Phil hadn't made it to share the experience with him. She explained how she had asked his professional advice about forthcoming Isis Mummers productions of Shakespeare. Her ambitions clearly lay way beyond the epic five-act, multi-actor love story of Antony and Cleopatra; the whole of Shakespeare's canon lay at our feet. Professor Webster Ferris was the answer. It was a monologue of undisguised hagiography.

What advice had he given her? How do you do even the simplest of the bard's works with a group of eight (if you're lucky), the majority of whom are over sixty and many of whom can't learn a few simple lines and say them at the right moment? I knew what he would have said, the same as me: "Don't."

She rounded off with the most absurd question yet. "I hope you don't mind my asking, but did your parents name you after the Jacobean dramatist John Webster? One of my ambitions is to put on a production of *The Duchess of Malfi*."

Phil snorted volubly at this impossibility, as he rammed a huge spoonful of creamy tiramisu into his mouth.

"I'm named after Barry Webster. He scored a goal for

Rotherham United in the first leg of the League Cup Final in 1961 on the day I were born."

Angela laughed. I think she thought he was joking. Webster gave Phil a disapproving look which confirmed quite clearly that he was not. The gloves were off. Angela quickly changed the subject. "I haven't asked you what you thought of *Still Life*? I didn't dare." She was obviously fishing for compliments, but I knew Webster would never pick up on that. He was plain speaking; he told it as it was. All eyes were on the professor.

"It's a creaky, dated old piece, in't it? The film were much better. I don't suppose anyone other than you lot has done it for a while and you can see why. It's difficult to put on anything, mind, when the talent you've got is limited." No one could quite believe what he had just said. The unpopular, blunt, uncompromising undergraduate, disliked in all quarters of the university, lived on. I had to admire and secretly celebrate that.

"What about Roni?" Phil demanded. "Was she rubbish too?"

"Had you bothered to come along, you'd have seen that, as usual, she was so much better than everyone else," he replied firmly. "She were always the best. That right load of toss that lad Roland put on in Cambridge – bollocks the lot of it. She were the one with stage presence, the person everyone watched no matter what garbage he had her saying."

If I'd had a pin I would have dropped it – just to see if what they say is true. Joy's face was a picture. No one used that kind of language in front of her. Not if they didn't want to be marched to the Head's office before being excluded and sent to a special secure gulag for disruptive pupils. But there was more to come.

"Even that fooking King Arthur crap, with only one pissing knight at the round table. Bugger me, what a pile of shite. Kids' show? Roland hoped they wouldn't notice the dross – a bloody dog would have seen that only Roni had any talent."

"That show was only at the Edinburgh Festival not in

Cambridge," Phil said. I could see the cogs whirring in his brain. "You weren't even there. You'd pissed off to the States to give the Yanks the benefit of your opinions by then."

"Well, that's where you're wrong, pal. I were there and I saw every bloody awful minute of it."

Nobody quite knew what to say or understood what was going on. Surely, despite the aggressive exchange and clear tension, Phil and Webster should both be happy to award me 'Best Actress' even if it was not necessarily true. Only Lanre and I had the full information which placed Webster Ferris and the conception of Arthur Spittal in the same city at the same time. I thought Phil was probably getting there.

There was silence. Everyone shuffled in their seat. Even Vernon knew he needed to shut up. "I'll make some coffee," Angela said eventually.

"Not for us," Phil stood up decisively. "If Roni isn't feeling well, then I should take her home."

31

Later that night

We travelled back in silence, me moaning occasionally in the vain hope that Phil might attribute my distress to illness. I was still unsure if he had drawn the obvious conclusion now he knew Webster Ferris had been up in Edinburgh at the festival that summer. Just one day. Just one encounter. What were the chances of conception?

Stupidly I still thought I might be able to avoid the inevitable. Selfishly my thoughts had veered swiftly from clean slates and a desire to be honest to self-preservation in the face of imminent discovery. If ever I doubted that I lacked strength of personality, or backbone as it used to be called, that car journey confirmed it.

We had to push against a great pile of what looked like unwashed clothes and single shoes to open the front door. The few items Arthur had removed from the car were strewn about the hall.

"For God's sake!" Phil kicked a lone trainer with such force it rebounded off the banister and nearly hit him in the face. This wasn't the time for a joke about Alex Ferguson and Beckham in the dressing room at Manchester United, though it did pop into my head as I stifled as giggle. "He hasn't even taken this crap up to his room. It's the last straw. As if arriving late and leaving the petrol tank empty wasn't enough." Anger was not something anyone associated with Phil but since the accident he had been progressing from slightly irritated through pissed off and annoyed to a splendid line in absolutely furious.

I followed him into the kitchen where he filled the kettle and got out the small tea pot and one cup. If I needed one, this was a signal that I was in trouble. He seemed to be collecting himself as the water boiled.

"I've often wondered," he began, "but I dismissed it. At first, I thought he looked like your Uncle Pat and your dad to a certain extent. He doesn't look like anyone on my side – but children often don't look like either or a combination of both parents, I know that." He spoke calmly, as he did when he patiently explained how to check the tyre pressure or relight the boiler. "I thought it was paranoia. I've always known about you and him. I've never asked particularly because I thought it was all over, finished, before we left Cambridge." He poured the water into the pot and popped the lid on definitively to illustrate his point. His back was still turned to me. "When Arthur grew into an adolescent and looked just like him, to satisfy that niggling doubt I had, I worked out what the rough date of conception must have been – during the festival, when we were together. The similarity in looks was a cruel irony, there to remind me that you had loved someone else before." He moved to the fridge to get the milk. "Now I discover he was in Edinburgh. He didn't go to America straight after graduation." I could see as he turned round that he wasn't calm at all but was struggling to contain his feelings.

"Phil, I want to…"

He interrupted me. "We're going to play a game, Roni. I've got some simple questions and you must answer ONLY 'Yes' or 'No' to them." I protested but he continued, his voice becoming louder. "Do this, at least. Don't muck about. Answer truthfully. Two rules: 'Yes' or 'No' and honesty. Got it?" He put the milk into the mug and started to pour his tea.

"Did you know he was going to be there tonight?"

A Feather Between the Lines

"No."

"Did you know he was coming to England before Mary's visit that day?"

"Yes, but…" He wagged his finger.

"My rules. Did you meet him in Edinburgh that summer?"

"Yes."

"Is there a possibility that Arthur is his son?"

"Yes."

"Was there ever a moment in the last thirty-seven or so years when you thought you should mention this to me?"

"Yes, I have been…"

"Uh, uh, remember the rules. I don't want excuses or explanation. Not at the moment." He paused, "Do you love me?"

"Yes."

"Well, I suppose that's something." He picked up the mug and walked to the door. "I assume you will be coming up in a minute. If you don't have other arrangements."

I wanted to explain myself, the youthful logic which had accompanied my own doubts at the time as to who was Arthur's biological father. Webster had left me. Phil was there. He too could have fathered this child – who did bear a resemblance to Uncle Pat and my dad. I'd just turned twenty-three, for God's sake. I had no job, no plans, no money – and no proof.

I thought I'd wait a few minutes for Phil to restore himself with the cup of tea and then go up and face the music. I put the milk back in the fridge and washed up the pot. When I turned round from the sink, Arthur was standing in the doorway.

"I was in the sitting room reading. I turned out the light when I heard you drive up. I didn't want to deal with Dad moaning on about the car." Understandably he looked shocked. Not for the first time I was unable to speak. It's been a feature of the last fifty or sixty years. "It explains a few things," he said charitably.

"Look," I said eventually, "I'm sorry you had to hear that.

Particularly in that way. Dad is your dad. He has cared for you from the time he knew you were coming, long before you were born. He has nurtured you, supported you and loved you. He has fathered you in every sense of the word."

"Not quite every sense," Arthur replied, with the frankness of his potential biological father. "Not if I followed what you were saying correctly."

"I don't know. I'm not sure. I had a boyfriend before Dad and at the very beginning of my relationship with your father, somewhat ill advisedly, I slept with him. Just the once and then he left and I didn't see him again until now." Somewhat ill advisedly? I sounded like a barrister trying to defend his guilty client's execrable behaviour. "You could find out, do one of those tests, if you really want to know, but honestly, I don't think it will change much. Dad is angry, but he's angry with me. It won't change how he feels about you."

"He's already got me down as an incompetent loser," Arthur replied. "I don't think he thinks much of me. I'm sorry about the petrol. I was in such a rush to get back I didn't look at the gauge."

"Oh, darling, he loves you." I moved to give him a hug. "We both do and we're both very proud of you and your achievements and how successful your writing has been."

Hugging my grown-up son always reminded me of embracing Webster Ferris. Same height and build, same hair and colouring. I had always tried to put this Pavlovian response right to the back of my mind. It seemed particularly wrong to think about Webster at that moment.

"Who is he, then, this man? Is he staying near here? Why did you meet him tonight?" It wasn't unreasonable of Arthur to ask.

"He lives in the US. He was a student at my college. We studied English Literature together. He is also a writer and an academic. He's in Oxford giving some lectures at the moment." I was hoping pathetically that this would be enough, but Arthur's mind was whirring. With the speed of analysis and connection of Professor Ferris and the detective-like sleuthing of Angela, he was beyond any airy-fairy, non-committal pronouncement I was trying to make.

"Not that dude doing the Shakespeare series?" Arthur's mouth was wide open with disbelief. "For fuck's sake, R.V. Ironside is my father? I was reading that book, *The Apparition of Love,* when you came in. Christ it's depressing."

He was shocked. I made him a cup of tea and got the bottle of brandy I use in the Christmas cake every year out of the cupboard. I poured him a glass. I had one myself. Fortification for my next encounter with Phil.

Arthur assured me he was OK. I was trying to own up to my deceitful and appalling behaviour, but I got the impression that this revelation was like a missing jigsaw piece for him. He had spent years trying to figure out why he was so different to his father and his sisters. He and I were always very close, something that was to do with the age gap between him and the girls. For nearly seven years it was just him and me, together in the playground, in the garden and at home, whilst we both matured. Arthur even writes under the name McNamara – though that is probably more to do with having the surname Spittal and being called Slobber at school. But Phil and Arthur? They are not alike in any way.

After some time, when I was sure he was feeling alright, we decided it was time to go upstairs. The light was out in our bedroom. Phil had got fed up with waiting for me or decided I wasn't coming. I crept into the dark. Although I tried to shut the door, undress and fumble for my nightdress quietly, I made an extraordinary amount of unintentional noise. Stubbing my toe on the leg of the bed as I climbed in made me shout in pain.

"Phil, are you awake?"

"I am now."

"I would have come up before, but Arthur was in the sitting

room. He heard everything. I've been talking to him. He's OK. He knows you are his dad and always will be."

Phil made no response. "I love you, Phil. You must realise that."

He was lying on his back. I tried to snuggle up to him, running my hand down his soft-skinned, downy arm, hoping to hold his hand as a prelude to intimacy and apology. He turned away, on to his side so his back was against me, an impenetrable barrier like the Berlin Wall, erected suddenly and solidly and not inviting efforts to breach it.

"No," he said decisively. "Not now." The subtext was that he might mean not ever.

32

The next day
Monday 22nd May 2023

I'd made a promise. Should I keep it? Things had changed. Should I add 'promise keeping' to the list of behaviours I was clearly unable to accomplish by the age of 60?

Phil didn't say anything before he went to work. Arthur had waited for the sound of him and his bike leaving before he got up. That first encounter between them was going to be difficult. My visit to Webster Ferris later in the day wasn't going to be easy either.

"You couldn't drive me to the station could you? I forgot I've got a meeting with my editor today. I'm supposed to be in central London by 11." Arthur was putting a packet of shortbread biscuits into one pocket and an apple and a banana into the other. Breakfast.

Given the bullet train isn't yet running from our local station, or indeed the main line at Oxford or Didcot, this was going to be a challenge. Poor timekeeping – another of my failings, this one passed to my son.

Guilt and indulgence: the combination which saw me driving my son to Oxford. Not only could I drop him at the station but while I was there I might as well drop in to see Ferris at his college. Turning things over in my mind, I recognised there was a possibility that Arthur would ask to meet him, so I needed to prepare the ground for that. I also recognised the futility of justifying my visit in my own mind. I couldn't even be honest with myself.

The Head Porter was holding court with another member of staff when I entered the lodge. He showed no sign of curtailing his conversation.

"I said to him 'I don't care how many letters you have after your name or how many medals and honours have been bestowed on you. You can publish as many papers as you like and write all the books you want, but you are not bringing that into the college without prior permission from the Master. Nothing less.' I think that told him."

Although the colleague was standing, the porter was sitting in a chair, leaning back. His feet were up on a desk in a private area beyond the front counter where access was undoubtedly strictly limited. It was an expensive-looking office chair, the type with wheels and the ability to spin round and round, with a lever under the seat which you can pull to lower it very suddenly. I suspected he allowed no one else to rule from this throne.

He was a master of this vehicle, I discovered. When he eventually decided to turn his self-satisfied grin and attention to me, he pushed off from the desk with his feet, speedily travelling to the centre of his office where, with a deft prod to the ground from one foot, he performed a ninety-degree turn arriving at the point on the main counter where I was standing. Such precise mobility must have taken hours of practice. The grace and accuracy of office chair manoeuvrability could give figure skating a run for its money at the next Olympics. Great Britain could be in line for a stash of gold medals, an accomplished selection of civil servants, local government staff and other office-dwelling desk slaves providing a crack team to represent us.

A Feather Between the Lines

"You'll be after Professor Ferris." I expressed surprise that he should remember me. "All part of the job, Miss," he said, performing a speedy sideways slide which also encompassed picking up the receiver of a telephone and pushing a couple of buttons as he came to a halt. Clearing his throat as he spoke into the apparatus, he announced, "Another visitor in the lodge for you. Miss McNamee." Then, casually chucking it back into the cradle as he rotated a full 360 degrees, he confirmed, "He is in residence. Lucky you. I suggest you wait in the quad, Miss. And all the very best."

I wanted to obliterate his smug, self-satisfied expression by telling him he'd got my name wrong. For once I managed to restrain myself. It was possible, I decided, that during his stay Webster Ferris had taken on this bumptious, self-important martinet. I sensed friction. Such types were attractive prey for him during his fists-and-black-eye period in Cambridge forty years earlier.

I wasn't his first visitor? Had Mary called in uninvited? Had he assumed she was me when he opened his door to find her accompanied by their progeny and the surprising news?

As I went into the quad, Ferris appeared from a door in a building on one side. He was alone and grinning madly, I was relieved to see. "You managed to get past the rottweiler then," he laughed when he caught up with me. "I was coming to rescue you. Are you up for summat t'eat? If you get in early there's less of a queue."

It sounded unlikely he was taking me to a Michelin-starred restaurant. He led me up a steep flight of steps to what turned out to be the dining hall of the college. We took a tray and queued up at the counter for our food, taking it, after Webster had paid at the till, to a long refectory table. "This is proper good, in't it? There en't many places you can get two meal for seven quid. Don't say I haven't spoiled you."

The seats were long benches and he sat next to me, not opposite, which wasn't where most people might have chosen to put themselves. Webster Ferris, I kept being reminded, wasn't like most people. Our fellow diners were earnest students, discussing their mornings' activities in the lab or developing points from the lectures they had just attended. They looked serious and intelligent. Where were the hooray Henrys and loud voices who had dominated the hall at our college? Still in bed perhaps. Surely there are some students left in Oxford who find the a.m. get up a strain.

"I never ate with you in college," I said. "Do you realise that?" At mealtimes Ferris sat with his political brothers discussing Labour Party business such as leafletting about the miners' strike in low, intense voices. Before I knew him, I'd noticed his solemn interactions with this group which I had no wish to join. Our relationship, when it began, was serious too, but furtive and not on display in public places. Ferris grinned. I was sure he remembered.

"Your Phil's gone right miserable, hasn't he? Proper aggressive."

"He had an accident before Christmas. He got run over by a bus." Ferris hooted with laughter. "Well, that's not strictly true: a bus knocked him off his bike and he hit his head. He hasn't been the same since. He was very lucky it wasn't worse." Webster made no comment. I couldn't see his face straight on, but I imagined his expression said 'a pity'.

"Do a lot of cycling does he?" Ferris asked eventually. "Do you go with him?"

"Don't be daft. He likes cycling on his own. He particularly enjoys it if there's hilly terrain and if it's cold and windy. He goes walking too, with his old college mates. They're trekking a path round the coast of Britain."

"What the fook for?"

"It's a hobby, I guess. Like birdwatching or being fanatical about a football team."

"Fair dos," Webster laughed. "You're obviously attracted to

A Feather Between the Lines

the neurodivergent type." I shut up. I'd said too much, and I'd probably been rude – about both of them. "Did you know I've got a fancy label these days? My therapist gave it me," he boasted.

As the hall filled up, more people sat at the table, squeezing up on the benches so that by the time we had finished our apple crumble and custard we were sitting quite close to each other. Our arms occasionally touched as we spooned up the delicious pudding. I wondered if Ferris had engineered this understated frisson of closeness. It was too public a place to tell him about Arthur, his surprise child.

When we went back outside, the quad had become busier, full of students meeting up at lunchtime. I knew we were both thinking the same thing, remembering being amongst them. It didn't seem that long ago.

"Takes you back, dun't it?" he suggested.

"You're in this kind of place all the time. You've never left university."

"Stanford's not like this," he replied, ignoring my jibe. "It's a huge campus, not mixed in with the city. Wasn't founded 'til the 1880s. There's nowt from the thirteenth century; the bed I'm sleeping on here is older than anything in Stanford University. The students travel around on electric scooters and skateboards and sit about in cybercafés and hotspots. I'm a dinosaur – it's amazing I'm still there. I reckon I'd have been cancelled b'now if anyone could understand what I'm saying." I caught his eye and we smiled at each other.

With some reservations but thinking it might make a better venue in which to break my news, I accepted an invitation to go to his room for a cup of coffee. It was in an old building in the college, up a twisty wooden staircase which smelled of beeswax. Inside it was plush – a freshly upholstered and comfortable modern relative of the set of rooms he had occupied in our last year at Cambridge.

"Good, eh?" he said. Tall stacks of books and sheaves of paper covered many of the surfaces, but there was a laptop open, suggesting that even Ferris had moved into the twenty-first century and partly abandoned his fountain pen. "I've got a coffee machine and a mini fridge." He pointed proudly to both and opened the door of the fridge. He was like an estate agent who indicates something obvious such as a cupboard just in case, despite being able to grapple with mortgages and conveyancing, you didn't know what one was. The fridge contained only a carton of milk. At least it might be fresh. That was some progress in the last forty years. More amazing still, he seemed to be able to operate the coffee machine. "Blue one or purple one?" he asked, showing me a choice of pods which he could use. "I don't know what the difference is. They both taste like coffee. Better wash a cup up, I s'pose." Ah. Not a complete transformation then.

Whilst he was fiddling about, I looked out of the window at the quad below. The grass was covered with the last of the hawthorn and cherry blossoms, a pink and white confetti which looked like a sprinkling of hundreds and thousands decorating one of Katie's green cakes.

A pair of students were walking hand in hand and stopped to kiss beneath one of the trees, uninhibited and carefree. Ferris was never so open with his affections. He kept even simple embraces, passionate but awkward, confined to his room. Our relationship was conducted only within the walls of his set. Until on that final day, when he had arrived unannounced and unexpected in Edinburgh and he had grabbed my hand in public and held me in the open air, oblivious to any audience assessing our connection. And then that almost unaccountable outdoor conjoining, the open-air sex which was the genesis of my years of deceit. How many times had I recalled him disappearing down the mound of Arthur's Seat, running away from me and my refusal to leave immediately and go with him over the sea to a foreign land?

A Feather Between the Lines

My last sight of him until our reunion at the Beaumont Hotel, just two weeks earlier. Almost thirty-eight years. It was hard to comprehend.

He brought me the cup of coffee and stood beside me looking out of the window himself.

"This is more like it, i'nt it?" I didn't respond. Did he mean, being here, in his room, was more like we used to be? I wasn't sure how to say what I really wanted to say. "There's no sugar," he added.

"Can't have everything." I was better at casual quips. Nothing emotional, nothing that might give any feelings away.

"Did you ever think about me?" he asked staring out into the quad, careful to avoid eye contact. "All these years, did you wonder where I were or what I were doing?"

This was my entrée. The moment when I could begin, 'In fact I did, because I have a boy and he looks just like you.' Like Lanre serving Mandy her lines, he'd played the shot for a perfect return. But I let it go. I remained silent on my side of the net.

"I thought about you. Probably every day. It didn't often make me happy. There's never been anyone else. You are the only woman I ever wanted."

"Oh, come on, Webster, you don't expect me to believe that do you? Nobody else, in all that time?"

Belittling him when he was trying to express his feelings was what had caused him to run away from me all those years ago. I realised that this wasn't the best reply, though I sincerely believed what he had said wasn't true. I knew that he had slept with Mary on our graduation day, for goodness sake. Another lucky strike – resulting in the production of Luke Featherstone. How many more Lucky Strikes all around the USA were there, testament to the tenacity of his sperm and the timing of a menstrual cycle?

"I didn't mean there hadn't been others. I meant I didn't care for any of them. I've had no long relationships. I've never been married." There was silence for a moment. "I told you, I'm not asking anything of you. I don't expect anything from you. I want to say I'm sorry if I made you unhappy." He stared out into the world beyond, seemingly focused on a collective memory somewhere in the college air. " 'She bid me take love easy, as the leaves grow on the tree; / But I, being young and foolish, with her would not agree'."

"You know just as much Yeats as me," I mumbled. I could feel him close to me, not touching but radiating that power that made me feel a combination of fear and exhilaration.

" 'She bid me take life easy, as the grass grows on the weirs; / but I was young and foolish, and now am full of tears'."

The tears were mine now. I tried not to let him see.

"I'm sorry, Roni, I don't want to upset you. I hope you're happy. I didn't want you to be miserable, ever. I wanted to see you, to check. To acknowledge my behaviour." This last phrase sounded like some psycho-nonsense from his therapist, something she had told him between giving him a diagnosis and a huge bill. "I've cocked it up again, as usual," he said quietly. "Still getting it wrong." I was sobbing loudly; I couldn't stop it. He put his arm round me, and I felt guilty at the pleasure his touch provided. "I've been running away from things for so long: problems, issues, difficulties – from myself really. It's been good to come back to England. I've seen you, seen my mam, seen my home and Rotherham, I've even seen The Millers." He paused. "I don't know if I could go back to Cambridge. Not yet. What was it like? When you went back to the reunion? Looked like you had a good time, from the photo – stuck some cocktail umbrellas in your hair!" he was trying to jolly me along.

"I wondered if you'd be there. I was hoping you wouldn't," I sniffed. "I didn't know how I would deal with that." We were both silent. He rubbed his hand up and down the top of my arm comfortingly. I turned and buried my head in his chest. I couldn't help myself. He put his other arm around me and pulled me close, resting his chin on the top of my head. Neither of us knew what to say. So much was unspoken, unexplained. It was yet another moment when, 'By the way, I think you are the father of my son,' was impossible to vocalise.

After a while he moved back a little. With a hand on each of my shoulders he looked me straight in the face. "You. The woman version of that girl I loved." He spoke softly, his gaze penetrating my eyes with such strength that I had to look down. "A mature and lovely Roni, the one I have been longing for for so long. I never stopped thinking about you, dreaming of a day like today when I could be with you, looking at you and touching you." He rested his forehead on mine. I could feel him gently breathing in and out.

I couldn't speak. I couldn't release my hands, clasped tightly against my chest. I daren't. This was Webster mark 2, a counselled and analysed version, in touch with his emotions and able to express them. I was the repressed one, conflicted by loyalties, unable to confront the truth. I couldn't look at him because I couldn't be responsible for what might happen. He took his head away momentarily before kissing me slowly and lightly on my forehead.

"We can't do this, Webster," I said eventually.

"I can," he emphasised. "You're the one with the husband."

I pulled away.

Phil. What a bloody mess I'd made of everything.

Webster realised he'd said the wrong thing, but it was too late. "I apologise," he muttered. "Forgive me."

There was nothing I wanted more than to return his embrace and feel the warmth of his body and touch of his skin. Neil was right. You can love two people but I doubted Phil could entertain that concept.

"I should go." I picked up my bag and looked inside for a

handkerchief to dry my eyes. Only a small, hard clump of pre-used, unabsorbent paper tissue was there.

"You'll have to use the back of your sleeve. I find that's as good as anything," he joked. "I've been summoned to a meeting. I'll walk down with you."

"You've not got yourself in trouble again, have you?" I tried to be as breezy as he was trying to be. Webster Ferris had been a regular in the Master's office as an undergraduate. "What have you done this time? You didn't beat up the Head Porter, did you?"

Webster chuckled. "Not yet, but I'm working on it as a parting gift to thank the college for their hospitality before I go." Mention of him returning across the Atlantic made us both reflective and we walked in silence to the lodge.

"Tomorrow and Wednesday. My last lectures. Please come. Don't let this be goodbye." He spoke quickly, immediately walking away towards the back of the quad. I watched him go. He didn't turn round. Who was running away now? Him? Me? Both of us?

"Did you have a good time, Miss?" the porter called out as I passed him on the way out.

"Piss right off," I shouted, and was pleased to see that he looked quite surprised.

When I got home, Phil was sitting at the kitchen table. "You're back early." I was trying to sound normal.

"I thought I ought to come back and have a little chat with everyone. Just did a half day." He didn't raise his gaze from the OS map that he had spread on the table in front of him. "When I got home – there was nobody here."

"You should've said. I could have come back sooner."

"Oh, I expect you've been busy. Been to Oxford have you?"

"I drove Arthur to the station. He's gone to London for a meeting with his publisher, or editor. Somebody." There was a bottle of wine on the table. "Where's that come from? Looks a nice bottle." It had a posh label.

A Feather Between the Lines

"Angela. She called in earlier," he explained.

"It looks a better one than the one we gave her on Sunday. Is it a hint to up our game next time?"

"It's an apology." His voice was flat and inexpressive. "She's very sorry, but she hadn't realised that I don't get on with your 'cousin'. She invited him to dinner as a surprise but should have worked it out. It's why you hadn't mentioned him and his lectures to her before or why you met him at the Beaumont Hotel not here at home. She hoped I hadn't seen him at the Marketplace Theatre and decided to go home then and there and not watch the show." I didn't know how to reply. "She should have been a private eye, not an English teacher. It gets worse and worse, doesn't it, Roni?"

33

Tuesday 23rd May 2023

There was a collection of black bin bags outside in the garden. Not garden waste – wrong colour bags. Phil wouldn't make such a refuse error. They did not contain all my possessions, I was happy to see, but the London-exiled detritus which had been clogging up the hall. In a way that suggested a return to the practicality and order of pre-pothole Phil, it was evidence that he had not wasted his afternoon the day before when no one was home.

He'd gone off in the car after our teatime encounter, stung by the revelation that I had been meeting up with Professor Ferris and passing him off as my cousin. He had not returned, and I had spent the night alone. Arthur too had called to say he was staying overnight and would be back in the morning. Even the cat was unwilling to curl up on my lap as usual and had taken herself off to purr elsewhere.

I'd started rereading *Vile Bodies* that evening. I'd hoped to choose a book which didn't touch in some way on my current situation. I remembered Waugh's flapper party-fest as amusing and light-hearted, but I'd forgotten it centres around a struggling writer and that the other characters, despicable hedonists who behave appallingly, are funny but ultimately unlikeable. Worse, I hadn't recalled the bleak tone of the latter part of the novel. I was deep into this second half, where things weren't going so well, when Phil returned late morning.

A Feather Between the Lines

He went into the kitchen without saying where he'd been and I didn't ask. He didn't look furious but propped himself up against the table with his feet crossed, one hand resting on his chin and his gaze averted from mine, studying the floor.

I started at the beginning and, delivering a monologue where fortunately I was able to keep my emotions in check, told him everything. Almost.

I began at the Edinburgh Festival in 1985 with Ferris's surprise visit and his exit, furious and at high speed, out of my life until just a few months ago. I explained my doubts when Arthur was born and afterwards when he was a late teenager and how I'd suppressed them, hoping it wasn't true. I told him how Ferris had got in touch after the photo in the college newsletter and why I'd contacted him. How I had intended to tell Phil, but the bike accident and the death of his father had made it more difficult. How one bad decision led to another and how sorry I was. How I loved him and hoped for his forgiveness.

Lying by omission: it featured in Gran's catalogue of sins. I'd committed a few over the years but this was the one which kept on coming. I didn't tell Phil about the open-air nature of Arthur's potential conception (too embarrassing), the exact details of my meeting the previous day (just too hard to admit) or how I was in love with Webster Ferris and always had been. How do you explain that concept: 'I love you but I love someone else as well'? You wouldn't believe it possible unless you had experienced it: Neil's theory of boundless love. You love your second and subsequent children as much as you love your firstborn, why not with love for a partner? Or two? I was hoping Phil did love his first child.

He listened without comment, sifting and analysing the information for veracity as well as assessing how reasonable any of my behaviours had been. He didn't let on his conclusions, if he had drawn any.

Eventually he turned to put on the kettle. He reached for the small pot again. I wasn't out of the woods. "I've been thinking," he began. "I'm planning my future." It didn't sound that promising. "I did as you suggested. I saw the GP this morning. A new one. She says I have made a marvellous recovery. No headaches, vision or speech issues. All good. Nothing to worry about – so you can stop trying to make out I've gone through some kind of personality change."

"I wasn't, but she's never seen you before, she doesn't know you. I just think you have been acting out of sorts."

He chuckled. "No surprise, really. You're hardly acting normally yourself. Perhaps it's catching." He popped a single tea bag into a mug and put the pot back. Old Phil was very particular about tea making; he always used a pot. More evidence of a casual disposal of years of routine.

"One thing the accident and Father's death have impressed on me is that I'm not going to be here for ever. I should make the most of things, do what I want to do. Live a little." I started to worry that this did not include me.

"My share of the sale of Meadowmead Close will help with retirement. I'm going to do more trekking and cycling and spend more time at Granny's cottage. Geoff and I were looking at the Camino de Santiago last night." He seemed excited suddenly. "There are several routes to Santiago di Compostela. From Italy, Portugal, France, Spain. We'll start with the French route. 680 kilometres."

So he'd been at Geoff's, planning my worst nightmare: hundreds of kilometres of Geoff, Malcolm and other assorted geeks, on foot, expanding their road game to continental highways along the route. St-Jean-Pied-de-Port to Santiago di Compostela – the final section – 100km on the A54 (Sarria to Santiago).

"Do I feature in your future plans?" I asked cautiously.

"You're welcome to come along. You can do as you please, though of course you have been doing that already."

A Feather Between the Lines

"I thought we might plan something together, now we will both be retired," I suggested tentatively.

"Such as a holiday to San Francisco perhaps?" He fished the bag out of the mug triumphantly, the timing of the perfect brew accomplished. "I think, Roni," he concluded firmly, "the time when you had an entitlement to share in decision making has expired."

At that moment Arthur arrived home. He looked uncomfortable when he found us in the kitchen together. This compounded my guilt – not only had I put him in an awkward position but the way in which he had discovered the news was awful. In a show of maturity which surprised me, he broke the ice.

"Hello, Dad," he said. "Are you OK?"

"Yes, thanks, son," he replied pointedly. Perhaps things were going to be alright between them. I left them to it, fearing I would make things worse.

After a considerable period of time whilst I sat anxiously next to the window only hearing the muffled sound of their conversation in the kitchen, I saw Phil and his bike leave and disappear along the lane. The hi-vis vest was back on. A sign of returning common sense and rationality? I hoped so. Arthur came in to see me.

"I told him," he explained, "he's my dad and always will be. This other dude, well, I've had thirty-seven years without him. He's not going to change anything."

"I'm sorry; all of this is my fault." I couldn't think what else to say, it seemed so inadequate.

"Mum, I can see it from your point of view. What were you to do? Katie and Jessica, they aren't like me, but then they're not like each other either. Jessica is like Dad I suppose, but Katie isn't. I don't think it matters that Dad and I are different."

He told me he'd been to see Tania the night before and discussed it with her. I was glad she had welcomed him. Perhaps she'd have second thoughts.

"You're being very grown-up about this." I hugged him close so that he couldn't see the tears brimming in my eyes.

"I am thirty-seven," he pointed out, offended perhaps that I should think he was still a child. I'd said the wrong thing yet again. "Can I ask you something?" I nodded. "Did having me spoil things for you? Did it mean you couldn't do what you wanted to because you had me to think about?"

I told him that my baby meant so much to me and that I had never, for a single moment, regretted having him. Not then nor at any point in the intervening years. And I was sure that Phil felt the same. "Professor Ferris is still here. Do you want to meet him?" I added tentatively.

"Does he know? About me?"

The reminder of the hideous prospect of having to tell Webster that Arthur existed made me feel ill. He didn't seem interested in my children. He didn't even know their names. I shook my head. I was hoping Arthur would say 'don't bother', but no.

"Perhaps you should just tell him there's a possibility," he suggested. "We could see how he takes it. See what he says. I could write to him after he goes back, and we could take things from there. Maybe."

"Good idea," I replied, thinking 'Oh crap'. I was going to have to do it, for Arthur's sake if not for anyone else.

"My meeting went well. They've given me a publication date. My agent came along. She held the fort until I got there. I told them what had happened – it kind of got me out of the poo for being late. She thinks it's a cracking story and that I ought to write about it. It's given me some ideas for my next novel."

Bloody hell. I hope he is going to use a pseudonym. Fortunately, most people I know are lying when they say they have read Arthur's work. It's an unspoken arrangement between us that they will say how marvellous it is and I won't quiz them on it, exposing the fabrication.

A Feather Between the Lines

In a despicable way I was miffed that there was no message on my phone from Ferris, asking why I hadn't been to his lecture that afternoon and begging me to come to the next one. I couldn't help it, although I hated myself for being so self-obsessed.

Surprisingly, Phil returned shortly bringing a take-away curry from the expensive Indian restaurant in the next village. He'd ordered all the dishes we like. It was a peace offering, I thought, as well as being a realistic way of getting something to eat when he had, correctly, assumed that I had nothing planned.

He'd got me my favourite – Nawabi King Prawn. I assumed it indicated that, whilst not entirely forgiven, I might at least be staying put and not be thrown out to share Mandy's spare room with offcuts of tartan wallpaper and a vicious-looking claymore that was too heavy and lethal to be hung on her wall. We ate together without mentioning the elephant in the room and Phil drank all of Angela's bottle of expensive wine without giving Arthur or me a glass. His prerogative in the circumstances.

34

The last lecture
Wednesday 24th May 2023

It's surprising what you can say with conviction if you have the nerve. It's a skill I've developed through years of turning up at the last minute.

When I arrived at the lecture hall, the doors were just closing. "Professor Ferris's assistant," I announced confidently, showing my bag as if it contained vital notes for the lecture. My lack of a ticket unnoticed, I was accompanied right to the front and shown a seat uncomfortably close to the gaze of the lecturer. I could see Angela and Joy, who'd arrived early enough to secure themselves a position close to the lectern by conventional means. Angela gave me a little wave and mouthed 'Hello'.

The fourth lecture: Shakespeare's last plays. Reconciliation and Forgiveness. Heavy duty concepts for my present circumstances. These plays feature characters apart for long periods and then brought back together with a lingering feeling of wasted time.

Webster had noticed me arrive; he couldn't have avoided it. I was like the bride's mother walking down the aisle just before her daughter's entrance dressed as a meringue. I thought I glimpsed a look of relief that I had come, but I tried not to catch his eye further.

It was almost as if our tale was one of Shakespeare's sources.

Hermione and Leontes in *The Winter's Tale*: suspected affairs and bastard babies, years wasted in separation, missing children and resurrected romance. Pericles, reunited with his estranged daughter after years of being apart. Cymbeline's daughter, Imogen, discovering her long lost brothers and reunited with her husband.

Banishment, misunderstanding, foolish jealousy and lengthy longing. All that our story was missing was violent storms, shipwrecks and being cast out to sea. We should have gone punting on the Cam and capsized over the weir at Mill Pond all those years ago to supply the whole story.

The Tempest, supposedly the last of all – a story of reconciliation brought about through repentance and forgiveness. Ferris cast his eyes towards me as he outlined the countless examples of 'cowardice, inaction and suppressing desire' in these final works.

"Letting 'I dare not' wait upon 'I would'": he emphasised the lecture series title as if it was an admonishment to us both. "The last plays are often categorised as problem plays or even romances," he explained pointedly, "and who would disagree that romance is often a problem for us all?"

Letting I dare not wait upon I would. That certainly applied to me. It's how I acted in 1985 and it was how I was behaving at that moment.

Ferris closed by quoting from *The Winter's Tale*. " 'Lead us from hence, where we may leisurely / Each one demand an answer to his part / Perform'd in this wide gap of time since first / We were dissever'd:....' " and then by encouraging the audience, as when, in the final scene of *The Tempest*, Prospero asks for applause to free him from his situation, " 'But release me from my bands, by the help of your good hands'."

The crowd obliged. The hall was filled with deafening clapping for the winner of the R.V. Ironside award for bleakness and misery tinged with the faint hope of better things to come. They loved him.

He left the stage and headed for me. "Quick, out by the side door." I could see Angela and Joy getting up and looking towards us, expectant that they could have a word with the professor, hoping that their flattering familiarity with the lecturer would be noticed by the rest of the audience. Webster pushed me through a door marked FIRE EXIT ONLY and we emerged into a side street. He headed off and I could barely keep up with him, knocking the battery of bicycles and tourists taking selfies out of his way as he went. There was no stopping him. We crossed the High, appropriately at very high speed, ignoring buses, taxis and kamikaze cyclists, then dodged down Magpie Lane, a thoroughfare luckily too narrow for motorised transport.

"Did you want to avoid Angela that much?" I asked. Webster was scowling. He didn't look happy. We went through a gate in some railings and eventually emerged at the back of some colleges near Christ Church Meadows. We stopped and I caught my breath.

"Are they after you? Have you finally killed the Head Porter? I can't hear any sirens." He didn't laugh. His face was serious.

"I'm glad you're here," he said eventually. "You didn't message me."

"You didn't message me either."

Some schoolboys were playing cricket on the playing field beside us, watched by a few desultory parents only pretending to be interested. A gaggle of mothers in deckchairs were exchanging gossip but one red-faced father was not hiding his anger because his son had just been given out lbw. "Come ON, ump!" he was shouting at the hapless elderly teacher in a dog collar whose misfortune was to be allotted the third XI fixture on a Wednesday afternoon.

Ferris watched the boys. I couldn't tell whether he was enjoying this bucolic English afternoon scene or whether he was working up to one of his former socialist rants. 'Don't you know about the miners' strike? And what Thatcher has done to Britain?'

A Feather Between the Lines

"I was distracted by something yesterday. I didn't message." He spoke slowly, watching a boy miss a dolly of a catch. The rest of the fielders groaned as the ball continued, barely moving across the grass, until it came to a slow-motion stop just over the chalked boundary.

"Are you in trouble with the Master? Did you get your wrists slapped? Are you being sent down?" Webster was not in the mood for silly banter.

"No. It wasn't the meeting."

We carried on walking until a park bench, invitingly placed by the side of the path, allowed me to sit down.

I told him why I hadn't been to the lecture the previous day, because Angela's visit had revealed that I'd told her Ferris was my cousin. I didn't elaborate but emphasised that I'd needed to stop at home to try and explain myself.

"Why did you tell her I was a cousin anyway? You could have told her the truth. Not that it's any of her fooking business."

This was a good point. I could have just said he was an old friend from university – why didn't I? Of course I knew. I was not just meeting an old friend to catch up. I was meeting someone who I'd been fantasising about for many years – and I'd been caught in the act and didn't think logically. I was pretty sure Webster had worked that out too.

"Phil got annoyed about that, did he? Took a day off? That's a bit disproportionate." It might have been – but if you added in a query over the paternity of his son and a wife who had been visiting an old flame (probably the boy's biological father) behind your back, taking time off to discuss it seemed almost mandatory.

I tried to change the subject. "Did Angela pester you yesterday after the lecture? Did Joyless give her opinion? Oh dear. Sorry."

"You could say there were a few things happened after the lecture," he remarked mysteriously. "How are things between you and Phil?" He was not to be diverted.

"Oh, you know…" I was trying to sound breezy. "We've been married for nearly thirty-eight years."

"I don't know. That's why I asked."

I made no reply. "Roni," he said. It sounded like he'd been building up to the next part of the sentence. "There's something I've got to tell you." Oh God. This is it. He's going to tell me he loves me and he's going to ask if I feel the same.

"In the audience yesterday was Mary Featherstone. Remember her? She had a chat with me afterwards." He was leaning forward, his arms resting against his legs, which were splayed apart. His head was hanging down. This was a confession, but not the one I was expecting.

Sure enough he told me about the way he had been so unhappy and upset on our graduation day that he had made love to her after the ceremony. A bizarre release of tension on his part, an affirmation that someone, at least, if not me, found him desirable, and an experiment on hers.

I couldn't respond partly because I already knew all this but mainly because I didn't know if she had included the additional information attached to this tale, the after-effect as you might call it.

"Oh well, got you out of the Master's awful sherry party." I tried to sound jovial.

"Is that your response? I've felt guilt about it for all these years." Webster was cross.

I felt awkward. "I just said that because I don't know what to say. It's all a long time ago. I apologise for making light of it. What were you expecting me to say?"

"There's more. She had someone with her. Her son. She says he's mine. I'm the only man she's ever slept with apparently. She's gay." As usual I was mute. "Going to think up a gag about that are you? That's not so funny is it? How about 'perhaps screwing me put her off men?' " He held his head in his hands. "And he

A Feather Between the Lines

certainly looks like me. Fucking hell. He's a professor. Here! English Literature."

"Are you pleased to have a son?" I asked after a while.

"All that time, she's never tried to contact me, she never thought to tell me. She knew where I'd gone. Am I pleased? Pleased? She comes up at the end of a lecture about Shakespeare's tragedies with the 'good' news and there are all these other people standing there. I'm glad you weren't one of them. I didn't want you to hear like that."

I put my hand on his shoulder. "Her timing could have been better, but you may find there are benefits to having a son. You've missed all the shitty bits. No nappies, no sulky teenagers, no awkward parent/teacher meetings. Straight to adulthood, fully formed, glitches ironed out. A convenient ready-grown human!"

"How can you be so bloody flippant, Roni? I don't want this." It was probably not the moment to slip in the additional information about the amazing co-incidence of the other possible offspring. "He's just written a book, that's the other thing, newly published. He wants me to endorse it. It would be 'useful' apparently to have a Stanford professor, an expert in Shakespeare, who has just discovered he is the author's father, to publicise it."

I thought of Arthur's agent, urging him to use the surprise father thing as inspiration. This was looking increasingly like even more of a disaster movie than the one I thought I was starring in.

"Was Mary at the lecture today?" I asked. "Is that why you were in such a hurry to leave?"

"I don't know. He may well have been, if not her. I didn't want to hang about to find out."

It started to rain very lightly. I suggested we walk down the path and see if we could find a teashop somewhere or shelter in Christ Church at the end of the Broad Walk. When the rain started to fall more heavily, we hurried up, he with his long steps outpacing me again. He held his hand out for me to grab, "Come on, me old duck," he called. "We'll get wet else." I wanted to hold his hand, despite what this might suggest and what it might lead to. It was warm and soft, familiar.

We turned into Christ Church and stood under the gateway, waiting to see if the shower might pass. A bowler-hatted porter approached us officiously and then looked obsequious and touched the brim of his hat when Webster flashed a lanyard at him and announced, "Professor Ferris." He had provided the right kind of password, an open sesame which sorted academics from the tourist revenue stream who needed to ship up £15 to get any further.

"There's something else," he said, as we emerged through the entrance into a grassy courtyard on the other side. Oh Lord, what was this? He's got a terminal illness? Or in order to get rid of them, he'd told Angela and Joy all the details of our romance? He'd described our parting copulation on Arthur's Seat but omitted to point out that we weren't in fact related?

"That meeting yesterday, it were about discussing a job they've offered me." He wasn't looking at me. He sounded unsure, as if he couldn't decide whether to tell me. "It's a part-time professorship. There's accommodation, membership of a college and some lecturing."

A panic alarm sounded in me. I'd tried not to think about him going back to the US and how we might navigate the future, particularly if Arthur decided he wanted to form some kind of relationship with him. I hadn't considered the possibility that he might return to the UK and be so close to home. That scenario was a dream, an idealised happy-ever-after screenplay in an unspecified location which conveniently ignored Phil, Arthur, the girls and even the cat. It just involved him and me: no arthritic toes, just the body and stamina of the twenty-three-year-old model of myself which I carried in my head and assumed in my reverie.

"Are you taking it?"

"I don't know. It depends."

"Let's go in the cathedral," I suggested. I liked to visit this place when I was in Oxford – I usually had to pay. "It's got some fine stained glass." There was a pleasure in being with someone who would appreciate the coloured beauty. Phil, if I could get him inside, was less interested in the Burne Jones trio, Faith, Hope and Charity, than the engineering of the vaulted chancel.

I took him to a side chapel where a large, highly coloured window depicted a man sheltering under a tree near a city. "This is my favourite. It's mostly painted glass, not stained, and it's 16th century so not the oldest here by far. But I love it. Do you know who it is?" Ferris shook his head. There weren't many times when I knew something he didn't.

"It's Jonah."

Ferris looked closely at it. "I'm buggered if I can see a whale."

"The whale is at the beginning of the story. God asked Jonah to deliver a prophecy but he didn't want to and tried escaping to sea. He was shipwrecked and the whale swallowed him. After three days he told God he was sorry and got spewed out." Ferris nodded. Everyone knows that bit – or they used to when schools bothered to teach children Bible stories. "The window shows the next part. Jonah in Nineveh. His prophecy was to tell its citizens God knew they'd been wicked – but he didn't want to because he thought they didn't deserve repentance. He sheltered under a vine with gourds whilst he thought about what to do." Ferris stepped back to view it properly. "But God made the vine die so Jonah felt the full heat of the sun and had to confront his reluctance." Ferris looked thoughtful but said nothing. "There are some advantages to having a zealous Catholic for a gran," I added. "The citizens took off their clothes, wrapped themselves in sackcloth and sat in ashes whilst they repented. My gran was always on about sackcloth and ashes: grief and repentance. She really made a party go with a swing."

Eventually he said, "Do you think I've done enough sackcloth and ashes? Have you forgiven me? 'The joy of love is too short and the sorrow thereof, and what cometh thereof, dureth over long'. Recognise that? *Morte d'Arthur* – the Thomas Mallory version not Roland's abbreviated bullshit." He smiled but looked sad. The tale of King Arthur. If only he knew. How ironic! "Seems to me Jonah got a second chance," he added.

"I don't think I'm really in a position to be doing any forgiving. I'm still sheltering under the gourds." I didn't expect Ferris to know why I said that. I hoped he might ask. He didn't, clearly thinking I'd shown him the window to suggest he needed to put in a little more grovelling – which wasn't the case.

We moved out of the chapel back into the main body of the cathedral. He looked contemplative. We were walking up the aisle – a symbolism not lost on me at least.

"What do you think then? Should I take it?"

"What?"

"The job. Should I come back?"

"It's not up to me!"

"Isn't it?"

There it was again. That sudden shift between light-hearted fun and an awkwardness which could descend between us at a moment's notice. The frisson: fear and excitement mixed. At the door of the cathedral, we stopped.

"Webster, you are the only one who can decide. You don't have to do it immediately do you? Do you want to come back here to live? Do you want to leave there? Does the idea of having a son make you want to experience that relationship? There's lots of reasons." I tried to make it sound casual.

"There's only one reason, Roni, that I would contemplate being so close to you." I flushed. His meaning was unequivocal. " 'No legacy is so rich as honesty'. You need to tell me. I need help to understand. What are you doing here? Why have you

A Feather Between the Lines

come? Today – the other days? I've been trying to work it out. You needn't have replied to my letter. We could have just met the once. You could have told me to piss off. But you didn't and I clung to that. You're not denying it are you?"

"You said you expected nothing of me, remember?"

"I don't expect. But I do hope. I want to hear it from you. If I come back to Oxford, are we going to see each other? Yes or no?" Bloody hell, it was Phil's confession game again.

"You've only just sprung this on me. Half an hour ago, I had no idea there was a possibility that you would return. What about Phil? What about the children?"

"Children! How old are they?"

"The youngest is nearly thirty," I said in a pathetically quiet voice. He shrugged his shoulders, dismissing that as a valid excuse.

"I will want to see you if I come back. If that's not going to happen then I'm not going to make life more difficult for myself than it already is."

We were looking out onto Tom Quad, huge, grassed and bordered by the honeyed stone and crenellated lodgings, which had been home to hundreds of students over the years. Christopher Wren's tall Tom Tower, with its famous shapely dome, visible from many parts of the city, was opposite us. It houses a bell which I imagined might be about to toll, solemnly and dramatically, sounding the death knell of our relationship. How ironic that this place, so reminiscent of that great rival institution in the Fens, might be the end of it all. Our alpha and our omega.

"The birdwatching is good in Northern California," Ferris said in a surprising departure in the conversation. Perhaps he was finding reasons to make staying there attractive. "There's a bird called the Californian condor. I'm always happy when I see one. They're endangered these days. It's got a huge wingspan, almost nine feet, dark plumage and, although it's clever with a good memory, it matures late. It's me, the Californian condor.

If I'm reincarnated, I'll come back as a bird. I'll be one of them. Monogamous, bonding with his mate and only pairing with her throughout his life. He displays a loyalty and commitment to his life partner."

I wanted to tell him that I'd like to be that partner but that almost thirty-eight years had passed and that things had happened, if not to him, to me. I had chosen a life partner. Much as I longed for a parallel universe where I could hop between our house and Phil and an elegant college room with Ferris, even I knew that this was unlikely to be a reality. Loyalty and Commitment. They were concepts I had to bear in mind, however much I wanted to touch him and enjoy the warmth and excitement of his embrace and feel the pleasure of the frisson he inevitably generated throughout my whole body.

"It's not easy, I can't…"

"It is easy. It's obvious for me and if it isn't for you… then I have got it wrong," he sighed. "Not for the first time."

What wasn't easy for me was speaking, discussing and displaying my emotions. He'd owned up to that. And he had made progress in overcoming it, but I couldn't and hadn't.

"'…but answer made it none'." As usual he had a Shakespearian quotation to hand, "OK. I understand." He began to walk away.

"Don't run off. Not again, I need to…" I called after him, but his pace just quickened. He'd been angry when he charged away down Arthur's Seat, frighteningly so, but this time he was just resigned. "Webster!" He continued to ignore me. I'd never catch up with him unless he slowed down to let me do so.

"I'm a respectable married woman with a husband and a home and three children," I bellowed this line out into the quad at the top of my voice, as much in agony and frustration as in the hope that he would stop and wait for me.

35

Later that day

When I eventually arrived home after a slow slog back in the car, Phil had the planner out on the table. Various highlighter pens were in use, blocking out great swathes of time in a colour-coordinated kind of way. "What are you doing?" I asked.

"It's quite complex," he said, waving one hand at me as if talking to me might distract his train of thought. I made some tea, pointedly using the larger pot and getting out two cups.

"Been out?" he asked after a moment, though it was obvious he knew the answer to that question.

"I said goodbye to the professor," I explained in an effort to be transparent. This wasn't entirely true but our parting had certainly had the feel of something final.

"No need on my part," he replied.

"He's going back to the States."

"I'm sure they are eager for his return." Phil, in this sarcastic, pretending-to-be-nonchalant kind of mood, was unbearable.

He pushed the planner towards me. "Green is Granny's Cottage, yellow is completing the British Coastal Path, pink is the Camino walks and then Geoff, Malc and I thought we might try and fit in a coast-to-coast hike or even start bagging a few Munros. I've got a blue for the coast, appropriately, and orange for the Munros. I'm struggling to fit them in. I'm going to have to get a planner for next year. I'm not even sure you can buy one in May."

My feet ached at the thought of this multi-coloured vision of hell. There was barely a clear white day in sight.

"Retirement is going to be busy," I suggested.

"Great isn't it! Being able to do just what you want. I can't wait." He smiled enthusiastically. "Good Lord, is that the time? I'm going over to Geoff's. We're having a planning meeting." He replaced the lids on all his pens and inserted them back into their plastic holder. "I'll need to take the planner, if that's OK. Perhaps we should get separate ones now I'm retiring. Not that you ever bother to fill anything in on it anyway." He got out one of his cycle panniers and carefully placed the pens and timetable of torture inside. "I'm taking the bike, so I won't be back tonight."

"What about your tea?" I put the cup on the table.

"No time for that. The car's yours, if you need it," he shouted as he went out of the room.

There was a strange stillness and quiet in the house after he left. I didn't like it. I hoped Arthur was upstairs, but he wasn't. I could see Mandy was back from work – her car was in the lane. I went and rang her bell. No one answered immediately, but just as I was about to go the door opened – not fully. "Aye?" asked a slightly aggressive and unmistakably male voice. Through the opening I could identify a stocky man whose rugged red beard obscured the lower half of his face. His bright blue eyes stared at me accusingly and his wild ginger hair was clashing alarmingly with a fluffy pink dressing-gown – the only item of clothing he seemed to be wearing. "Whit kin ah dae fur ye?"

"Are you Iain?"

"Ah might be. Wha wants te ken?" He looked suspicious.

"I'm Roni. I live next door. Is Mandy in?" As I said it, I recognised that the cosy evening I thought I might be able to persuade her to share was unlikely to be on the cards. Not unless

Iain fancied a threesome. I wasn't sure I did – even if the offer was there.

"Mandy's a wee bit busy just noo. Ah'll tell 'er ye were askin' efter 'er."

As he started to close the door, I heard Mandy's voice call out from somewhere upstairs, "Who is it?"

"Och, it's just an auld wifie sayin' she's frae next door."

Mandy, at least, was having fun. The auld wifie went home and rang Lanre. I thought he might be talked into an evening at The Railway Tavern with someone of his mother's age.

"I'm sorry, I was going to call you," he apologised, sounding sheepish. "That was quite an evening at Angela's. That Webster fella doesn't mince his words. What happened when you got home?"

He couldn't meet up to find out – he was packing to go on holiday. But he was interested enough to have a quick chat on the phone whilst he was cramming his swimming trunks, sunglasses and a precautionary supply of ibuprofen and Pepto Bismol into his case. He was going on a singles holiday to Greece. "Next time I think I'll be coming with you," I said.

I told him about Phil working it all out and about Angela's helpful visit with the wine present. I could imagine Lanre regaling my story as an amusing anecdote whilst he was sipping a cocktail at the bar. I couldn't blame him; I would have done the same.

"Did you tell him?" Lanre asked. "Did you tell the prof how you feel about him?"

"I didn't tell him about Arthur."

"That's not what I asked."

"I've blown it. It's too late. I've missed my chance."

"Not necessarily. This is your last chance to avoid having to come with me on a singles holiday next year. If that's not an incentive, I don't know what is! Remember my line?" Lanre switched to his clipped Alec voice. "Mightn't it be weak and not strong at all to run away from such tremendous longing?" I wasn't sure he was right.

I put on the TV. It was difficult to find something to watch which didn't make matters worse. I thought a programme about huge concrete buildings erected by the Nazis might be devoid of a plot and certainly wouldn't embrace any romance. How stupid. Within three minutes I was immersed in the misery of the slave labourers forced into constructing them. The news on a twenty-four hour loop? More depression, death and disaster. For once I didn't want to read. I ended up half-watching the excursions of a jolly couple from Oldham looking at properties in Spain to buy for their retirement. The apartments may have been soulless and basic, but the sun was shining and they were clearly excited about and looking forward to the next chapter in their joint adventure.

The cat, at least, came and sat on my lap as if she knew how miserable I felt.

36

25th May 2023

Next morning, Arthur had reappeared and was performing the coffee symphony when I came down for breakfast. "You're up late, Mum," he commented. I smiled weakly. He was looking particularly Ferris-like. Having spent time recently with Webster, their mannerisms and body language were so similar that there was no longer a shred of doubt in my mind. "Good news!" He grinned. "Dad offered to pay for my car to be repaired. I'm paying him back, of course, when I can." At least things between them were looking promising.

Things were looking up slightly for me too – I got a cup of the black-beaned nectar without having to plead for it.

Arthur was scrolling through his phone. He can do this simultaneously with many of life's other necessities: typing on his laptop, eating, drinking, having heated conversations. I hoped that driving wasn't one of them. His phone is an extension of his body, one he keenly misses if he is parted from it. Only he can touch it and he visibly panics if I want to hold it when he invites me to look at something on its screen.

"Fuck me!" he announced. "Good God." I waited for an explanation, but none came. He was clearly shocked. "Look what's come up on my feed." He didn't actually mean look, because I can't see to read the screen without holding the device and that is verboten. "I've been searching Professor Webster Ferris."

I waited to hear what he had learned. A report of the lectures? The murder of the Head Porter? Ferris had been arrested last night, drunk and disorderly after succumbing to a bender after twelve years of abstinence – and all because of me?

" 'Published today by Oxford University Press. *The Townley Mystery Cycle: who was the Wakefield Master?* by Professor Luke Featherstone.' There's a bit about the book, then it says, 'To coincide with the launch, the author, who, when appointed, was the youngest ever professor of English Literature at Oxford University, has revealed that he has discovered who his father is for the first time. Professor Webster Ferris, renowned Shakespearian scholar of Stanford University in California, is currently visiting Oxford to deliver a series of lectures…' "

As usual, I said nothing. This time it was because I just didn't know where to start. "Mum, that woman who brought the lecture leaflet was called Featherstone. Is that her son?" I nodded. "There's a picture too. Fuck it, he looks like me! Is it true?"

"I think it probably is," I admitted, shamefaced.

"He's the same age as me. Old Ferris dude must have been knocking you both off at the same time!" This wasn't really the language he should have used when speaking to his mother, though in the circumstances I could hardly reprimand him. For once the phone was out of his hand, discarded onto the table as if, as the bearer of shocking news, it might contribute to more information-overload than he could deal with.

"Does Dad know about this, Mum?" he asked eventually.

"No. And please, unless it crops up in conversation, please don't tell him, not yet."

"I definitely think I might want to meet the randy old goat at some point," Arthur announced.

Estrangement from his phone didn't last long. Presently he was searching for more information. "There's more about this bloody book. It's everywhere. OUP have gone to town on the

A Feather Between the Lines

publicity angle. 'Professor Ferris's academic pedigree is clearly continued by his son as this volume, with its groundbreaking scholarly research, ably demonstrates.' I'll certainly write to Ferris. I'm not letting Luke Featherstone get all the publicity."

Amazing, isn't it? He'd had a half-brother for a mere ten minutes and there was already sibling jealousy and professional rivalry.

I was a little disconcerted at Arthur's attitude to all these revelations. Was it easier for someone who lives his life through the sensationalised narrative pedalled by the internet and whose life experiences are formed by a type of modern fiction which presents the worst of life and its misfortunes as the norm? He's not naïve but I had expected more angst, disbelief or even anger from him. Perhaps he is just well balanced and rational. Thirty-seven years of Phil have had some effect.

If Arthur was going to contact Ferris, even if not immediately, there was something I needed to do. We may have parted in a less than desirable way, yet I needed to tell him in person. He probably didn't want to hear the news, but I owed it to him not just to write an impersonal letter.

I'd drawn this conclusion a long time ago, of course, and had been trying to do it every time I'd seen him, miserably failing at each opportunity. I couldn't avoid it any longer. The chance to see Ferris again, maybe really for the last time, was, of course, another motivation, although I couldn't quite admit it to myself.

Back to the city and a nervous walk along Broad Street to the Porter's Lodge. I stood outside the gate for a long while, running through the script I had written so that I didn't say the wrong thing.

The Head Porter, clearly still alive and just coming to a halt having pirouetted a full 720-degree double rotation, saw me and fixed me with a glare. He pointed to a new sign on the counter. 'The college will not tolerate bad language or threatening behaviour towards its staff and reserves the right not to admit visitors and residents who fail to comply with this regulation.'

"I've come to see Professor Ferris," I announced nervously.

"No doubt," he began. "Can you read?"

"Yes, thank you." I decided I needed to grovel if he was going to allow me through. "I'm sorry about last time. We had had a tense meeting and I was a bit annoyed. With him."

"Understandable." I wondered if the sign had been created after my potty-mouthed farewell last time or because of Ferris. The female acolyte was back, standing, of course – there was no way she had earned the right to a static chair yet alone one with movement. She nodded her head sycophantically and it wasn't entirely fanciful to imagine she had had first-hand experience of Webster's invective.

"The professor is very popular this morning. You're not the first to be asking for him." He gave me a knowing look.

"The Oxford Student and Cherwell have been here," the girl chipped in.

"Those are student newspapers, of course, not the proper press. We've had the phone going too. The woman from the local radio is very persistent. I had to tell her to stop calling, no point – he won't be speaking to any of them. I wouldn't be surprised if the local TV lot don't show up. They like a story with a bit of sex. It beats potholes and campaigns against new reservoirs. You don't get a fatal crash on the A34 every day." He seemed animated, carried away and over-excited by his new role as gateway between Ferris and the media.

"There's not much sex," the girl corrected. "Just the once, ages ago, by the sound of it. It's more of a long-lost relative story really. Like that programme on telly where someone from Australia finds an aunty in Reading they didn't know about." The Head Porter ignored her.

I wondered how Ferris was coping with being outed as Luke's

father, presumably without his consent. I doubted there'd be a rush in Blackwell's for an academic book on medieval mystery plays as a result of this information, but it was a sensitive (and officially unproven) confession for Webster himself to have to deal with.

"Could you tell Professor Ferris that I'd like to see him. Roni McNamara."

"I could," he said tantalisingly, "but I'm afraid that's not going to be possible, on account of the fact that the Professor is not at the college."

"Did he say when he'd be back?"

"Between you and me, Miss, I'm hoping not for a long time."

A paralysing fear crept over me.

"Of course, you'll appreciate that his whereabouts, in the present circumstances, are not in the public domain. I'm afraid I cannot divulge as to where his location might be."

"I reckon he's gone back to America," the woman announced triumphantly. "He had a big suitcase."

"I can confirm," the Porter added, irked, "that he has left the college on a permanent basis."

It hadn't crossed my mind that Ferris would return so soon after his last lecture – or was he running away again? From me, from Luke Featherstone and his thoughtless announcement and ball-breakingly dull academic tome, from the Oxford student press hacks and from making a decision about the faculty's job offer? From the future?

I stumbled out into Broad Street and ran along to the junction with Magdalen Street, where I leant against the railings bordering the graveyard of the church. I sobbed – in an uninhibited way, as if crying loud and long would dry up my tears forever. A young student, probably only about twenty or twenty-one, came and spoke to me.

"Can I help?" she asked. I shook my head. "Are you safe?" she continued. "Can I call someone for you?"

I've noticed young women of this age are very supportive of other women. They bother to approach people in distress. They ask if they are OK. When I was twenty-one, I would have run a mile from a crazed old bat bawling her eyes out. I thanked her and as she walked away, glancing back at me occasionally as she disappeared amongst the other pedestrians, I wished I was her. Twenty-one again, ready to start over and avoid the mistakes I'd made, supported by a sisterhood which would have enabled me to take time to make decisions which would affect my future life.

37

A short time later
25th May 2023

I was walking back to the bus, slowly down George Street, when my phone rang. It was Lanre. "Roni?" he said. His voice was quiet and whispery.

"Speak up. I can't hear you. I'm outside."

"Rni, I cnt spk up." It was a terrible line. I asked him if he wanted me to call him back. "I'm gn to the arprt."

I sheltered in the doorway of a restaurant and put my spare hand over my other ear.

"Have a lovely time. I wish I was coming too. Next time!"

"I'm on the bus. He's hre. He's gng to Hthrw too." Despite the reception and Lanre's attempts not to be overheard, I knew who he meant. "He didn't see me whn he gt on. He's at the frnt. I'm nr the bck. Did you tell hm?"

"No. I'm in Oxford. I just went to find him – and he'd gone. I was too late."

"D'y wnt me to tlk to hm?" I didn't know how to respond. "There's a spare seat next to him. I'll move." Lanre was speaking normally now. He'd abandoned the stage whisper. "I'll tell him to hang on at the airport. You can come and talk to him yourself. Get round to Gloucester Green bus station and on the next Airline bus. They leave about every twenty minutes or so. Hurry up. If you go now you'll be there in time." I could hear the excitement and scheming in his voice and he was unable to keep up the subterfuge. He wasn't going to make a career as a spy.

"I can't."

"No such word, my mum used to say. Get yourself on a blimmin' bus and meet us at the airport. I'll tell him." He hung up. I had no opportunity to argue or come up with a flimsy excuse.

I was close to the bus station. Phil said we should do what we want. I wanted to see Webster Ferris – so I ran along the road, into Gloucester Green, found the next bus departing for Heathrow and bought a ticket from the driver.

Before long, in a madly impetuous, post-bus-and-pothole-Phil kind of way, I was passing through Oxford, past Christ Church and Tom Tower, along the High and beyond the city, through the dreary between-the-wars ribbon development of Headington and then speeding along the A40 (City of London to Fishguard, Wales) towards London.

I felt as if I had boarded a roller coaster but had second thoughts. Unable to get off, yet fearing the unpredictable journey and experiencing a dramatic loss of self-respect and all control as I hurtled towards the loop of the M25 and our final destination. I wanted to get to the end for the sole reason that it would then be over.

Somewhere near High Wycombe I got a text from Lanre. 'Have swapped seats and spoken. Unconvinced but will wait for you if you get here in time. Luckily he's in plenty of time for his flight. He's terminal 5 like me.'

The coach arrived and I called Lanre from the stop for an update. "Level three, departures, lurking near the check-in desks," he told me. "Don't hang about."

When I got there, Lanre was standing in the middle of a cavernous, grey and white modern space which was curiously not

A Feather Between the Lines

very busy. He was alone. I'd missed Ferris or he didn't want to wait.

"He's not happy," Lanre reported. "I don't know what happened between you. I told him what you think of him and persuaded him to wait but…"

"But what? What did you tell him? How do you know what I think?"

"It's obvious," Lanre laughed. "I'm surprised he needed telling. He wouldn't have stayed otherwise. We've both checked in but I'm going to have to go through or I'll miss my flight. So annoying. I'd like to watch from afar." I was very glad Lanre was going to have to make an exit. "Let me know every detail. He's in the café." He threw me a thumbs up before he headed towards the sign saying SECURITY.

I could see Webster now, his face scowling. He looked up when he saw me – but he didn't smile. He had two empty coffee cups in front of him and his leg was jiggling with the same impatience, possibly anxiety, that it had that very first time we met in Dr Bennett's study at Cambridge.

"I didn't know you were leaving today." He said nothing. "I went to the college; the Head Porter's sidekick told me you'd gone." He frowned and exhaled.

Eventually he replied. "I changed my ticket. There were no point in staying. Didn't know you were interested."

"I've got something to tell you." He didn't invite me to sit down, but I pulled up a stool to the small table and started my rehearsed speech. "I've got three children, two girls and a boy." Ferris raised his eyes to heaven. Presumably he was anxious to proceed to the departure lounge, away from people reading OUP press releases or Luke Featherstone waving a large, boring tome at him. Me giving the same excuse about why I couldn't see him again was increasing his chances of being dragooned into an impromptu book signing.

"The boy is called Arthur. He's just had his birthday. He's 37 now." There was no reaction from Ferris. "He was conceived in Edinburgh, at the Festival, in August 1985. I'm sure he is your son."

For an uncomfortable moment, Ferris was silent. "Fuck off, Roni, what is this?" He didn't smile. He didn't even seem surprised. He just looked angry. "Is this another of your flippant jokes?"

"I've been trying to tell you. I couldn't do it. It never seemed the right moment. Now Mary has got in first."

"This isn't what your mate told me you were chasing along the motorway to tell me." His voice rose as he stood up. "I don't want to be a father. I have never wanted to be one and now not just one of you but two of you want to make me one."

"I don't want to make you one, you are one. You don't have to do anything about it, but I thought you ought to know. It didn't happen to me by myself. You were there. Fifty percent of his DNA is yours."

"And it's taken you, both of you, until now, thirty plus years on, to tell me. Well fuck you!"

"You did," I said loudly and firmly and immediately regretted it. People were looking at us: a free cabaret, two buskers performing their schtick. We could have passed a hat round.

"I've got a plane to catch," he announced, moving towards the entrance of the café. "I've waited here long enough." His voice showed irritation. He left, striding purposefully out into the grey and white space. I couldn't let him get away this time. I followed him out on to the concourse.

"Webster, stop! Don't run away again." He was heading for the check-point where I, without a boarding pass, had no access. "Please!" He stopped but he didn't turn round. I approached him. "Arthur wants to write to you. You don't have to answer, but if you do come to feel you want some contact, I've written our address

A Feather Between the Lines

here. He's come back to live at home for a bit – girlfriend troubles." I handed him a scruffy piece of paper I'd found in my pocket on the coach. On one side was a shopping list but I'd scribbled our address on to the other with a barely working Biro borrowed from the man in the seat next to me.

He didn't look at me directly but just held the scrap of paper, his gaze on that instead. "You never told me where you lived. I thought you didn't want me to know." He was breathing deeply, in and out, in and out, audibly, as if he was trying to control his emotions.

"Well, I do want you to know. I want you to know where both of us are."

"Arthur's Seat," he said quietly.

"And I want to tell you something else as well." He carried on looking at the paper. I was grateful for that because I wasn't quite sure where to look myself when I told him the next bit.

"I love you, Webster. I've never really stopped doing so. I tried to put it to the back of my mind, to ignore it, but it's always been there. Seeing you again this last couple of weeks has been difficult, I won't deny that, but I'm glad it's happened. Maybe we'll see each other again…" I couldn't continue. I'd run out of words.

A huge man wearing a checked shirt and chinos came hurtling towards us. For a brief moment I thought he was a mugger or a plain-clothed policeman who was going to tell us to hit the deck because a bomb was about to explode.

"Hey, Webster dude," he shouted, slapping Ferris on the back with a force so strong it almost knocked him to the floor. "You on the British Airways flight? I didn't know you were over here too. Come on, we need to move, or it'll be taking off and our bags will be in San Francisco without us." He grinned, showing an impossible number of bright white teeth in the process. "I've been meeting guys at some school called Wor Wick. Jesus, what a dump. Can't wait to get back." He nodded his head slowly, expecting us to agree with him. "I checked in and then, well, let's say I had a few last things to do and was kinda enjoying them and now I gotta rush." He winked lasciviously. My mind boggled at the thought of what he might have been doing and, more worryingly, where.

"You flying?" he asked me. I shook my head, aware I was looking on the verge of tears. "Way to go. Last goodbyes then." He whooped and pumped his fist in a kind of power salute, reminiscent of Donald Trump on a podium. He didn't show any signs of giving us any privacy for our farewell.

Webster tucked the slip of paper into the inside of his jacket. In exchange, he pulled out something and placed it into my own pocket as he kissed me. First on one cheek and then on the other.

"OK, man, let's move," said his colleague, pulling at him. "We gotta clear security and find our gate. Maybe we can get them to change things around so we can sit together." Webster's expression did not suggest that an eleven-hour flight next to Mr Loud Irrepressibly-Energetic was what he had in mind.

Webster kissed me again. This time on the lips, lingering just long enough to ensure that I knew that it was meant with feeling and that this embrace wasn't just a performative farewell.

"OK, let's go!" his travelling companion shouted, dragging Webster by his sleeve. They both headed at a fast jog towards the uniformed woman checking boarding passes, the point of no return. I followed up to the place where I was not allowed to go any further.

"Please come back," I shouted after him. "Even if you don't take the job." Webster didn't turn round. He carried on. But, as they rounded a corner, just as I could no longer see them, he raised his hand. I wasn't sure whether it was a wave or a stop sign.

It was a slow journey back to Oxford. The M25 was beginning to clog up. Out of the bus window, up in the sky, I could see the steady stream of planes taking off, heading west. One of them, disappearing up into the clouds, might have Ferris onboard. Was

A Feather Between the Lines

he looking down from a window seat, getting his last views of England, planning to return, or was he bidding a definitive ta-ra? I sat very still and closed my eyes. I tried to get that picture of Ferris out of my mind, his back turned away from me, his arm raised in perhaps what was a final farewell, the last view I would ever have of him. A line from *Still Life*, spoken by Dolly, the friend who interrupts the last goodbye, came to me as I thought about the events of the previous few months. 'It might have been smoothed over perfectly easily and no one would have known anything about it'. Surprisingly I fell asleep and when I woke we were back on the A40 nearing the approaches to Oxford.

I remembered that Webster had put something into my pocket. I felt for it; it was so small that I almost thought I'd lost it. I brought out a small manila envelope, about two inches square. It was old and creased and its flap had been sealed with Sellotape as if it had been opened and shut several times in the past. I slid my nail under the tape, which, having been there for some time, was easily unstuck. Inside the package was a thin and cheap-looking plain gold ring, worn away in parts as if it had once been a regular adornment on a finger. I turned the envelope over. On the front, handwritten in cursive script, it read, 'for collection by W. Ferris', and along the bottom the printed words, 'J H Clark and son, Funeral Directors, Rawmarsh, Rotherham'.

38

Five weeks later
30th June 2023

Alone in a crowded room, like the singer of that song. The Railway Tavern was packed. Phil's retirement party was in full flow, the hired room thronging with colleagues from work all celebrating his release from almost thirty-eight years at the same company. An assembly of engineers and support staff, none of whom I wanted to talk to and most of whom had nothing to say to me, were laughing and enjoying each other's company.

Arthur had returned to London, car repaired, back to Tania's flat but without the bulk of his chattels, which were still taking up floor space in his bedroom at home. I'd moved Pedro in there too, the outsized straw donkey, the fifth Spittal P. If the entire carpet was covered then there was no need to go anywhere near it with the Hoover, I decided. The black bin bags were still in the garden where Phil had put them – the tempting prospect of a rehoming at the dump something which he was, for the moment, resisting.

It had turned out that my interpretation of Arthur's banishment was wrong. I'd assumed that Tania had reached saturation point with the lack of steady income and my son's inability to live like a proper adult. She had given him an ultimatum – but not one involving the need to grow up and get a proper job. She

A Feather Between the Lines

wanted a child, and he didn't. Not initially. Like Cyril Connolly he had feared 'the pram in the hall' as likely to stifle his creative endeavours. But he had come round and had returned to her to participate, I assumed, in the joyful process of making one. I wondered if the revelations about his own creation had prompted his change of heart. I didn't dare ask. Maybe I might become a granny after all. I didn't want to scupper that one by sticking my oar in.

In the background that song was playing again, the one with the lyrics about the girl frozen in time. But unlike her, the process of thawing out the twenty-three-year-old me had begun. It had started nine months earlier with the arrival of the first letter: co-incidentally the same period of time as the gestation of a baby that Tania might be hoping to grow. My rebirth was imminent.

Arman, the postman, had recently brought me another envelope, my address written on it in the spidery handwriting I recognised immediately. This time, instead of hiding the letter, I carried it with me so I could look at it in moments like these. Something to clutch at when I wondered how I was going to cope with this new reality. The multi-coloured, fluorescently-highlighted stretches of time when Phil would be elsewhere were displayed on the planner in the kitchen. The time when we would be apart was clear. Most of the time.

I went to sit outside in the pub garden. It was a warm evening and still light enough to read the letter, although I knew its contents by heart already.

Dear Roni,

There were some benefits of an eleven-hour flight trapped in a seat beside The Incredible Hulk disguised as a colleague from the computing department at Stanford. Unsurprisingly, he and I have little in common. I had to pretend to be asleep for most of the journey to prevent hearing too many details about his sordid affair with a technician from Warwick University. I had plenty of time to think about the events of my own visit to the UK.

It is now two weeks since I left Oxford and I have been thinking of nothing but you and our own relationship. I made knee-jerk decisions in 1985 and was in danger of doing so again this time. However, I have made some personal progress since then. Now, in 2023, I can, with reflection, see things from others' viewpoints. Like a Californian Condor, it's taken me a while to mature.

'Men at some time are masters of their fates: The fault… is not in our stars / But in ourselves.' (Julius Caesar)

Initially, in panic and anger, before I left, I told the English faculty that I was not interested in their offer. Returning to Stanford has put things into perspective. I don't want to stay here forever; I want to come home. I have recently spoken to the university (Oxford) and smoothed things over. The offer is extant.

I'm considering how I might be able to cope with being near to you if we don't see each other or if our meetings are sporadic. I am hoping that your final admission to me at the airport means there is some possibility that we might find a way forward. 'Only in the agony of parting do we look into the depths of love' (George Eliot).

How I deal with the other purported child I'm supposed to have fathered – the one with a professorship in the same department and a book he wants promoting – I don't really know. I've yet to figure that out. If Arthur wants to write to me, tell him to go ahead. One son at a time.

The ring, as you may have worked out, is my mother's wedding ring. I carried it with me that day when we met in Edinburgh, intending to give it to you. I have wondered so many times what might have come about if I had not been so

A Feather Between the Lines

blinkered in my understanding of your feelings and situation. I brought the ring back to England on my visit because I had thought of returning it to my mother by burying it at her grave. By the time I visited Rotherham, you and I had seen each other again and I couldn't leave it, alone amongst the weeds, if there was some chance, however slim, that we might reunite. Foolish perhaps but, as I told you before when we stood atop Arthur's Seat and watched the sun about to set over Edinburgh, you are the only woman I have ever loved apart from my mother. That is still true today, so I want you to have the ring. If you feel that is inappropriate, perhaps you will give it to the boy. Something from me, a connection with the grandmother and grandfather he will never know.

Knowing about Arthur as I do now, I have worked out why you married Phil so soon after I left. Pride and Prejudice – I was guilty of both. Like Elizabeth Bennett, 'Vanity not love has been my folly'.

I enjoy watching Canada geese in the Bay area. Some of them fly thousands of miles across the Atlantic to Northern Europe. Migrating birds always return if they survive the perils of the trip and make the journey safely.

'I wish you all the joy you can wish.' (Merchant of Venice)

With love, Webster x

I'd already sent my reply. Just three words, WAITING FOR YOU, written on the back of a postcard of the dreaming spires of Oxford.

I could hear the muffled sounds of music and chatter at Phil's party from the pub garden, but I preferred to be outside with my letter. My phone rang.

"Roni, it's Angela. Please have a word with Lanre. He'd be such a marvellous Antony and you have to play Cleopatra. She is in you. I've worked out how we can do it – no need for the

Nubian slaves and I can get round many of the other characters by doubling up. What do you think?"

We all have the thing with feathers, a little bird, in our soul singing the promise of hope.

Author's Note

If you enjoyed *A Feather Between the Lines*, please tell your friends and book group. I'd love you to leave a review on Amazon, Waterstones or Goodreads.

You can follow me on Facebook and Instagram for all my book news by going to the following links or scanning the QR codes:

Instagram: https://bit.ly/KathCrew_Instagram

Facebook: https://bit.ly/KathCrew_Facebook

Do you want to know what happened in the first book? *A Cactus Called Ironside* is the first in the series, available now on Amazon: amzn.to_4dpmVxu

About the Author

Kath Crew has been telling stories since she could first talk and writing them down since someone showed her how to use a pencil. Her active imagination has occasionally landed her in trouble over the years.

She was President of Cambridge Footlights in the 1980s and wrote for and performed in revues whilst at university. As a teacher she wrote for her students and has been a contributor to various publications.

Now she is free of children, her own and those belonging to other people, she is enjoying writing at length for a larger audience. She hopes to entertain with humour whilst not being entirely flippant or lightweight.

Originally from London and a townie at heart, she now lives in Oxfordshire with her husband. She is trying hard to fit in with life in the country and extend her classification of the natural world beyond a basic 'bird', 'flower' or 'tree'.

Acknowledgements

Thanks to Pippa, Georgie, Mike, Belinda, Kath and Caroline for their advice and support.

And to Jen at Fuzzy Flamingo who has made the realisation of this book possible.

Endless gratitude to Nick, whose dedication to the removal and replacement of commas and continued help and encouragement is unwavering.

www.ingramcontent.com/pod-product-compliance
Lightning Source LLC
Chambersburg PA
CBHW020359080526
44584CB00014B/1095